Adolescence in the 21st Century

Constants and Challenges

Adolescence in the 21st Century

Constants and Challenges

edited by

Frances R. Spielhagen
Mount Saint Mary College

Paul D. Schwartz
Mount Saint Mary College

INFORMATION AGE PUBLISHING, INC.
Charlotte, NC • www.infoagepub.com

Library of Congress Cataloging-in-Publication Data

A CIP record for this book is available from the Library of Congress
http://www.loc.gov

ISBN: 978-1-62396-496-2 (Paperback)
       978-1-62396-497-9 (Hardcover)
       978-1-62396-498-6 (ebook)

CONTENTS

Foreword vii

David Elkind

Preface ix

Frances R. Spielhagen and Paul D. Schwartz

PART I

EXAMINING THE ADOLESCENT IN THE 21ST CENTURY 1

Frances Spielhagen and Paul Schwartz

1 Seeking the Right Fit: From Training Bras to Self-Identity as
   Adolescents Search for Self 3
   Susan Riemer Sacks

2 "Talk to Me . . .": Communication Between Mothers and Young
   Adolescent Daughters 23
   Debra A. Hrelic

3 Parental Religiosity and Adolescent Educational Attainment:
   The Role of Noncognitive Skills 39
   Gregory M. Eirich

4 Adolescent Literacy Development and the New Literacies:
   Challenges and Possibilities 63
   J. David Gallagher

5   Sociopsychological Problems among Youth in the Modern
    Russian Family...87
    Olga E. Lomakina and Tatiana I. Gustomyasova

PART II

CONSTANTS: PURPOSE, AGENCY, MOTIVATION   101

Frances Spielhagen

6   Service Learning as a Tool for Developing Emerging Adults
    into Productive Employees and Citizens............................. 105
    Moira Tolan

7   Doing Social Justice: The MYTI Program and Inner City
    Students.. 125
    Rosaria Caporrimo and David Kerner

8   Autism in Adolescence: Facing the Challenges..................... 141
    Irene Van Riper

9   Education of Peacemakers: Raising College Students'
    Awareness of and Respect for the "Other" 155
    Margaret Murphy, O.P. and Diane Bliss

PART III

CHALLENGES: ADOLESCENCE AND EMERGING ADULTHOOD   167

Paul Schwartz

10   The Challenge of Acceptance: Digitalk and Language as
     Conformity and Resistance.. 171
     Kristen Hawley Turner

11   Homeless Adolescent Mothers: Engaging Strengths Emergent
     in Parenthood.. 187
     Alexandra Jordan, Marina Mazur, Aurelie Athan, and Lisa Miller

12   Prenatal Cocaine Exposure—Two Decades Later: A Case Study .. 199
     Rae Fallon

13 My Body, My Biography: The Use of Narratives of Self-Injury
as a Path for Healing..209
Susan Anne Conte

14 Music and Emotion Regulation among Emerging Adults
in College...225
Janice C. Stapley

About the Contributors..239

FOREWORD

David Elkind

Life's transitions are never easy, but adolescence, the transition from childhood dependence to adult independence, is perhaps the most difficult of all. It is made even more hazardous today when technological and social changes are occurring at a more rapid pace than ever before in history. The adaptive challenges for the adolescent, for his or her parents, teachers, peers, and co-workers are greater and more varied than ever before.

This book is a testament to these challenges. It is also an acknowledgement that in many respects psychology is still at the natural history stage of inquiry. Many of the chapters in the book are qualitative interview investigations. And necessarily so. There are simply no units of humanity comparable to the units in physics, or in biology. I believe it was a wise, and in many ways, daring decision to celebrate qualitative research at a time when there is an academic bias towards experimentation.

The range of issues facing contemporary youth is so vast that the editors, of necessity, had to be selective. They have chosen to illustrate the diversity of the topics rather than a comprehensive treatment of a single theme. The problems chosen range from the communication between adolescent daughters and their mothers to the problems of Russian youth to issues of literacy in a communication age.

The chapters are uniformly well written and supported by both research and interview data. I believe the book will be of interest to all those who

Adolescence in the 21st Century, pages ix–x
Copyright © 2014 by Information Age Publishing

work with adolescents and to those who teach courses dealing with this age group. The book does a real service to the field by illustrating the many different ways contemporary society is impacting on youth.

PREFACE

Frances R. Spielhagen and Paul D. Schwartz

At its root meaning, the word *adolescence* implies developmental change and growth, the transition from the innocence of childhood to adulthood and its concomitant responsibility. The timing, parameters, and cultural variations and expressions of this transition have varied from generation to generation and culture to culture. In the Judeo-Christian tradition, age 13 has denoted the assumption of adult status through bar/bat mitzvah and confirmation ceremonies.

In the 19th century across the globe, children assumed their adult status also around age 13 when they finished formal school and/or entered the work force on farms or in factories. Adolescence as a developmental period that separated childhood from adulthood was not in existence. In the early 20th century, child labor laws, compulsory education mandates and the juvenile court system in the United States prohibited youth entering the workforce full time before age 16, hence rendering them incapable of assuming the independent stature of an adult. It was during this time that the term "adolescence" entered the American lexicon, and with it came the founding work of the father of adolescence as a field of study, G. Stanley Hall, who began the scientific study of this "new" developmental period.

By the 21st century, what used to be a brief period of transition, the teen years 13–19, began to become elongated at both ends of the paradigm. This new paradigm, *extended adolescence*, became the topic of conversation and scientific study among adults concerned with the young people in their

Adolescence in the 21st Century, pages xi–xiii
Copyright © 2014 by Information Age Publishing
All rights of reproduction in any form reserved.

lives, whether personally or professionally. The period of adolescence started earlier than the teen years, with the early onset of puberty as young as age 9 or 10, and extended beyond the teen years into the early and mid 20s. The expression "failure to launch" became a common refrain among parents and among educators, and with Dr Jeffrey Arnett's seminal work, the term "emerging adult" entered this adolescent paradigm as a newer developmental period. Other writers have uses the term "the Odyssey years" to describe the continued quest for identity and autonomy found among today's young adults.

In 2009, soon after the economic meltdown that affected the social and financial outlook for many across the globe, the Center for Adolescent Research and Development of Mount Saint Mary College set out to explore the current phenomenon of adolescent development under the umbrella title, *Adolescence in the 21st Century: Constants and Challenges.* CARD invited scholars across the U.S. and from abroad to submit their own research-based proposals on the forces affecting adolescent development in the current social, political, economic, and educational environment. CARD then organized and implemented three interdisciplinary research-based conferences, in an attempt to provide as many lenses as possible to explore the phenomenon of adolescence today.

In 2010, David Elkind kicked off the conference series with an overview of adolescent development throughout the latter half of the 20th century to the present day. Elkind, a prolific and seminal scholar in the area of adolescent development, and the author of the hallmark work, *The Hurried Child,* challenged the audience to continue the conversation in the coming months and years. In 2011, William Damon, director of the Stanford University Center on Adolescence spoke of his own research on civic engagement and purpose among adolescents today, and how he saw today's youth as drifting without an apparent moral compass. Finally, in 2012, Jeffrey Arnett spoke of his work on emerging adulthood and delayed adolescence and the issues that this developmental change had on the culture as a whole.

At all three conferences, scholars from the social sciences, education, business, and philosophy presented their findings to a large audience of academics, professionals working with adolescents, parents, and graduate and undergraduate students. This volume presents a rare interdisciplinary collection of research that explores the phenomenon of adolescence in the changing and fast-paced world of the 21st century. We have invited key researchers from the three CARD conferences to bring to light and to life the voices of the adolescents and young adults in their studies. For it is these voices that will inform the reader of both the unique and perennial concerns of this generation as it moves forward into adulthood. In this book, the intersection of the lenses of psychology, education, nursing, business, and philosophy, provides a comprehensive look at the lived experiences of adolescents today.

The Greek philosopher Plato is reputed to have bemoaned the manners and mores of the younger generation. Such concern is a constant of the adolescent experience. The challenge is to look behind the adolescent persona to what is really happening in their lives. This has been true in any time in history, but it is especially important in the opening decades of the 21st century, when so many sea-changes have affected the lives of those living in these tumultuous times.

The editors are grateful to the contributors for their willingness to lend their expertise to this volume. In addition, we extend our gratitude to Dr. Amanda Maynard, Dr. Sarah Uzelac, Dr. David Shaenfield, and Mrs. Kathleen McCoy for their work on the annual CARD conferences. We also would like to thank our graduate research assistants who have worked behind the scenes over the last several years and who promise to contribute in their own ways to future generations of adolescents: Lauren Kroll, Daniel Cantor, Matt Kimmerle, Jennifer Gregory, and Lauren Henry. Finally, without the support of Mount Saint Mary College and the vision of Father Kevin Mackin and Dr. Iris Turkenkopf, the Center for Adolescent Research and Development could not have accomplished this substantial contribution to our understanding of adolescence. We are grateful for the vision, support, and commitment to scholarship that the college has provided.

EXAMINING THE ADOLESCENT IN THE 21ST CENTURY

Frances Spielhagen and Paul Schwartz

This volume is the product of the collaboration of the scholars who shared their work at the three CARD conferences, under the umbrella theme of *Constants and Challenges.* We have divided the volume into three sections, with editors' introductions for each section.

Section 1 contains five chapters that deal with the constants of adolescent development. These chapters address a range of topics that explore the perennial stresses facing adolescents and contemporary responses to those stresses. In Chapter 1, "Seeking the Right Fit: From Training Bras to Self-Identity in Adolescents' Search for Self," Susan Riemer Sacks examines one of the universal and historical constants of adolescence, the development of a sense of a new and multidimensional identity. Through retrospection ("where have I been?"), introspection ("who am I now?"), and prospection ("where am I going and where do I want to end up?"), the adolescent/young adult solidifies an operating framework and personal identity that will serve him or her in adult life for the future.

Adolescence in the 21st Century, pages 1–2
Copyright © 2014 by Information Age Publishing

Communicating with an adolescent is often a daunting task at best. Chapter 2 further examines adolescent interactions with adults, specifically girls and their others. A recent title for a book on adolescence was titled, *I'd Listen to My Parents If They'd Just Shut Up* (Wolf, 2011). Such a title clearly illustrates the convoluted logical thinking, if you can call it that, of a typical adolescent. Debra Hrelic helps us see some parameters of the process of communication in Chapter 2, "Talk to Me.... Mothers' Experience of Communicating with their Young Adolescent Daughters."

In Chapter 3, "Parental Religiosity and Adolescent Educational Attainment," Gregory M. Eirich explores the role of religion and religiosity as potential variables in the adolescent's sense of identity and educational attainment. In particular, he examines here how parental religiosity affects the development of noncognitive skills and the intersection of those skills with educational attainment.

Another historical and cultural constant regarding adolescent development is change. Adolescents will always challenge the status quo and carve out their own culture with its own unique artifacts. In Chapter 4, David Gallagher discusses how technology and other variables have created a new cultural literacy among adolescents.

Finally, it is useful to examine the phenomenon of adolescence in environments outside the United States in the current shrinking global environment. With an ever-increasing recognition of the interrelatedness and blurring of cultural boundaries, CARD invited visiting Fulbright scholar Olga Lomakina to provide a cross-cultural examination of adolescence in post-Communist Russia. In Chapter 5, Dr. Lomakina and her colleague, Tatiana Gustomyasova, summarize the sociopsychological problems among youth in Russia in the new millennium.

These five chapters provide an interesting intersection of lenses on the phenomenon of adolescence in the early years of the 21st century.

REFERENCE

Wolf, A. (2011). *I'd listen to my parents if they'd just shut up.* New York, NY: Morrow.

CHAPTER 1

SEEKING THE RIGHT FIT

From Training Bras to Self-Identity as Adolescents Search for Self

Susan Riemer Sacks

The years between 11 and 21 represent a dramatic developmental decade. The pivotal years from early adolescence to young adulthood are exemplified by a range of physiological, sexual, cognitive, and psychological changes. It is common to describe this adolescent period as one of identity crisis, rebellion, self-consciousness, sexual exploration, peer engagement, promise and hope, anxiety, searching, and experimentation. In whatever terms adolescence is identified, it is a time in life that is marked by a quest for individual identity. The prevailing questions—Who am I? Who will I become?—permeate the mind and soul of adolescents, and whether or not these questions are answered with ease or with a battle remains each individual's "coming of age."

Theoretical paradigms from Freud to Mead to Erikson to Gilligan provide a framework to examine adolescents' search for their self identity. This chapter examines female college students' reflective writing about their teen years. During this critical time in their development, they cite many

Adolescence in the 21st Century, pages 3–21
Copyright © 2014 by Information Age Publishing
All rights of reproduction in any form reserved.

challenges as they negotiate between duty and desire, parental values and peer pressures, the mores of the times and the ways of their cultures. Fundamental life questions are raised, posed by various tensions, perceived and real. The young women present the essential dilemmas which challenge them: puberty, menarche, body image, transitions to new school levels, peer groups. Building on earlier studies, the chapter presents student voices that detail major concerns about "fitting in," "looking good," and "becoming an adult."

Grappling with a growing sense of oneself as a sexual being and searching for answers to "Who Am I?" and "Who Will I Become?" are challenges that necessarily reflect one's gender, race, economic status, ethnicity, and sexual preference. One of the more vexing dialectical characteristics of the teen years is the tension between "being like all others" versus "being unique and 'just me'." The chapter explores the relationship of emerging self-identity and the capacity for female adolescents to anchor themselves in activities through which they claim their place and sense of selfhood. The growth from preoccupations with training bras and physical development emerges to an analysis of social and emotional aspects of female identity and aspirations.

Adolescence occurs today in increasingly connected contexts, constantly broadening beyond the relationship of self and family to include connections to peers and multiple, social institutions. With technology, these connections may include all parts of the world, and whether or not the widespread use of technology will make identity formation more or less complicated remains to be examined a decade hence. Finding one's voice and one's sense of self are central to the developmental tasks of the adolescent decade. The argument in this chapter is not whether the period of adolescence exists, but rather that the tasks of the adolescent decade are complex aspects of an ever-evolving process of becoming a whole person.

Do the voices of today's women enlighten adolescent struggles? Over eight years from 2005 to 2012, 119 senior college women enrolled in an adolescent psychology seminar and began the class responding to the stem, "As an adolescent I..." All were teenagers during the early 21st century and are currently emerging into young adulthood. Understanding how they identified their struggles and the strategies they used to find strength in their selfhood may provide a path for others in their adolescent years.

Of the 119 women, nearly two-thirds (72) identified early adolescence as the most memorable time in their lives. The ages from 11 to 13 years preoccupied their current reflections with issues of personal development, both physical and familial, of interpersonal concerns with girl friends and boys, and of structural changes such as the move to middle school with new academic pressures. Preoccupation with puberty, differential rates of physical development, and the arousal of sexual desires led to being self-conscious, awkward, confused, insecure, easily distracted, conflicted, and competitive. The years from 11 to 13 were the transition years: new bodies, new schools, new friends, new goals. Without hesitation and no prompting, several women identified this early adolescent period as one of desire for physical development from training bras to real bras, to growing up!

Fewer of the seniors (17) cited the middle teen years from 14 to 16, and the dominant concerns of that period were challenges to parents' curfews and obtaining a driver's license. This was a period of testing the boundaries and of experimenting with drinking, drugs, piercings, hair dyeing. There was only a peripheral concern with responsibilities and relationships and the beginning of "thinking about consequences." One labeled these years as "a brief period of respite" between the emotional roller coaster of the early adolescent years and the stresses of the later ones.

By the late teens, between 17 and continuing, the focus begins to shift to the future, to college applications, to performance issues, to defining a "deeper identity." Interpersonal issues of friendship seemed less preoccupying and issues of "managing all aspects of my life" took over, as cited by 25 of the women. This latter shift in emphasis led to intrapsychological feelings of insecurity and questioning one's self and self-esteem. Tensions exist between the recognition that "I am not a child anymore" and the knowledge that "I am not an adult either." Several women focused on the experience of two worlds and two "homes"—one at school and one with family. The experience of sexual relationships and one's sexual identity took on deeper, more considered, and profound meaning. Five women identified the "teen years as tense" and overall difficult times for "finding" themselves.

Over the decade covering the teen years, the women identify their move from centering on their physical, sexual, and social development to broader relationships with peers, schools, and the future to the internal struggles that emerge between dependence versus independence. The women experienced their adolescent decade with their own voice and means of expression. For each there were intrapersonal foci on appearance, on body image, on self-identification. Anna Freud (1969) identifies the internal struggles, a serious reorganization of one's psyche. Interpersonally, family, peers, and friends were central, and for most the major struggles of identity seemed to take place in the community of others. In the larger scheme, there were concerns, and sometimes conflicts, with "the system" as the social structures were signified. Economic and cultural mores played a role in the aspirations and goals of the women as they moved toward adulthood.

BEGINNING THE QUEST OR WAITING TO GROW UP

This notion of "waiting" seemed to best represent the first theme expressed in one's evolving identity. One wrote:

> When I was an adolescent, I was perpetually waiting until I was no longer an adolescent.... There were no instruction manuals, so I didn't know when you were supposed to start wearing a bra.... The strange thing about adolescence is that I remember simultaneously wanting to be unique and individual—but with things like bras or periods, I wanted to be exactly on par with everyone else. Mainly, my adolescence could be summed up as an attempt to forge an identity that was unique, individual, and above all creative, while still remaining enough under the social radar so as not to be deemed strange or weird.

Another suggested, "I am a work in progress."

A plethora of identities emerged as the women responded to their adolescent selves. The following terms self-identify the women as they reflect on the tensions of their adolescent years: rebel, juggler, perfectionist, goody-goody, chameleon, caterpillar, alien, fantasizer, roller-coaster rider, and "an ugly duckling who becomes a swan." At any moment and for any length of time, a metaphor to express self-identity is embraced. As one stated, "I had a very hard time balancing who I thought I should be, who I thought I was, and how I saw others' expectations and perceptions of me." A second felt she "led somewhat of a dual life, happy on the outside and miserable within." A third felt "lost in my own skin." Finally the struggle, conflict, and tension were summed up: "I was many different people—never quite sure who I truly was or who I truly wanted to be."

THE "FITTING IN" DILEMMA

To *fit in* occurred as a major need over and over again in the voices of the women.

> As an adolescent I was a hundred different things, often all at the same time: lonely, depressed, exuberant, popular, unpopular, angry, ambitious, courageous, loyal, and both a good and bad friend.... The only one adjective that could consistently describe my adolescent experience would be self-involved.... Adolescence was a struggle for me to figure out who I was and where I fit in.... Adolescence was most notably in my mind the period during which I figured out what type of person I wanted to become and the time I hated most.... I was confident in the future, unhappy in the present, and thought that I was suffering more than anyone else had as an adolescent.

She sums up the tenderness, confusions, and longings of herself as a young adolescent. She reflects here the desire to *fit in* but is uncertain what she wants to fit in to. Her longings are part of the struggle for identity shared among her peers, even if she thinks she is "suffering" more than all others. And others do voice the same feelings:

> I remember how important it was to me to be wearing the right clothes, so that I could fit in.

> I think that "fitting-in" was a big challenge for me...and something that caused me a lot of anxiety.

> Others around me seemed to effortlessly maneuver the complicated social world of middle school and high school, while I wondered constantly what I was "supposed to" be doing to fit in.

> I was constantly trying to figure out who I was and decide whether or not I wanted to keep being that person.

> I did not fit in ethnically...(but) after a few months of therapy, I realized there was nothing wrong with me.

For adolescents who could not decide how they *fit in*, there was often a dramatic identity worthy of embracing. This is a period in life, wrote one,

> ...during which I struggled to create my *self* and my identity, eventually succeeding in balancing all these conflicting parts of my personality. What I have learnt is that inner stability can be achieved in the realization that one's individuality is always evolving.

The issue of "fitting in" dominates many of the responses, and the concern to be like all others versus being unique challenged all of the women. Erik Erikson (1950) set forth the questions that seem to occupy the students' reflective thoughts. The fundamental questions—Who am I? and Who will I become?—governed the adolescent period for this diverse group of college women. Some wrote that the quest continued as part of a process of growth; many believed that the major adolescent traumas were resolved by the time they were writing this essay as 21-year-old college seniors.

For female adolescents whose identity revolved around "fitting in" and physical development, time and maturation resolved some of their dilemmas. Today, the peak of pubertal change occurs at 11.5 years for girls and 13.5 years for boys. Whether early or late or part of the norm, once girls achieve menarche, the preoccupations about their physical development diminish as they progress physically.

DRAMA AND MERCURIAL EMOTIONS

Emotions often accompanied the *fit in* quest. This reflection stated the conflict experienced in this woman's adolescent years:

> ...filled with tension and anxiety.... I spent hours overanalyzing every single detail of all situations and became overwhelmingly self-conscious. Every aspect of life was stressful.... everything about my life was an extreme... disappointment and failure were my biggest fears.... My identity was at stake with each decision I made.... Each day and each year seemed as though they were forever.

"Hypersensitive about everything" was someone else's experience of the teen period. She wrote:

> I was always crying about something—my appearance, my weight and my social life. These sensitivities led to insecurities, the source of all of which were my parents and my older brother.

Her voice was seconded by:

> I hope when I am older I still remember how I catastrophized [sic] events because everything really is a big deal as a teenager.... I hope... to remember the struggles I went through and the pressures I faced to fit in and find a place for myself.

In his summary of adolescent storm and stress, Arnett (1999) cites numerous studies that supported the mood disruptions of adolescents. Expressions of emotional extremes appear to be more frequent among adolescents. The "beeper method" research indicated that adolescents reported feelings of self-consciousness, embarrassment, awkwardness, loneliness, invisibility, and nervousness more frequently than either adults or pre-adolescents. Some attributed the mood swings to cognitive and environmental factors because of adolescents' expanded capacities to reason abstractly and hypothesize about outcomes. While some of the women in this group recalled retrospectively experiencing mood changes, for many others, the period of adolescence was marked more clearly by other concerns.

THE BODY

The developing body dominated many a female's challenge to "fit in," and it extended the struggle to figure out her physical place among peers. All phases of puberty writ large became the teens' focus: body changes, its appearance, its image in the mirror. Voices ranged and raged:

> I was incredibly awkward. My body changed, I was not only taller than all the boys, but we had to wear bras and my boobs began to grow so I could no longer wear certain favorite shirts or fit into the pants I had bought only a few months ago . . . like your body was changing, you were changing, and you had no control of any of it. Your own body was morphing inside you, betraying the lines and shapes you had known your whole life . . . everything seemed to betray me.

> I was one of the first girls in my class to hit puberty. . . . I was becoming aware of my body. . . . I developed "breasts" [and] I was teased for the small lumps beneath the wool sweater vest of my school uniform. . . . I was beginning to look different. . . . I was uncomfortable in my own skin. It didn't seem to fit me. It felt fake. *I* felt fake.

> I vividly remember the overwhelming sense of preoccupation, if not obsession, with my weight, hair, and clothes. Every morning I stared at the mirror wishing that I were thinner, or that my hair was straighter and longer.

In navigating adolescence, the girls needed to feel control. The body issues took over their sense of control and empowerment. Until they got their voices back, until they felt that they fit in their own skins, the struggle was often overwhelming. Feeling to be a "fake" or an imposter indicated a diminished identity and was painful to acknowledge. The power of the need to belong, to conform, led the adolescent to "assume that everyone was staring at me . . . and whispering about it (my appearance) in the stalls of the girls' bathroom." To avoid this discontent, one woman expressed her empowerment,

> I began to exercise and diet compulsively, determined to control and perfect my body as I could not the rest of my life. . . . Though it was a constant struggle, the intense satisfaction I felt from depriving myself made everything worth it.

Body image, on the other hand, remained a concern of the women into adulthood. It was mentioned in passing in their writing and in discussions and was expressed as an awareness of self-presentation, style, weight, and dressing up for interviews. While this focus is not the same as the earlier preoccupation with one's physical development and almost obsessive concern to "fit in," it remains important in young women's lives.

COGNITION PROPELS DEVELOPMENT

For some adolescents their intellects saved them from a negative path. A wide spectrum of supports "saved" the adolescent girls for whom physical developmental issues were not mentioned as salient. Biology did not govern their reflections. One represented adolescence as a time of growth, less painful and more expansive in retrospect. She experienced adolescence as an exploratory time

> ...where I was able to find out a lot about myself—my personal wishes, desires, goals, and values. I also found out a lot about the world around me: friendships, relationships, and a deeper understanding of text and philosophical thought....The road from adolescence into young adulthood was not completely bumpy. My curiosity raised many questions, but allowed me to find many answers...and to examine social and philosophical thought....I am thankful that I had a strong support system of friends, family and teachers who helped guide me through both a rough and beautifully developing time in my life.

Relying on family and friends boasted her confidence to use her cognitive ability to seek and solve answers to "who I am and what I will become." The culture of her society became part of her development and spurred her to broaden her thinking. Jean Piaget (1947) identifies adolescents in the "formal operations" stage of cognitive development where the individual can reason abstractly and think hypothetically. During this period, meta-cognitive analyses can take place, and the adolescent can think about how she is thinking, postulating, and reflecting. Within the cocoon of "a strong support system," her intellectual curiosity guided the adolescent's path.

Two others came to self-realization about their cognitive development:

> Eventually, being smart was cool, as long as you weren't the type to ostracize yourself....In junior high school...the choice was between being cool and being smart. In high school, I was much less reserved about being intelligent.

And,

> I devoted myself to school and other intellectual activities. The few hours per day that I was alone, I spent most of the time preparing for school. Thereby, I gained a lot of self-esteem.

The strength of being smart and using one's smarts buoyed the self-identity of several of the teenagers as they began to take strength from their minds.

FAMILY

One's family provided a core support or a serious problem. A teen's family life can lead to stress, and one's "self-esteem issues regarding self-worth" emerged from "instability within my home." Abuse may occur. Or the home can foster attitudes and values cherished later:

> I was open minded in regards to sexuality. I was raised in ... a liberal town with a prominent homosexual community. My constant exposure and inter-actions with families and friends with two moms, two dads, or transgender parents made me accepting and in support of the "non-traditional" fam-ily.... [F]oster(ing) a natural tolerance for "difference" (as determined by society and cultural "norms") is something that I am incredibly grateful for today.

For some, the roles and responsibilities they had to assume in the family led to a resistance to think about self-development. Many experienced self-pressures that were internalized from external burdens. Responsibilities were often expressed by oldest daughters, girls who were the first in the family to go to college, females who needed to work to help the family finances. These challenges led to being "socially awkward and angst-ridden," wrote one teen of an "immigrant single mother in New York City." Another started working and earning money when she was twelve years old, and she felt, "I had no clue how to interact with my peers, and because of this I never went through a lot of experiences... [like] parties, pressure to drink or do drugs." These women do not associate loneliness with social anxiety, but rather recognize a different set of experiences and desires.

RELATIONSHIPS MATTER

Beyond family, one close friend, either boy or girl, can help to settle the ambiguities of the adolescent years for others. One wrote, "I got the courage to ask an acquaintance (a boy) from middle school to walk with me to school every morning.... I was very comfortable and took part in many clubs and organizations.... I built up a lot of confidence and self-esteem." She needed to accommodate the physical, mental, and social changes before she "was capable of shaping who I am." Connecting to another person in a deeply companionable manner and building stable relationships helped propel the adolescent toward maturity.

The concepts of relationship and connection advocated by Jean Baker Miller (1976) and Carol Gilligan (1982) form the lasting bond that enabled many teens to forge their own identities. An only girl in a family of five brothers, another felt "lost in the shuffle" in a "turbulent male household."

Friendships with girls became the source for respite and modeling and the path through adolescence.

> Luckily, I had three best friends throughout my adolescent years whom I could rely on to listen to my complaints and offer support.... Those crazy, turbulent years were always softened by the caring and support those wonderful girls provided.... Whenever my life seemed out of control or incredibly unfair, I could always turn to my dear friends who could always put things back into perspective for me.

The power of chumship and close friendships signaled the development of new social relationships as the individual moved from childhood to adolescence. Harry Stack Sullivan (in Muuss, 1953) proposes the significance of relationships, and his theoretical work coupled with Gilligan's understandings of women's voices shaped the context for understanding this adolescent's safety net of girlfriends.

Rising self-awareness was also reflected by "I was starting to understand my*self* during this process.... Others' perspectives were becoming a variable in how I defined myself." Rising cultural awareness was gained by a Caucasian/Cuban teen who wrote,

> I was different in the way I enjoyed spending my time, the food I ate, and what I was allowed to do.... It wasn't until my third year in high school that I embraced these differences and allowed myself to be different from most of my classmates. Being myself was a sort of relief.... I became much more confident and happy.

In many cases the teens found support when they "realized my parents, my grandparents and the past traditions I tried to overlook helped me find myself in light of the new world I lived in." Another found a "boy who save[d] me from drowning in my own (social) phobia." Yet another was anchored by "my friends, unconditional love and support. I needed to explore and discover myself, without the fear of rejection." Friends provided support "to gain independence from my parents" who over sheltered her "due to my traditional South Asian upbringing." Finally, one of the few of the 119 women who mentioned a teacher wrote of the power of "a very close relationship with my piano teacher ... the only adult that I really trusted." The teacher saved this teen from feeling alone and seeking a negative lifestyle. Of all supports mentioned by the women, friends dominated their writing, while family members were frequently included as well.

Risk behaviors occur more frequently among adolescents than other age groups, but pushing the boundaries in some form seemed to be part of the transition to adulthood. Norm-breaking and antisocial behaviors were not uncommon in the areas of substance, drug, and alcohol use. Risky driving was less frequent among these women, many of whom came from an urban environment where driving among teens is not as common as for those in the suburbs or rural areas. In the high schools where programs are initiated for abuse prevention, the risky behaviors have been reduced. In the area of unprotected sexual activity as a risk behavior, warnings about AIDS and HIV from family members, teachers, mentors, group and religious leaders, and peers have had a significant influence and impact among these women.

Nearly all of the young women agreed that they struggled from time to time during their teen years, but that the vacillations were shared by others around them, were anticipated and even expected, and were merely part of the developmental process. It is important to acknowledge that these women are writing reflectively as young adults at a selective university. They represent a broad economic, racial, ethnic, and religious group, but are generally characterized as women with an independent mindset, willing to buck trends, take a stand for their beliefs, and live in New York City and thrive. It was important to consider what propelled them forward when considering their verve during the adolescent years.

PILLAR FOR EACH

Strategies and passions emerged to help the teens move to a new level of identity development. In addition to support from family, friends, and an occasional teacher, religious leader, or therapist, the adolescents found strength in organizations. For someone "between various worlds: black and white, social and asocial, desirable and undesirable," a channel was open in the Black Student Union and the Diversity Committee. For an athlete, being on two varsity teams led one to say, "Thank god for sports." Sports could well be substituted for art, dance, drama, music, camp, books. For the journalist and thespian, editing the yearbook and "acting in one of the lead roles in my school play" brought "comfort. To deal with "social anxiety... and translate that anxiety into action and to work to help other adolescents get through theirs," one became a "Student Government officer and later a Peer Advisor." In the end, she wrote she satisfied the two parts of her personality: "the scared child that seeks to understand those around her... and the active doer who believes that through understanding systems and taking action, things can be fixed [and this is] also why I majored in psychology and political science." Often, adolescents form or join groups to take action for a cause. These groups may even take the shape of cliques or gangs with the power to intimidate as well as to move for positive good. For the teen, however, they serve the purpose of identification and relationship.

Other women found solace and support in the passions of their lives. Totally immersed in physical or athletic commitments, three women found support to grow through physical training. From the age of 12 until late in her junior year in high school when she "retired," one devoted herself to gymnastics. "I was a fiercely determined and dedicated young woman hoping to qualify for the Olympic games in rhythmic gymnastics," she wrote. Then when the coach was forced to retire, she felt "as if I had been stripped of my identity." In reflecting, she found that "if it weren't for faith, I wouldn't have been able to get through that time." She also found a love of dance and used "dance to heal both myself and those who are watching." An early passion, even when thwarted, can transform the adolescent's dreams and help her find a focus.

Another "loved classical music and books for adults, and I was very involved in Classical Ballet." Abandoned by both parents and raised by an older sister in Switzerland until she was 15, she grew up "very fast." "Dancing provided a home for me . . . based on a scholarship to a ballet academy in London." Settled and alone in London, the void of family was filled by ballet and the camaraderie of the corps. Whether ballet or gymnastics, both of these teens found strength and identity in the physical discipline of their passions. Physical endeavors have been the source of identity for many of the young women.

Athletics has long been the province of boys as a developmental outlet. But in 1972 the U.S. Congress passed Title IX of the Education Act to make women's athletics more equitable. One's adolescence in California was defined by softball: "Having a team to which I 'belonged' as a group with a common goal, was a terrific experience." The positives were profound in terms of team friendships, of staying physically fit, of traveling together with teammates. Nevertheless, these strengths were sometimes challenged because the boys in her classes viewed her as "one of the guys," not as a partner for the "slow dance on Saturday night." She grew beyond her social anguish and captained her softball team to a winning season. Long overlooked as a domain to develop identity, sports strengthened the girls in the transition to adulthood.

From loneliness and aloneness to belonging, even initiating, teens gain self-awareness and the self knowledge for healing, for growth, and for identity solidification. Though some escaped for a time into drinking and drug-taking, these women fundamentally turned anger, hurt, confusion, frustration, and rebellion into education, career, and relationships. Self-realization and a sense of freedom and confidence usually emerged late in adolescence: "I realized I was in charge of the changes I want to make and the person who I wanted to be."

Through the auspices of school and its activities, several of the women found the structures that guided them through adolescence and into adulthood. One wrote:

> I got involved in theatre...was exposed to an entirely new set of possibilities...to flout rules and give voice to dissent....I managed to be a rebel and a good girl at the same time....I maintained excellent relationships with my parents and never did anything that really disappointed or worried them.

Like sports and physical activity, theatre and a unique group of friends showed her how to be "different" and yet driven to succeed. Finding that delicate balance of merging the good girl and the rebel in an individualized way demonstrated strength and courage.

Other pillars were anchored in one's religious commitments. One found the "reason for being in my faith." Her feelings during adolescence were that her friends became her family, "and my own family were my enemies...I was lost and I knew it, but I couldn't help it....I think a lot of my adolescent years were focused on looking for answers and searching for ways to be 'un-lost'." Feeling lost is another aspect that leads adolescents to search for meaning in life. The power of spirituality changed this teen's life, her path, and her power. Her voice took on a keen and clear trajectory, and she found a "shield" for grappling with growth and change. As James Fowler (1981) suggests, faith answers the fundamental questions for some seekers: "What is the point of all this? What is worth living for?" One woman wrote, "I found my answers in faith...and since that moment of 'conversion,' I never turned back." The strength of faith focused the direction of the believer.

One summarizes the teen years as she experienced them: "I was a well-rounded kid who enjoyed those teenage years—for the most part." She remembers "experiencing moments of extreme emotional highs and lows" with friends, family, and school activities. She found learning as her direction and was guided by her passion that "education is the only thing that lasts. Once you learn something, no one can take it away from you. It's the power that can change your life." Reflecting resiliency and dedication, she represents the persistent adolescent who succeeds by excelling in school and extracurricular activities and by avoiding or circumnavigating the negative distractions and pitfalls.

She embraced protective factors and avoided risk factors in her poverty environment to graduate from college. She worked diligently, dreamed big, stayed focused, set standards, kept her "eyes on the finish line and refused to become distracted by negative things on the sideline." Her strength lay in learning and "resiliency, a deep determination to succeed—even in the presence of adversity...resiliency is a state of mind, an act of being that allows individuals to set and exceed their own expectations by defying all odds." This philosophy served as her mantra and thrust her into maturity. The philosophy helped many a teen to walk through the arc of the teen years.

COMING OF AGE AND BALANCING STRESSES

Toward the end of the high school years, most confessed, as one wrote, that "adolescence was a struggle to figure out who I was and where I fit in . . . but I had unwavering confidence in the future." Another wrote, "Instead of trying to become someone else, I have been constantly trying to become a better me." Or, "I merely began to discover my true self, I realized that sometimes it is best to act your own age. After all, there is no rush." Some used the adolescent years as "a time of finding myself, of exploring, and of just being." Another thought, "I have grown to accept myself, and I see my adolescence as a long, painful period of self-discovery, without which I would not have found the self I have become." A true sign of freedom for one preoccupied with "constantly trying to figure out who I was and deciding whether or not I wanted to keep being that person" was the decision to stop "blow drying my hair and let my curls be free, a symbol of my commitment to being myself."

To embrace and accept one's unique identity, though challenging, is part of the maturing process. The adolescents began to accept segments of their identity that they had earlier dismissed when they were preoccupied with peer acceptance and approval.

> I knew that authentic was better than fake, but I was being bombarded with words and images telling me otherwise. Straightening my hair is one way that my young self dealt (and didn't deal) with these adolescent struggles.

Identity covers a broad sweep among the women and must be self-defined by each. Whether one learns to cherish her curly hair or her nerdish ways, her athleticism or her faith, her culture or her race, this became an articulation of self. During adolescence, family and friends often supported and reinforced characteristics of self-identity, but all along the person was evolving her own selfhood.

Many sources provide attachment for adolescents to pull themselves through the decade of potential *strum and drang*, as G. Stanley Hall identified the period in his work *Adolescence* (in Muuss, 1916). Hall argued that development and behavior occur in an inevitable, unchangeable, and universal way. *Sturm and Drang* served as the motto for Hall's adolescents, vacillating between bursts of joy and exuberance and deep valleys of doubt and anxiety. Yet the adolescent voices recorded here envisioned the period as increasingly one of process, of control, of multiple experiences, and of strengthening challenges. Many found their adolescence shaped or influenced by the social environment of family, peers, school, religion, and community. Some considered adolescence as part of the ups and downs of development, others reflected on survival in a toxic world, others turned to a multiplicity of supports. They seemed to concur that it is a period of challenges and some extremes, and they did believe that all girls everywhere must find the right fit—but each would assert that it must be the right fit for her!

No one questioned whether or not there was an adolescent period, and all agreed that the decade exists with particular growth and with personal "coming of age." Without question, the earliest period of adolescence became the focus of young adult memories, and the early teen years evolved in clear relief. These were the times when relationship with parents may have caused the most conflicts. As the young adolescent struggled to define herself, she sought independence from her parents and their boundaries. Studies by Laursen, Coy, and Collins (1998) concluded that parental conflict frequency was highest in early adolescence and its intensity the greatest in mid-adolescence. Nevertheless, in reflection, parents did matter, and the more they were willing to engage their adolescents in conversation, the better the outcome, according to William Glasser (2002). Glasser advocated that parents "give up direct control" over their adolescents and the gain would be "more indirect control...through a stronger and happier relationship" (2002, p. 111). Adolescents pushed the boundaries just far enough to see where the walls were, as noted in remarks above. Somehow maintaining the connection remains the key parental role and probably will remain so for the entire 21st century. However, the connections may come via technology.

IDENTITY ACHIEVEMENT, OR WE ARE NEARLY THERE!

By late adolescence, these women knew they were college bound, they had direction, they had determination, and they possessed a sense of self often gathered through relationships. The struggle of identity development no longer centered on figuring out who "I might be," but in letting everyone know "who I think I might become." It was not as though identity was fixed, but rather it was *imagined* more clearly. What seemed really to matter varied from person to person, but what propelled each and every one of the women was an attachment to something. Regardless of economic status or race or sexual identity, the women's passions developed during their high school years and shaped their identities. Whether faith, ritual, sport, theatre, school activities, writing, or social action, the women found friendships and formed deep relationships that helped to build their identities.

These women did not have to hide their voices under a calm demeanor; rather, they found supporters for their emotional identities. Comfort in relationships led to comfort in achievement identity.

Erikson (1950) long ago suggested that industry precedes intimacy in his developmental stages. But his subjects were male and they clarified "Who am I?" and "Who will I become?" by focusing on achievement and success. Once clear about his identity, the male adolescent would form an intimate heterosexual relationship, according to Erikson. Miller (1976), Gilligan (1982), and Martin (1996) question this trajectory for females and have argued that deep relationships are the foundation for women's achievement identities.

RETHINKING ADOLESCENCE

In this chapter I posit that the characteristics which traditionally embrace the period of adolescence must be more openly defined. The changes which occur during the years from 11 to 21 are many and powerful. Physically, sexually, physiologically, psychologically, cognitively, and socially—the decade is one of profound development.

But it is not for each and every person a period of struggle and stress. Nor is it a smooth sail. Rather than box adolescents by adult definitions, the argument is for more elastic, even fluid, boundaries, so that as new skills and understandings are learned and mastered, the boxes have "give."

Stereotypes are dangerous (see Steele, 1997, for full discussion). At a vulnerable time of searching and seeking, adolescents must not be cast into roles or singular identities. Not all boys are aggressive, not all girls are attractive, not all Asian students are math whizzes, not all adolescents living in poverty are poor performers, and not all "jocks" are academically inadequate. Adults nod and agree not to stereotype, but so often do. It is extremely important for the influential adults—whether parents, leaders, teachers, or any significant others—to open and expand their perceptions about expected performance. During the transition period of adolescence, even the girl with purple and orange hair and the boy with over-sized baggie pants can outsmart the adults with their wit and abilities or their sensitivity and compassion, if given a chance. Piercings may represent expressiveness, and rap may be poetry if adults listen carefully. As one of the "model minorities" stated, "It makes me feel so angry about the stereotypes that some [Asian] adolescents are trying to uphold in our society and believe they are failures when they are not fulfilling their academically brilliant 'role'." Deviant does not equal bad. Society can accept, or at least tolerate and surely understand, those behaviors that "do no harm."

The most serious problem with a narrow vision for the adolescent experience is that there are costly consequences when unresolved adolescents enter adulthood. Mental illness and self-harm are outgrowths of thwarted identity development. The broader the definitions and the more diverse the possibilities, the greater the chance is that each adolescent will find the "right fit" for herself or himself. There are many phenomena involved in identity formation and its continuation during adulthood. In contemporary times, many contextual issues must be considered to understand each individual's development. As one's identity grows and shifts over a lifetime, the "right fit" will re-form itself.

In contemporary, Western society, adolescence is a powerful developmental period. Adolescents are cognitively ready to think abstractly and reflect and remember during this period of life, and its influence on adulthood is gripping. Looking back, people just do not forget 8th grade or 11th grade! There is no perfectly smooth path. For some, the teen years are peaceful, full of developing competence, confidence, connections, character depth, and compassion, along with the positive sense of making a contribution to society. For others, the years are full of mood swings, emotional highs and lows, risk-taking, and stress with family, friends, and school. For most, however, there is a balance between peaceful periods and stormy ones, and this is the "normal." On the other side of adolescence is the formed identity of "Who you are!" and "Who you may still become!

NOTE

Graduates of Barnard College and Columbia University from 2005 through 2012 who were enrolled in a seminar, Adolescent Psychology, gave permission to quote from their papers. However, no names have been used in the chapter. These women are the source of my inspiration to teach adolescent psychology and to try to understand adolescents. To each I am most grateful. It is with much appreciation that I acknowledge Emily Thomas, a 2011 graduate of Barnard College, who assisted with identifying quotations chosen for this chapter.

REFERENCES

Arnett, J. J. (1999). Adolescent storm and stress. *American Psychologist, 54*(5), 317–326.

Erikson, E. H. (1950). *Childhood and society.* New York, NY: Norton.

Fowler, J. W. (1981). *Stages of faith: The psychology of human development and the quest for meaning.* San Francisco, CA: Harper and Row.

Freud, A. (1969). Adolescence. In *The Writings of Anna Freud* (Vol. V, 1956–1965). New York, NY: International Universities Press, Inc.

Gilligan, C. (1982). *In a different voice: Psychological theory and women's development.* Cambridge, MA: Harvard University Press.

Glasser, W. (2002). *Unhappy teenagers: A way for parents and teachers to reach them.* New York, NY: HarperCollins.

Hall, G. S. (1916). *Adolescence* (Vol. 1–2). New York, NY: Appleton.

Laursen, B., Coy, K. C., & Collins, W. A. (1998). Reconsidering changes in parent–child conflict across adolescence: A meta-analysis. *Child Development, 69,* 817–832.

Martin, K. (1996). *Puberty, sexuality and the self: Girls and boys at adolescence.* New York, NY: Routledge.

Miller, J. B. (1976). *Toward a new psychology of women.* Boston, MA: Beacon Press.

Muuss, R. (1996). *Theories of adolescence* (6th ed). New York, NY: McGraw-Hill.

Piaget, J. (1947). *The psychology of intelligence.* New York, NY: Harcourt, Brace.

Steele, C. (1997). A threat in the air: How stereotypes shape intellectual identity and performance. *American Psychologist, 52*(6), 613–629.

Sullivan, H. S. (1953). *The interpersonal theory of psychiatry.* New York, NY: Norton.

The following books contain additional perspectives

Atkins, D. (Ed.). (1998). *Looking queer: Body image and identity in lesbian, gay, bisexual and transgender communities.* Binghamton, NY: Harrington Park Press.

Austin, W. (2003). *First love: The adolescent's experience of amour.* New York, NY: Peter Lang.

Belenky, M. F., Clinchy, B. M., Goldberger, N. R., & Tarule, J. M. (1986). *Women's ways of knowing.* New York, NY: Basic Books.

Brock, R. (2005). *Sista talk: The personal and the pedagogical.* New York, NY: Peter Lang.

Brod, H., & Kaufman, M. (Eds.). (1994). *Theorizing masculinities.* Thousand Oaks, CA: Sage.

Bukowski, W., Newcomb, A., & Hartup, W. (1996). *The company they keep: Friendship in childhood and adolescence.* New York, NY: Cambridge University Press.

Cote, J. (2000). *Arrested adulthood: The changing nature of maturity and identity.* New York, NY: NYU Press.

D'Augelli, A., & Patterson, C. (Eds.). (1995). *Lesbian, gay and bisexual identities over the lifespan: Psychological perspectives.* New York, NY: Oxford University Press.

Gardner, H. (1993). *Multiple intelligences: The theory in practice.* New York, NY: Basic Books.

Garrod, A., Smulyan, L., Powers, S. I., & Kilkenny, R. (Eds.). (2012). *Adolescent portraits* (7th ed). Boston, MA: Allyn and Bacon.

Gilligan, C., & Brown, L. (1994). *Meeting at the crossroads.* New York, NY: Ballantine Books.

Graber, J., Brooks-Gunn, J., & Peterson, A. (Eds.). (1996). *Transitions through adolescence.* Mahwah, NJ: Lawrence Erlbaum Associates.

Jordan, J., Kaplan, A. G., Miller, J. B., Stiver, I. P., & Surrey, J. L. (1991). *Women's growth in connection.* New York, NY: The Guilford Press.

Kantrowitz, B., & Springen, K. (2005, April 25). A peaceful adolescence. *Newsweek,* 58–61.

Klass, P., & Costello, E. (2003). *Quirky kids: Understanding and helping your child who doesn't fit in—When to worry and when not to worry.* New York, NY: Ballantine.

McLaughlin, M., & Heath, S. (Eds.). (1993). *Inner city youth: Beyond ethnicity and gender.* New York, NY: Teachers College Press.

Miron, L., & Lauria, M. (1998). Student voice as agency: Resistance and accommodation in inner-city schools. *Anthropology and Education Quarterly, 29*(2), 189–213.

Moran, J. (2000). *Teaching sex: The shaping of adolescence in the 20th century.* Cambridge, MA: Harvard University Press.

Moshman, D. (1999). *Adolescent psychological development: Rationality, morality and identity.* Mahwah, NJ: Lawrence Erlbaum Associates.

Root, M. (Ed.). (1996). *The multiracial experience.* Thousand Oaks, CA: Sage.

Savin-Williams, R. C. (2005). *The new gay teenager.* Cambridge, MA: Harvard University Press.

Scherer, M., (Ed.). (2005). The adolescent learner [Special Issue]. *Educational Leadership, 62*(7), 1–96.

Suskind, R. (1998). *A hope in the unseen.* New York, NY: Broadway Books.

Tatum, B. (1992). Talking about race, learning about racism, *Harvard Educational Review, 62*(1), 1–24.

Taylor, R., & Wang, M. (Eds.). (2000). *Resilience across contexts.* Mahwah, NJ: Lawrence Earlbaum.

Ward, J. V. (1996). Raising resisters: The role of truth telling in the psychological development of African American girls. In B.J. Leadbetter and N.Way, (Eds.). *Urban girls: Resisting stereotypes, creating identities* (pp. 85–99). New York, NY: NYU Press.

Way, N. (1998). *Everyday courage: The lives and stories of urban teenagers.* New York, NY: NYU Press.

Wilson, B. L., & Corbett, H. D. (2001). *Listening to urban kids: School reform and the teachers they want.* Albany, NY: State University of New York Press.

CHAPTER 2

"TALK TO ME..."

Communication Between Mothers and Young Adolescent Daughters

Debra A. Hrelic

ABSTRACT

Communication between mothers and daughters has long been described as tumultuous, and often unpredictable. The mother–daughter relationship itself is one that changes throughout life, and adolescence is often anticipated with trepidation as a period of development. An often negative connotation is "well supported" in the popular media and may be responsible for mothers approaching communication with their adolescent daughters with a preconceived tainted view. Communication is characterized as difficult, even before it occurs. This leads one to question the phenomenon of mother–adolescent daughter communication, and to ponder whether the experience is indeed a common negative occurrence.

In response to these implications, earlier research (Hrelic, 2002) studied the issue of communication between mothers and their older adolescent (13–19 years old) daughters. That study portrayed positive relationships and good communication, in contrast to popular belief. Mothers described a "sharing connection" with their daughters and a "trans-generational growth and

Adolescence in the 21st Century, pages 23–38
Copyright © 2014 by Information Age Publishing

23

development" as relationships between mothers and their adolescent daughters evolve.

An implication for further study was to explore communication with mothers and young adolescent daughters to determine whether conflict is more likely to be found with this age group. The original study (Hrelic, 2002) was replicated with mothers of younger adolescent daughters between 11 and 13 years of age and in the 6th–8th grade in school. This study reflects the unique perspective of mothers living the experience of communicating with their young adolescent daughters.

BACKGROUND

Scientific and popular literature abounds with sources related to parenting issues, adolescents, parent–adolescent relationships, and in particular, communication regarding sex or sex-related topics—pregnant adolescents—and "teen moms." However, intensive literature reviews throughout the past 15 years have revealed large gaps in knowledge pertaining to mother–adolescent daughter communication, and even less regarding mother–young adolescent daughter communication. The research and studies cited in this work, though older than preferable in scientific research, remain valid and reliable.

A mother–daughter relationship is a complex phenomenon that dynamically changes throughout one's lifespan. During childhood, mothers and daughters often share an intimate and special bond with one another. This relationship becomes more fragile during adolescence. Mothers as well as their adolescent daughters must adjust to this naturally occurring ebb and flow. When mother–daughter relationships are viewed as harmonious and supportive, adolescent daughters are more likely to successfully handle the challenges of adolescence and develop greater self-esteem (Gross & McCallum, 2000), showing fewer symptoms of depression (Hales, 1999). It is believed that "a mother's self-esteem has more influence on a girl's self-confidence than any other factor" (Hales, 1999, p. 148).

Communication is a crucial element of role adjustment, mutual trust, and shared understanding (Yowell, 1997). Approximately 15–20% of adolescents aged 12 through 17 years experience parent–adolescent communication problems (Reed & Dubow, 1997). Mothers and daughters use differing conversational styles and therefore experience conflict in communication efforts with each other (Beaumont, 2000). Mothers often overestimate their knowledge regarding their teens' friends and activities, as well as the actual amount of information their daughters chose to disclose to them (Orell-Valente, Hill, Alegre, & Halpern-Felsher, 2007). A social psychologist and author from Cambridge University, Teri Apter notes in her book *You*

Don't Really Know Me: Why Mothers and Daughters Fight and How Both Can Win (2004) that a typical adolescent girl will experience a conflict with a parent (mostly her mother) every two and a half days.

Much of the existing research in the area of mother–adolescent communication focuses on issues of sexual communication and family dynamics in general (Coffelt, 2010; Meneses, Orell-Valente, Guendelman, Oman, & Irwin, 2006; Rosenthal, Feldman, & Edwards, 1998; Stiffler, Sims, & Stern, 2007). Recent research (Aronowitz & Agbeshie, 2012) investigated the nature of communication between African American mothers and their adolescent daughters regarding verbal and nonverbal sexual communication. Findings indicated that by reacting less and becoming more knowledgeable of their daughter's responses, mothers can create an environment more emotionally conducive to positive communication. This in turn can lead to more comfortable initiation of sexual communication by adolescents. Other research confirms that both male and female adolescents were more likely to discuss sexual topics with their mothers than with their fathers, stressing the importance of fostering good and comfortable communication between parents and adolescents about sexual issues (Dilorio & Hockenberry-Eaton, 1999). In family communication, the mother is often identified as the primary communicator about sexual issues, regardless of the adolescent's gender (Miller, Dorsey, Forehand, & Ham, 1998).

Gross and McCallum (2000) explored the relationship between mother–daughter "synchrony" and its affect on an adolescent girls' self-esteem and academic ability. This study acknowledged that good communication between mother and daughter is necessary to establish a synchronous relationship that leads to attachment and mutual support (Gross & McCallum, 2000). The concept of "maternal acceptance" has been longitudinally examined (Hare, Marston, & Allen, 2011) as a predictor of emotional disclosure in adolescent communication with their mothers. Findings supported that adolescents' perceptions of emotional disclosure during communication is an ongoing and important process that can be supported during early adolescence. Maternal perception of influence was not found to be predictive of emotional disclosure. An earlier study looked at mothers' perceptions about themselves and parenting, an area infrequently explored in recent research (Riesch, Coleman, Glowacki, & Konings, 1997). Mothers identified differences between putting their ideals about parenting into practice, identifying their own upbringing and adolescence as influential to mothering and the desire to seek out additional knowledge and skills to improve mothering as important to them. This research showed that mothers used decision-making methods and trying to understand their child's perspective as the basis of their parenting styles (Riesch et al., 1997).

Often, the mother–adolescent daughter relationship is portrayed as tumultuous (Dellasega, 2001; Pipher, 2002; Shandler, 2002). This very

negative connotation is understandably undesirable and may be responsible for mothers approaching communication with a tainted view. Communication is often characterized as difficult, even before it occurs. This leads
one to question the phenomenon of mother–young adolescent daughter
communication, and to ponder whether the experience is indeed a common negative occurrence. In contrast to these implications, earlier research
(Hrelic, 2002) studied the issue of communication between mothers and
their adolescent (13–19 years old) daughters. That study portrayed positive
relationships and good communication, in contrast to popular belief. An
implication for further study was to explore communication with mothers
and young adolescent (11–13 year old) daughters to determine whether
conflict is more likely to be found with this age group. Another author offers a possible explanation for the positive findings of Hrelic (2002).

> By the end of adolescence, they (adolescent girls) emerge from the long
> metamorphosis into womanhood as bigger, stronger, smarter versions of their
> former selves. What we—mothers, fathers, loved and loving ones—can offer
> as they make their way through this sometimes daunting passage is our faith,
> even at the darkest moments, in the strong, resilient, and wiser women they
> are in the process of becoming. (Hales, 1999, p. 149)

A developmental difference between young adolescence and older adolescence is often clear. The answers to the questions raised about younger
adolescent girls, in relation to communication with their mothers, can only
be revealed by exploring the phenomenon and by conducting scientific and
scholarly inquiry. The act of communication involves not only verbal discussion, but also nonverbal expression of one's thoughts and feelings. This research will include any form of communication between mothers and their
young adolescent daughters deemed worthy of mention by participants.

STUDY DESIGNS AND METHODS

Study Design

A descriptive qualitative approach, influenced by phenomenology, was
used to explore the experience of mothers communicating with their
young adolescent daughters. Descriptive phenomenology aims to study the
lived experience as it is experienced.

This study was an exploration of communication practices between
mothers and their young adolescent daughters, from the mothers' perspective. Communication in this study referred to information shared or
exchanged between mothers and daughters. Communication could be verbal—using words or sounds, or nonverbal—using touch, eye contact, or

action. Written communication would also be a form of nonverbal communication. Young adolescents for the purposes of this study, were defined as 11–13 years of age and in 6th–8th grade in school. There were no age restrictions on the mothers in this study. Institutional Review Board (IRB) approval for this study was obtained.

Participants of this study were required to be mothers of young adolescent daughters. Mothers needed to be currently living the experience of communication with their young adolescent daughters, and be able to verbalize that experience. Participants were required to be English speaking. There were no restrictions as to the number of children they mother, or the birth order of those children. A nonrandom, purposive convenience sample of mothers with young adolescent daughters who met the above stated criteria was sought for this study. Participants were queried about meeting the stated criteria and their interest in participating in an interview regarding the phenomenon of study. Selection of participants was purposeful in relation to the age limitations of the young adolescent daughters. Participation in this study was entirely voluntary, and informed consent was given.

Data collection consisted of one-on-one guided interviews with participants. Individual interviews were audio taped, for the purpose of accurate transcription. Data were collected, interviews were transcribed, numbers were assigned to each interview, and once transcribed, audio tapes were then destroyed. Confidentiality was maintained.

As a descriptive qualitative study, data collection and analysis were influenced by Colaizzi's (1978) descriptive phenomenological method. Colaizzi holds that participants are co-researchers in the inquiry of the lived experience. The dialog between the researcher and the "co-researchers" permits the discovery of the true essence of the lived experience (Beck, 1994; Colaizzi, 1978; Sanders, 2003). Colaizzi also states that the participant is the expert of her own reality and is the best qualified to validate study findings (Beck, 1994; Colaizzi, 1978; Sanders, 2003). In descriptive phenomenology, meaning lies in the experience as it is revealed.

Methodology

Each participant's interview began with this research statement: *"Please describe for me your experience of communicating with your young adolescent daughter. Describe for me your thoughts, feelings, perceptions surrounding this experience until you feel that you have nothing left to discuss about it."* Interviews continued until the participant felt that she had nothing left to say about her experience. There were no time restrictions on the length of interview. Data were collected until saturation was reached and no new data were revealed. Interviews averaged between 30 and 60 minutes each.

Data analysis began when each transcript was read repeatedly, in addition to being transcribed by the researcher, in an effort to gain a true grasp of the experience being studied. Significant statements directly related to the experience of mothers communicating with their adolescent daughters were extracted from each interview and then numbered. The researcher went on to identify formulated meanings for each significant statement. Formulated meanings are statements that discover and illuminate the hidden meanings found in the various contexts of the phenomena, which allowed the data to "speak for itself."

Review of formulated meanings allowed for identification of recurring themes, emerging from and common to each interview. Thematic analysis involved a return to the transcripts for further confirmation and validation. At this time, any discrepancies among or between the themes were noted and corrected. As per Colaizzi's (1978) method of data analysis, all existing data were then organized into an exhaustive description of mothers' experience of communication with their young adolescent daughters. By presenting all participants with this description of the phenomena, they were able to validate that findings captured the true essence of their experience. No additional information was provided, and participants confirmed the accuracy of the emerging themes.

Saturation was the criteria for discontinuing data collection. To ensure qualitative rigor, credibility, fittingness, and auditability were addressed. Credibility was achieved by participant validation and confirmation of the exhaustive description of the phenomenon being studied, and how vivid the description of the data was to the experience itself. Fittingness was addressed by seeking out participants who have lived the experience being studied and were able to speak about it. Interviews, which were audio taped, and transcription of interviews were completed by one researcher shortly after the interview took place, allowing for optimal recall of events. Data analysis, involving identification of common themes and formulated meanings allowed the data to speak for itself and helped to assure the study's auditability. Utilizing Colazi's methodology of data analysis allows for auditability, when other researchers can follow research "decision trail" and arrive at comparable results given the same data and circumstances. Additionally, participants took part in the final validation of the data analysis as a true description of their lived experience, once again addressing the fittingness of the study and qualitative rigor.

Findings

A total of nine interviews yielded 355 significant statements. From these statements, 355 formulated meanings were generated. Data were then grouped into six theme clusters. The six themes were common to all participants, and will be presented individually along with direct quotes and appropriate metaphors.

Theme 1: "Timing is everything"

Timing of communication between mothers and their young adolescent daughters appears to be a crucial element of success. Mothers describe the necessity of recognizing whether a time is conducive or obstructive to open communication and feel the need to be ready to communicate when the opportunity arises, or the moment will be missed and communication may never take place. One mother explains, "We can't always talk it out because she puts up a wall. Then when it is a good time for her, she'll bring it up. No matter what else I'm doing, I have to stop and talk to her when she is ready." Finding the time to communicate honestly with their daughters is a priority. Mothers agree that "communication takes time, and it can't be rushed . . . it can be frustrating." There also appears to be an intuitive aspect of achieving the "right" timing. "It comes down to feelings. I can just feel it when it's not a good time to talk. It needs to be the right time. She has to be in the right mood." Another mother adds, "If she is not in the mood to talk, we don't communicate. If she is upset, or tired, we don't communicate."

Mothers agree that the best time for communication with their young adolescent daughters is when they are alone together. Good communication appears to require the full attention of both participants and is difficult to accomplish with distractions. One mother believes that her daughter "picks the times when she doesn't have to compete for my attention." Daughters do not always choose the most convenient time to communicate, but when discussions are initiated by the adolescent, mothers generally try to give their daughters the time and attention they seem to need.

In conclusion, mothers agree that timing is essential for successful communication to take place. The best communication occurs when each party is attentive to the other, and when they feel safe and comfortable.

Theme 2: "Walking on eggs . . . it's not always easy"

Mothers acknowledge that communication with young adolescent daughters "can be rather difficult" for a variety of reasons. One mother states, "There are times when I'm not really even sure that communication takes place. Communication is a two-way street, and my daughter holds a lot inside." But the general consensus among individual mothers was that issues, regardless of their difficult nature, need to be addressed. "Sometimes we talk about it, and sometimes we don't. But we always need to acknowledge it."

Confronting the issues related to "growing up," "body changes," and "sex" led mothers to uncharted waters. Mothers described being unsure of themselves and uncomfortable with topics. When mothers are not comfortable talking about the subject matter of sex with their adolescent daughters, communication regarding related issues is not likely to take place.

Mothers also describe their young adolescent daughters as practicing poor listening skills, which can impede communication. Daughters are also described as being "stubborn," "self-centered," and "uncompromising." Mothers describe the experience of communication as being "difficult" and "frustrating." Listening appears to be selective and directly related to the young adolescent's agenda.

Literature describes adolescence as a period of emotional turmoil, and this was supported by mothers participating in this study. "Emotions play a big part in our communication, or lack thereof. Her emotions, and mine. It's hard to talk meaningfully when someone's crying. If she's angry she'll cry. If she's sad she'll cry. In front of anybody, she'll cry. She's quick to show her emotions, but then it's over. It's forgotten. She's moved on."

Mothers acknowledged that regardless of intent, communication can be shut down when one party pushes too hard. Anger is another obstacle to good communication. Young adolescent girls were described by their mothers as often "moody," "unapproachable," and "hormonal." Mothers also universally acknowledged that they too may exhibit these same traits, all of which can "make or break communication." Communication between mothers and daughters cannot be forced.

Mothers frequently feel responsible when good communication does not occur. One mother states that "Sometimes it's like I'm walking on eggs around her. Because I don't want to upset her. I want her calm, but I want information. I don't even know sometimes what I said that was wrong. I just know that I blew it." Mothers not only assume responsibility for poor communication, but will change their behavior in an effort to enhance communication. This process is often described as "trial and error."

Theme 3: "When it works, it works"

Mothers can identify opportunities and approaches that encourage communication with their young adolescent daughters. Approaches vary from mother to mother, and each mother reports individualizing attempts at conversation to the receptivity of their daughters at any given time.

Mothers understand that in order for communication to be meaningful it must be understood by all participants. This includes recognizing their daughters as individuals and relating to them in a way that is comfortable to both. Mothers recognize that communication involves being open with each other, and they often compare their communication efforts with those of their own mothers. Along this same line, mothers recognize that communication involves being ready and able to hear what is being said, no matter how difficult. Mothers reported that anticipating events, feelings, reactions, and so on aids them in the communication process with their young adolescent daughters.

Making an effort to address issues regardless of disagreements is important to good communication. One mother sums it up by stating, "On some subjects, we just agree to disagree." Another mother finds it helpful to use her own experiences to open the lines of communication with her daughter. "One thing we talk about is what I was like at her age." Mothers strive to make their young adolescent daughters feel comfortable about communication, particularly concerning difficult issues. They report that communication is best when it is initiated by their daughters. Unfortunately, young adolescent daughters are not always forthright in their disclosure.

Regardless of the approach taken by mothers in communicating with their young adolescent daughters, it is the consensus of the participants in this study that good communication requires attention and effort. One mother describes it this way, "Talking about things brings them to a different level of awareness. Putting them into words kind of forces an acknowledgment of all the things you just do, but don't really think about."

All of the mothers reported that when communication is successful, it is worth the hard work. They all expressed a desire to be involved in their daughter's lives and to be informed (preferably by their daughter) when daughters are concerned or upset. Good communication is sensed by both parties. In the words of one mother, "There are times that I know we have really connected. I can tell that I've really gotten to her, or maybe I've really listened to her and I know what she's feeling. Those times there is just a bond that couldn't be any better."

Theme 4: "Listening to the sounds of silence"

Mothers describe an intuitive understanding of the context of adolescence, enabling effective verbal and nonverbal communication. They understand that it is often what is left unsaid that is the most important message. It is this intuitive sense of their young adolescent daughters that often helps mothers to recognize that communication needs to take place.

Each mother described in a variety of ways the nonverbal communication they share with their young adolescent daughters. One mother describes it this way: "She communicates without saying anything sometimes. It's the stomping around, and the grunting and groaning. Her attitude seems to be yelling at people, when she actually doesn't say anything."

Anticipation of their daughter's reaction to a given situation also helps mothers in their unspoken quest to attain good communication. Maternal perception is not limited to "mood swings." Mothers found it helpful to use nonverbal communication to anticipate when verbal communication would not be well received by their daughters. "We don't need to talk about it directly. She'll be tired, and probably irritable, and I try to avoid conflict when I know she'll be that way."

Mothers seem to interpret silence from their daughters as an unspoken understanding or mutual agreement about a particular topic. "In terms of communication with [my daughter], I guess just understanding the changes she is going through and her sudden need for privacy, or her concerns about her appearance, are all a form of communication between us. We don't really talk about it, but it's understood."

The nonverbal communication or unspoken sensing of the other's thoughts and feelings is not a unilateral occurrence. It is a reciprocal experience between mothers and their young adolescent daughters. "It is easy for me to tell when things are going good for her, and when they are not. I think she can tell the same for me, when I've had a good day or a bad day. That intuition is something we have developed." To further clarify this sentiment, one mother describes her daughter as being "wise enough to know when to stay out of my way. She'll take one look at me and she'll know." Another mother adds, "Her mood, and my mood, can make communicating hard to do. And I can tell when she's in a bad mood, or she's had a bad day. And I think she can tell with me too."

How does this nonverbal communication evolve? How does it work? One mother may have the answer to that question when she states, "When we're together, she'll observe me, she'll watch me, and then determine how receptive I'm going to be to her. I guess it works both ways really." Mothers and daughters rely on "a mutual understanding." As one mother adds, "Sometimes the best communication is no communication. Sometimes all I can offer her is to listen to her, and commiserate with her."

Mothers believe that they understand the context of being female and being an adolescent, thereby allowing them to identify with their daughters. "Being a woman is very helpful to our relationship and our ability to communicate. She will address things with me that she won't with her father. We have a different kind of understanding of one another." This understanding of context is appreciated by young adolescent daughters.

Mothers repeatedly take the blame when good communication does not happen or nonverbal clues are missed or misinterpreted. "If there is a miscommunication it's because I have misunderstood something about her. She seems to always get what I'm thinking, but sometimes I just don't get what she's thinking." In addition, mothers realize that reacting in a negative manner is not conducive to good communication.

All mothers agree that when good communication happens with their daughters, whether verbal or nonverbal, intuitive or behavioral, it is felt by both themselves and their daughters. "We communicate by talking to each other, or just being with each other, respecting the silence." Good communication is motivational: "When it does happen, it makes all of our unsuccessful efforts worthwhile. It keeps me trying." Another mother concludes, "We seem to really connect on a good level. Things go unspoken, but we both understand that we love each other, no strings attached." A mother's love is unconditional.

Theme 5: "The truth, the whole truth and nothing but the truth"

Mothers value open and honest communication with their young adolescent daughters. As with other issues, mothers compare the openness of communication with their experience as adolescence. One mother expressed a common feeling: "I'd like to think that I'm more open with her than my mom was with me." Mothers appear to understand the importance of open communication with their daughters and are willing to work hard at it. An essential component of open communication is being open to discuss any topic. Mothers also spoke about the fear related to adolescent activities and pressures, and how their daughter handles it. "We always have talked in our house about sex or alcohol, even from when they were little. . . . The language is not something they are uncomfortable with. . . . We don't hesitate to talk about the stuff we are trying to get them to avoid." Good communication also involves a mutual trust. One mother explains, "With her, I have to really gain her trust. I need to be consistent in what I say and do. And I need to hold her revelations to me in confidence. She needs to know that I really want to know what she is thinking and feeling."

Mothers agree that being open, honest, and trustworthy lays the foundation for good communication. One mother states, "All I can do is be open and honest and supportive. Listening is probably the most important part of communicating with my daughter." The participants also discussed the reciprocal nature of communication. "Talking about things gives her an opportunity to see how I feel." In good communication, the thoughts, feelings, and opinions of both parties contribute to the value of the communication itself.

While each of the mothers admit that communication with their young adolescent daughters is important and valued, it is not always easy to accomplish this goal. "It's not always easy getting her to talk honestly to me. And honesty is so important. Without it there is no trust. I feel that when she tells me things I almost have to double check the facts with someone else just to be sure I have the story right." Mothers admit that they "feel bad when we can't sit down and talk things through." One mother put it this way: "It would be nice to be able to break the pattern, and open up communication with my daughter. I'm going to keep working on it. And keep hoping that our communication will get better."

Mothers describe honesty as a precursor to good communication, but acknowledge that their daughters may be less than forthcoming in their communication efforts. One mother admits that her daughter is "honest about the basics," while implying that she may not be honest beyond that. Mothers also described having to "pull teeth" to get their daughters to talk about issues of importance, but feel that their persistence pays off. In addition, mothers optimistically felt that open, honest communication will eventually occur.

Mutual respect and consideration is also valued. Mothers spoke about the honesty of their daughters, and also acknowledged their dishonesty, stating that "trustworthiness" of what their daughters tell them is often in question. Mothers voiced the opinion that "keeping communication open and trying to anticipate conflicts before they happen is helpful." In summary, "Trust, honesty, respect, and love. They all have to work both ways, and they are all needed for good open communication."

Theme 6: "Change . . . can a leopard change its spots?"

Mothers recognize that communication changes before and during adolescence. One mother states, "She is harder to talk to now than she was last year." Mothers acknowledge the relationship between behavior changes and changes in communication. "She is definitely changing. She's quieter and more private." One mother states, "In 6th and 7th grade, though, it was really kind of scary. She was quiet and wouldn't open up about things." She goes on to add, "In 8th grade, she has become more open with me. I sometimes have to ask and ask, but I will eventually find out what is going on." Another mother states, "In the last few months she seems to be quieter and less responsive to me. Sometimes she just 'yeses' me to death."

When discussing the actual changes that are taking place, most mothers agree that communicating about personal issues "is like pulling teeth." In addition, mothers describe the emotional volatility of adolescence. Tone of voice and attitude were commonly identified as changes during adolescence. Adolescents were described as "fresh" in their responses to communication efforts. Recognizing this change, one mother notes, "As a parent, I need to come up with a different way to handle things, to be creative in how I talk with her."

Mothers describe the frustration and challenge of mothering young adolescent daughters. "Talking with [my daughter] about things is not always easy. If I asked her a direct question, she is very good at turning things around completely without answering. She often leaves me wondering why I asked the question in the first place. It's frustrating." Daughters are often less than obliging about the disclosure of issues in their lives. Mothers also report that communicating with their daughters can also be "unpredictable." Mothers admit to differences of opinion with their daughters and try to handle that situation in the way that would be best received. One mother summarizes it by saying simply, "We have changed the way we talk about things."

Other mothers describe communication with their young adolescent daughters as "easy right now," yet these mothers voice an anticipation of changes to come. In addition, communication appears to be valued more as daughters age: "I don't feel like our communication has really changed much, just that perhaps we value it differently as she gets older."

Mothers also describe communication with their daughters as a learning experience: "It is always getting better, especially with her. She's more willing to share as she gets older, or more able, whatever. Maybe I just ask the right questions now." One mother describes a realization, "I need to see things from my daughter's perspective. I guess communication is about learning as you go along." Mothers describe the process of learning as reciprocal.

Mothers acknowledge "There is security in being the mom, and having all the answers. Or I should say, having your daughter think you have all the answers." This changes as girls become adolescents. Mothers express a "desire to go in and fix things. And the hard lesson that I've learned is that I can't always fix things. Sometimes things have to work themselves out." One mother describes it this way: "Communicating with my daughter is constantly changing. There are a bunch of bumps or hurdles to go over. Some days are good and some aren't. I really want to know what is going on with her, so I just have to keep at it." In addition, mothers recognize that communication will continue to change as their daughters get older. "At times I really fear that we won't be able to communicate with each other." Another mother comments that her daughter "has brought me to a different level as a mom. In her own accomplishments, and through our communication, I have grown too." Mothers of young adolescent daughters agree that "communication is still changing" and "it's a challenge," yet they reiterate their commitment to communication with their daughters

The findings of this study reflect the unique perspective of mothers currently living the experience of communicating with their young adolescent daughters. The themes that consistently emerged from the data add to the clarification and knowledge of the phenomenon studied. This information can be used to assist families experiencing this developmental stage and to avoid the difficulties that are sometimes inherent in mother–daughter miscommunication. Identifying areas of maternal concern, patterns of communication, and the trials and tribulations associated with this particular phenomenon add to illumination of family dynamics. Through discussion of this process, mothers revealed strategies and behaviors that both helped to encourage good communication and those that did not. This information contributes to overall knowledge and the care of families. Sharing personal experiences is a value to oneself and others.

The implications of this research are numerous and valuable to those in clinical practice. Care of families involves an insight into relationships and interactions between family members. Providers need to identify actual or potential problems from the perspective of all involved. Knowing mothers' perception of communication with their young adolescent daughters opens for the professional a window into the dynamics involved in family interaction. Enhancing mother–young adolescent daughter communication can assist families to achieve a smooth transition through this challenging period of development. Existing research fails to sufficiently address mother–young adolescent daughter communication. Findings from this study demonstrate the richness of data in this area and indicate a need for further research in this area.

Mothers are often concerned about their ability to communicate successfully with their adolescent daughters. Previous research has identified this as a tenuous time for mothers and daughters, and supports anticipatory guidance. Acknowledgement of the difficulties that communication may entail, and the possibility for perpetuation of a "negative cycle" of poor communication, helps to validate the experience for mothers. It is also beneficial to relate a mother's communication experience to that of others during similar times or turmoil.

Issues and concerns that are important to mothers of adolescent daughters have been highlighted in this and previous studies (Diem, 2002; Hrelic, 2002; Riesch et al., 1997) and can be used to develop guidelines meant to assist families with communication through preadolescence and adolescence. Intervention directed by the actual experiences of this population may lead to increased satisfaction with family systems and open communication between mothers and daughters (Riesch et al., 1997). Practitioners in a variety of healthcare settings, are in a position to effect and enhance family communication, and in particular mother–young adolescent daughter communication. Healthcare providers can assist families to achieve a smooth transition through this difficult and well-documented period of development. In particular, the challenge is to embrace factors related to communication between mothers and young adolescent daughters that are authentic and based on the real experiences of this population. An increase in knowledge opens the door for more meaningful interpersonal communication.

REFERENCES

Apter, T. (2004). *You don't really know me: Why mothers and daughters fight and how both can win.* New York, NY: Norton & Co.

Aronowitz, T., & Agbeshie, E. (2012). Nature of communication: Voices of 11–14 year old African-American girls and their mothers in regard to talking about sex. *Issues in Comprehensive Pediatric Nursing; 35*(2), 75–89.

Beaumont, S. L. (2000). Conversational styles of mothers and their preadolescent and middle adolescent daughters. *Merrill-Palmer Quarterly, 46*(1), 119–133.

Beck, C. T. (1994). Reliability and validity issues in phenomenological research. *Western Journal of Nursing Research, 16*(3), 254–267.

Coffelt, T. A. (2010). Is sexual communication challenging between mothers and daughters? *Journal of Family Communication, 10*(2), 116–130.

Colaizzi, P. (1978). Psychological research as the phenomenologist views it. In R. S. Valle, & M. King (Eds.), *Existential foundations of psychology* (pp. 48–68). New York, NY: Oxford University Press.

Dellasega, C. (2001). *Surviving Ophelia: Mothers share their wisdom on navigating the tumultuous years.* New York, NY: Perseus Publishing.

Diem, E. (2002). Balancing relationship and discipline: The pressing concern of mothers of early-adolescent girls (Abstract). *Canadian Journal of Nursing Research, 31*(4), 87–103.

Dilorio, C. K., & Hockenberry-Eaton, M. (1999). Communication about sexual issues: Mothers, fathers, and friends. *Journal of Adolescent Health, 24*(3), 181–189.

Gross, P., & McCallum, R. (2000). Operationalization and predictive utility of mother–daughter synchrony. *School Psychology Quarterly, 15*(3), 279–289.

Hales, D. (1999). *Just like a woman.* New York, NY: Bantam Books.

Hare, A. L., Marston, E. G., & Allen, J. P. (2011). Maternal acceptance and adolescents' emotional communication: A longitudinal study. *Journal of Youth and Adolescence 40*(6), 744–751.

Hrelic, D. A. (2002). A Caucasian mother's experience of communication with her adolescent daughter. Unpublished manuscript prepared for University of Connecticut (Storrs, CT).

Meneses L. M., Orell-Valente, J. K., Guendelman, S. R., Oman, D., & Irwin, C. E. Jr. (2006). Racial/ethnic differences in mother–daughter communication about sex. *Journal of Adolescent Health, 39*(1), 128–131.

Miller, K. K., Dorsey, S., Forehand, R., & Ham, A. Y. (1998). Family communication about sex: What are parents saying and are their adolescents listening? *Family Planning Perspectives, 30*(5), 218–235.

Orrel-Valente, J. K., Hill, L. G., Alegre, K. M., & Halpern-Felsher, B. L. (2007). Adolescent girls' increased mobility and autonomy, and change in mother–daughter relationship and communication. *Journal of Adolescent Health, 40*(2), S30–31.

Pipher, M. (2002). *Reviving Ophelia: Saving the lives of adolescent girls.* New York, NY: Ballantine Books.

Reed, J. S., & Dubow, E. F. (1997, February). Cognitive and behavioral predictors of communication in clinic-referred and nonclinical mother–adolescent dyads. *Journal of Marriage and the Family, 59,* 91–102.

Riesch, S. K., Coleman, R., Glowacki, J. S., & Konings, K. (1997). Understanding mothers' perceptions of what is important about themselves and parenting. *Journal of Community Health Nursing, 14*(1), 49–66.

Rosenthal, D. A., Feldman, S. S., & Edwards, D. (1998, December). Mum's the word: mothers' perspectives on communication about sexuality with adolescents. *Journal of Adolescence, 21*(6), 727–743.

Sanders, C. (2003). Application of Colaizzi's method: Interpretation of an auditable decision trail by a novice researcher. *Contemporary Nurse, 14*(3), 292.

Shandler, N. (2002). *Ophelia's mom: Loving and letting go of your adolescent daughter.* New York, NY: Crown Publishers.

Stiffler, D., Sims, S.L., & Stern, P. N. (2007 August). Changing women: Mothers and their adolescent daughters. *Health Care for Women International, 28*(7), 638–653.

Yowell, C. M. (1997). Risks of communication: Early adolescent girls' conversations with mothers and friends about sexuality. *The Journal of Early Adolescence, 17*(2), 172–196.

CHAPTER 3

PARENTAL RELIGIOSITY AND ADOLESCENT EDUCATIONAL ATTAINMENT

The Role of Noncognitive Skills

Gregory M. Eirich

ABSTRACT

Recently, scholars have found that parental religiosity—measured as frequency of religious service attendance—is associated with higher levels of children's educational attainment in the United States. This chapter examines a key mechanism that may explain this relationship: adolescent noncognitive skills, which are socially valuable ways of conducting oneself regarding tasks and interactions with authorities, usually involving effort and a pleasant demeanor. Using data from the National Longitudinal Survey of Youth (1997), this chapter first confirms previous suggestive evidence that parental religiosity increases a host of adolescent noncognitive skills. Parental religiosity seems to equip children with these noncognitive skills mostly through a religious socialization process whereby highly religious adolescents develop a conscientious and prosocial *habitus* because they have adopted the high religious attendance patterns of their parents. Ultimately, however, this paper

Adolescence in the 21st Century, pages 39–61

makes a surprising discovery: While (some) noncognitive skills are shown to be very important predictors of adolescents completing high school and starting some college, they are not the mechanisms by which religious parents enhance their children's educational chances. Overall, this chapter highlights the critical role religion can play in altering adolescent behavior, failure, and success, but also the difficulty in tracing the exact pathways by which religion comes to alter adolescent life chances.

INTRODUCTION

Over the last two decades, scholars from a variety of disciplines have looked for fresh answers for why some adolescents succeed and others do not, and one answer they have increasingly settled upon is "noncognitive skills" (Farkas, 2003; Heckman & Krueger, 2003). These skills get their rather infelicitous name as a way to separate them from "cognitive skills," which most economists and many psychologists had considered the main determinants of academic and labor market success (Heckman & Krueger, 2003).

 A growing chorus of researchers has argued that adolescents can bolster their academic chances though more than having a high IQ or exceptional innate intellectual ability (Farkas, 2003). Adolescents can improve their academic performance by utilizing their noncognitive skills, which are *socially* valuable ways of conducting oneself regarding tasks and interactions with authorities, usually involving effort and a pleasant demeanor. DiPrete & Jennings (2012) elaborate on what types of traits fall under this heading: "'Cognitive self-regulation' includes planning, sustaining attention, effortful control of attention or action, task persistence, and inhibition of impulsive responses. 'Emotional self-regulation' includes the ability to control anger, sadness, joy, and other emotional reactions, which predict both externalizing and internalizing problem behaviors" (p. 1). There has even been a very successful recent attempt to rebrand popularize the notion of noncognitive skills as "grit" (Tough, 2012).

Given the growing interest in the noncognitive skills of children and adolescents, it is important to provide additional context around these skills. This chapter, therefore, investigates where noncognitive skills come from, why some adolescents have more of them than others, and if these noncognitive skills are really as critical for educational attainment as previous scholars have suggested. I will use as my research site a nationally representative cohort of American children who were young teens in 1997 and follow them through their adolescence and into their early 20s; their experiences are captured in the National Longitudinal Survey of Youth of 1997 (NLSY97) dataset.

I take as my starting point a surprising recent finding in the sociology of education: At least for recent cohorts, parental religiosity—measured as frequency of religious service attendance—is associated with higher levels of children's educational attainment in the United States (Eirich, 2012; Stokes, 2008; Yeung, Duncan, & Hill, 2000). Focusing on noncognitive skills, this chapter asks three broad questions. First, might parental religiosity increase adolescent children's levels of noncognitive skills? Second, if parental religiosity is associated with higher adolescent noncognitive skills, how does this happen? Is this mainly the result of parental practices of monitoring and social control, or is it due to a socialization process whereby religious parents provide their children with unique motivations to act in more socially valuable ways, even without being monitored? Lastly, does some of the educational advantage that children of religious parents receive operate through their parents' ability to provide them with greater noncognitive skills?

This will be the first explicit attempt to link noncognitive skills, religion, and life chances together. On the one hand, much of the existing evidence concerning religion's impact on personality traits and habits comes from psychology, which generally does not examine socioeconomic factors or outcomes, or even control for socioeconomic and demographic characteristics. Psychologists are mainly concerned with highlighting personality traits per se (Hood, Hill, & Spilka, 2009). On the other hand, sociologists and economists have failed to make the connection either. For instance, Farkas (2003) in his oft-cited review of the literature, notes that certain cultural resources can enhance noncognitive skills, whether racial/ethnic communities (e.g., Asian-American or Caribbean-American) or high-culture activities (e.g., music or dance classes). Yet he does not even mention religion as a possible valuable cultural resource that parents can use to help instill noncognitive skills in their children. A focus on these "soft skills" is critical for education researchers, who have hypothesized the importance of noncognitive skills in children's achievement but have not fully catalogued their sources, especially cultural ones.

RELIGIOSITY AND NONCOGNITIVE SKILLS

While I define noncognitive skills as socially valuable ways of conducting oneself regarding tasks and interactions with authorities, usually involving effort and a pleasant demeanor, many other definitions are available in the literature. As DiPrete & Jennings (2012) note about the definition of noncognitive skills: "The lack of standard terminology reflects the multidimensional character of these skills as well as the multidisciplinary collection of scholars who study these skills and their consequences" (p. 2). Researchers historically have taken a rather commonsense approach to what counts as a noncognitive skill.

For students, the noncognitive skills include things like "homework, class participation, effort, organization, and lack of disruptiveness" (Farkas, 2003, p. 545). They stand in contrast to standardized test scores of youth, which more closely approximate "natural" aptitude, though how innate cognitive ability is, is quite debatable (Bowles, Gintis, & Osborne, 2001).

A highly fragmented, but growing literature has speculated that religious people have higher levels of psychological traits and life habits that are associated with agreeableness and conscientiousness, which "are considered by many theorists to be the basic personality substrates of self-control" (McCullough & Willoughby, 2009, p. 86). From a psychological perspective, in a recent review of part of this literature, McCullough & Willoughby (2009) conclude that "there is strong evidence for our proposition that religion is positively related to self-control" (p. 86). What traits and habits are linked with religiosity varies from study to study, but they can best be characterized as noncognitive skills, whether measured in behaviors like putting on seatbelts and going to the dentist or in terms of the Big Five personality profiles. Their review is consistent with the extensive literature on "conscientiousness" in psychology as well (Saroglou, 2002).

Looking at adolescent religiosity, Muller and Ellison (2001) have come close to testing for a relationship between religion and noncognitive skills. They adopt Coleman's (1988) social capital framework, finding that adolescent religiosity improves "attitudes, effort, and conceptions of self" (Muller & Ellison, 2001, p. 160, quoting Coleman, 1988). These concepts come close to what is now placed under the rubric of noncognitive skills. They find that an adolescent's religiosity predicts some of these skills and behaviors, including a higher locus of control, greater educational expectations, more frequent conversations with parents about academics, more homework, and less class-cutting.

Unfortunately, Muller and Ellison (2001) rely on adolescent religiosity measures alone for all of their analyses, and so they cannot rule out the possibility of spuriousness. Specifically, the positive relationship between adolescent religiosity and noncognitive skills may be due to some unmeasured variable of such adolescents that makes them more likely to be *both* more religious *and* more conscientious. As they themselves admit: "If some adolescents reject manifestations of conventionality, such as religion and school, then the apparent religious variations in academic attitudes and behaviors...may reflect unobserved selection processes" (Muller & Ellison, 2001, p. 176). It is important to move beyond this type of analysis to better understand the full range of inputs into adolescent religiosity and their "social capital," or noncognitive skills.

A fine piece of research that does not suffer from the methodological flaws outlined above comes from Bartkowski, Xu, and Levin (2008). Using the Early Childhood Longitudinal Study (Kindergarten Cohort), they find evidence that among very young children, parental religiosity increases teacher and/or parent evaluations of those children for a number of noncognitive outcomes, including measures of self-control, social interactions, interpersonal skills, sadness/loneliness levels, internalizing problems, impulseness/overreactiveness, and externalizing problems. There is also a measure of school readiness that assesses the child's approaches to learning, and there too, parental religiosity is helpful. Their sample is of kindergarten and first-grade students, however, and so it is too early to know if these documented positive noncognitive effects continue into adolescence.

Religion researchers have indeed found some things that seem to amount to a religious *habitus,* which is "an acquired, trained disposition to engage in certain modes of activity when encountering particular objects or situations," usually tied to the social position of one's parents (Lizardo, forthcoming, p. 1). For instance, in adults, Ellison (1992) finds that among a nationally representative sample of African Americans, religious people are considered nicer by interviewers. Likewise, Swidler (2001) finds that religious Christians generally spoke of love in a way where their religious identity provided a benchmark for their actions, even if only in relatively superficial ways, like never using curse words. It is important to try to catalogue a number of these noncognitive skills all together in one place to see if parental religiosity matters for some more than others.

Despite the fact that no scholars have exactly investigated this relationship, it is reasonable to expect that increased parental religiosity will enhance adolescents' noncognitive skills.

PARENTAL RELIGIOSITY, PARENTING SKILLS, CHILD SOCIALIZATION, AND NONCOGNITIVE SKILLS

Some of adolescents' noncognitive skills may result primarily from superior parental control of children' actions. In particular, parents may be partly responsible for their children appearing to exert effort, by checking on homework and providing advice on which classes to take. Muller and Ellison (2001) find that religious children talk to their parents more about school, do more homework and take harder classes, and some part of this might be owed to greater parental concern. Parents can produce a sense in their children that they (the parents) are always monitoring them (the children). With a greater sense of surveillance (or parental knowledge of their whereabouts and interactions), children may be more inclined to exert effort and appear pleasant in more situations. More generally, parents can behave in ways that promote their children's noncognitive skills by interacting with their children in ways that make children trust and respect parental authority.

Partway between overt social control and socialization lie rewards and punishments. Parents can use rewards and punishments to induce their children to perform better in school and to show greater levels of noncognitive skills. In fact, Fejgin (1995) finds that part of the academic advantage that Jewish students have comes from being rewarded for good grades by their parents. No similar study has looked at other religions. Nelsen and Kroliczak (1984), building on Nunn (1964), find strong support among a sample of Minnesota fourth- through eighth-graders that the students whose parents have gotten them to believe that God punishes children who act badly have higher levels of self-blame and obedience. There is surprisingly very little research beyond this on how parents differ in their use of punishments and rewards based on their religion, with the notable exception of corporal punishment (Ellison & Sherkat, 1993; Ellison, Bartkowski, & Segal, 1996). It is at least plausible that more religious parents will use greater incentives, both positive and negative, to get their children to act respectfully and to show effort in school, but the evidence is not here yet, nor can I directly test for it here because I do not have the data.

At the other extreme is the idea of religious socialization, which I can test. Under this model, parental religiosity only matters because it transmits religiosity to children, and once children become religious themselves, parental religiosity becomes a redundant resource (Regnerus, 2007; Smith, 2003b). In this case, since most noncognitive skills are not directly under the control of parents, it is hard for parents to directly force their adolescent children to be polite or positive, or to try hard at school. Noncognitive skills are not easily subject to parental intervention or structuring. Under the socialization model, parents instill values, habits, and expectations in their children, and for religious parents, more of those skills will inhere in their children.

Following the model elaborated by Lareau (2003), social control gives way to the creation of an underlying *habitus* for children, partly made up of noncognitive skills. In fact, there is a way in which religion acts as a form cultural capital for parents of all socioeconomic status (SES) backgrounds in a way that is analogous to what Lareau (2003) labeled as "concerted cultivation" among higher-SES parents. She argues that upper-class parents provide an environment for their young children dominated by adults (mainly parents) and full of structured activities (like sports and arts). This environment and structure help the child develop—as they get older—a set of assertive but respectful dispositions toward authority, which coheres into a high-class *habitus*, or way of being in the world. By contrast, she finds that low-SES parents favor a philosophy of "accomplishment of natural growth," and do not organize their children's lives as much or as consistently, and children are encouraged to interact mainly with peers.

It is quite possible that something similar is going on with respect to parental religiosity. Lareau (2003) found that "concerted cultivation" became a way of parenting for higher-SES people largely in an unconscious way, meaning that her parents did not think that they were obliged to treat their children this way *because of* their class status. This is in contrast to how parental religiosity is usually shown to operate, as an explicit and quite conscious identity. Religious parents, *by virtue of thinking of themselves as religious,* value their children's nonacademic time, at-home obedience, and activities differently from other parents (Wilcox, Chaves, & Franz, 2004) and actually treat different behaviors as acceptable or unacceptable (Smith, 2003a). Religious parents do not necessarily think they are advantaging their children by promoting noncognitive skills like deference to authority, but they do somehow think that such behaviors are a part of what being religious means. As Smith (2003b, p. 22–23) notes, "A... major way that religion can influence the lives of youth is by increasing their competence in skills and knowledge that contribute to enhancing their well-being and improving their life chances."

That said, looking to children's religious service attendance as an indicator of adolescent religiosity is somewhat problematic because parents may still be able to compel their children to attend religious services to some degree, even if the children themselves do not want to go. Therefore, our measure of adolescent religiosity may be contaminated with parental influence to some degree because the amount of compulsion felt by children to attend religious services itself may be a function of parental SES (and other) factors, as suggested by previous research (Gunnoe & Moore, 2002). Estimates of the effect of children's religious attendance on academic success may be somewhat upwardly biased, and we should keep that issue in mind.

It is important to investigate which of these two mechanisms—parental behaviors or youth socialization—is more responsible for the high noncognitive skills that children of religious parents are likely to display.

ADOLESCENT NONCOGNITIVE SKILLS AND EDUCATIONAL ATTAINMENT

There is some evidence that noncognitive skills enhance educational attainment. Farkas (2003) notes that, often, noncognitive skills can largely explain GPA or educational attainment differences between groups based on race/ethnicity, gender, or socioeconomic status (SES). He also notes that noncognitive skills frequently rival IQ in terms of magnitude of contribution to educational achievement. These noncognitive skills are generally based on assessments by teachers of the adolescent's effort, friendliness, and self-control. These nonscholastic skills heavily influence the grades teachers give out, naturally.

Farkas' initial conclusion has come under scrutiny in recent years, as more researchers study the topic and use new data to answer these questions. As Hsin and Xie (2012, p. 7) note:

> The academic literature is...mixed. Some studies demonstrate that traits such as self-control explain much more of the variation in children's academic performance than cognitive abilities (Duckworth and Seligman 2005; Wolfe and Johnson 1995)....In contrast, other studies show that "hard" skills trump "soft" skills as determinants of academic success...(Duncan et al., 2007)

Moreover, few studies have looked at the role of noncognitive skills not on grades, but on actual attainment of educational credentials (Farrington et al., 2012).

Overall, within the current educational system, as "merit" is usually defined, students still need to exert effort, take a set of challenging classes, and get by in school to be in a position to attend post-secondary education, much less graduate from a college of some kind (Wong, 1990). Despite the unsettled nature of the literature, I still expect that adolescent noncognitive skills will explain at least some of the educational advantage children of religious parents have.

A NOTE ABOUT RELIGIOUS AFFILIATIONS

This chapter focuses on parental religiosity, not parental religious affiliation. This is because previous research (Eirich, 2012; Stokes, 2008) finds that what particular religion or religious tradition that parents belong to is not a strong predictor of most academic outcomes, once demographic and socioeconomic factors have been taken into account. For that reason, no hypotheses are generated about religious denominational differences.[1]

RESEARCH STRATEGY

Dataset

I use the NLSY97, a nationally representative survey of households with young people between the ages of 12 and 16 in 1997, designed to provide information about the determinants of their labor market outcomes. NLSY97 provides information on both the adolescents and their parents from each source independently. One parent (usually the mother) was interviewed in 1997. The adolescents have been re-interviewed every year since 1997.[2]

Analytic Plan

My research strategy has three parts. Part 1 tests the relationship of parental religiosity and a host of noncognitive skills. Part 2 examines what explains why religious parents increase the adolescent children's stocks of noncognitive skills. Specifically, I test which matters more: (1) parenting skills and style, or (2) religious socialization via high child religiosity? Part 3 examines whether greater noncognitive skills can account for the positive effect of parental religiosity on children's educational attainment.

Variables

Descriptive statistics for the main variables are listed in Table 3.1.

TABLE 3.1 (Unweighted) Descriptive Statistics

	Obs	Mean	St. Dev.
High School Completion	1,607	91%	
Starting Any Post-Secondary Schooling, Given High School Completion	1,464	71%	
Completed BA in a Timely Manner, Given Any Post-Secondary Schooling	388	11%	
GPA, net of IQ—8th Grade	2,537	–0.07	1.43
GPA, net of IQ—High School	2,184	0.05	1.41
Child's Optimism	2,493	11.43	1.93
Child's Effort on an IQ Test	2,377	4.14	1.05
Child's Cooperation	2,955	9.14	0.93
Noncognitive Skills Score	2,184	0.02	1.26
Max- Parental Religious Attendance (1997)	3,816	4.26	2.00
Child's Religious Attendance (2000)	3,816	3.56	2.17
Authoritative Parenting Style	1,744	32%	
Authoritarian Parenting Style	1,744	23%	
Indulgent Parenting Style	1,744	25%	
Negligent Parenting Style (reference)	1,744	20%	
Max-Know Child's School	1,744	2.70	0.82
Max-Know Child's Close Friends	1,744	2.58	0.72
Max-Know Child's Friends' Parents	1,744	2.07	0.83
Max-Know Who Child is With	1,744	2.84	0.81
Max-Child Wants to Be Like Parents	1,744	2.83	0.84
Max-Child Enjoys Being With Parents	1,744	3.32	0.65
Child Always Turns to Parents	1,744	17%	

Ultimate Dependent Variables

Educational Attainment: Three transitions through the educational system are modeled: *High School Completion* means finishing high school either through graduation or GED; this provides the most inclusive measure of educational success to start with. *Any Post-Secondary Schooling* refers to attending any training program, 2-year, or 4-year college at all for any length of time, conditioned on having completed high school. *Earned a BA Degree* means that the child finished a 4-year college program in a timely manner (by the age of 22 or older), given that the child started some post-secondary schooling.[3]

Intermediate Outcome Variables—Noncognitive Skills

- Indirect Measures of Effort
  - *Child's 8th-Grade GPA, net of IQ*. The residual from a regression predicting 8th-grade GPA—which originally ranged from "mostly below Ds" (value of 0) to "mostly As" (value of 8)—controlling for the student's age-adjusted percentile on the Armed Services Vocational Aptitude Battery (ASVAB) math and verbal test subsections. This residual can be thought of as a crude measure of the value students add to their grades that is not attributable to superior natural intelligence or test-taking ability.[4]
  - *Child's Average High School GPA, net of IQ*. Constructed in exactly the same way as the 8th-grade residual, with the only difference that this variable is averaged over multiple years of high school
- Direct Measures of Effort
  - *Adolescent Effort on the ASVAB test*. Answer to 5-point Lickert question if the adolescent tried to do their best on the ASVAB test, ranging from strongly disagree (1) to strongly agree (5).
  - *Adolescent Cooperativeness*. The NLSY surveyor rating of how cooperative their interviewees were on a scale of 1 to 10, with 10 being very helpful and informative; scores were averaged over all the years.
- Adolescent Optimism. A summed index of adolescents' agreement on a 4-point scale to the Lickert statements that: they expected the best in uncertain situations; often good things happened to them; they are optimistic about the future; and they usually expect things to go their way; Cronbach's $\alpha = 0.31$, which is low but still preferable to dealing with each item separately.
- Overall Composite Noncognitive Score. This variable is generated from the first factor score from a principal components analyses of the five factors enumerated above. The Eigenvalue on the first principal component is above 1 (1.62) and accounts for a sizeable amount of the total variance (32%). As such, it forms a reasonable scale of effort and positivity (Cronbach's $\alpha = 0.44$).

Key Independent Variables

- Maximum Parental Religious Attendance. An 8-category ordinal question about how frequently the parents attended religious services in the previous 12 months, ranging from "never" to "every-day." I use the score from whichever parent had the highest level of attendance; parents include both biological parents and residential ones (i.e., step-parents and partners).
- Adolescent Child Religiosity. Measured same as for parents above; this was asked in 2000.

Control Variables[5]

- Standard Sociodemographic Characteristics:
  - *Maximum Parental Educational Attainment* (from whichever parent had the most)
  - *Log of Total Household Income*
  - *Log of Total Household Net Worth* (total family assets minus liabilities)
  - *Child Lived with Both Biological Parents until at least Age 12* (0 otherwise)
  - *Southern Residence* (0 otherwise)
  - (6) *Rural Residence* (0 otherwise)
  - *Number of Siblings*
  - *Child's Race/Ethnicity* (indicators for African-American and Hispanic race/ethnicity, with non-black, non-Hispanic as reference)
  - *Female* (0 if male)
  - *Child's Age in 1997*
  - *Religious Affiliation* (indicators for 8 religious affiliation categories, using a modified version of Greeley & Hout's (2006) schema: Conservative Protestant,[6] Roman Catholic, Mainline Protestant,[7] Jewish, Mormon, Muslim, no affiliation, and "other" affiliation).[8]
- Typically Unmeasured (Control) Variables:
  - *Parental School Involvement* (summed index of how frequently either parent volunteered at the school and/or attended a parent-teacher organization, ranging from never (0) to often (2); Cronbach's $\alpha = 0.55$).
  - *Tidiness of Interior and Exterior of the Home* (summed index of NLSY surveyor ratings of how well kept the parent's home—inside and out—was in 1997, ranging from very well kept (0) to poorly kept (2); Cronbach's $\alpha = 0.82$).
  - *Parental Optimism* (measured same as for adolescents above; Cronbach's $\alpha = 0.49$).
  - *Parental Cooperativeness* (measured same as for adolescents above; the score is only from Wave 1).

Parenting Behavior Variables

- Parenting Style: A series of indicator variables for: *Authoritative* (where the adolescent characterized his/her parents as both highly supportive and strict[9]); *Authoritarian* (strict, but not highly supportive); *Indulgent* (highly supportive but not strict); or *Negligent* (neither highly supportive nor strict).
- Parental Knowledge of Children's Daily Lives, Social Networks and Whereabouts: *Maximum Parental Knowledge of Child's Teachers and School.* Adolescents were asked to estimate how much each parent knew about who their teachers were and what they did at school, with answers ranging from the parent "knows nothing" (1) to "knows everything" (4). Four waves of data were averaged, and the maximum of either parent was then taken.
  - *Maximum Parental Knowledge of Child's Close Friends.* Calculated the same as above, but about how much each parent knew about the adolescents' close friends—in particular, who they were.
  - *Maximum Parental Knowledge of Child's Close Friends' Parents.* Calculated the same as above, but about how much each parent knew about their close friends' parents—in particular, who they were.
  - *Maximum Parental Knowledge of Who the Child is With When Not Home.* Calculated the same as above, but about how much each parent knew about who they were with when not at home.
- Affection and Respect for Parents from Adolescents: *Child Sees Parent As Role Model (Maximum).* Calculated the same as above, but about (on a 4-point Lickert scale) how strongly they agreed that each parent is a person they want to be like.
  - *Child Desires To Spend Time With A Parent (Maximum).* Calculated the same as above, but about (on a 4-point Lickert scale) how strongly they agreed that they really enjoyed spending time with each parent.
  - *Child Always Turns To a Parent First.* Children were asked, if they had an emotional problem or personal relationship problem, who they would first turn to for help. This was asked for the first four waves. If they mentioned any of their parents for all four waves, they were given a value of 1, otherwise 0.

Estimation Technique

The hypotheses for this chapter are all investigated using ordinary least squares (OLS) regression, which is premised on the idea of predicting some outcome (Y) on average as a linear, additive function of parental religiosity

(*X*), additional characteristics of the parents or adolescents (*Z*), and with some amount of error (ε) in our prediction, in this form:

$$Y = \alpha + \beta_1 X + \beta_2 Z + \varepsilon$$

Generally, our interest is in β_1, which is the independent effect of parental religiosity on some adolescent outcome, controlling for other factors in *Z*. I will sometimes present and discuss a Beta$_1$, which is just the former β_1, but standardized, such that it is a scaled effect of parental religiosity, where all of the variables in the model, including *Y*, have been put on the same scale (of standard deviation units), such that we can compare the relative importance of one independent variable against another.

While for some of our variables, other regression models would be more appropriate (given the distribution of our dependent variables, specifically binary and ordinal logistic regression), I will simply report OLS estimates from these models, to ease interpretability and provide consistency; results are comparable using more complex methods (results available upon request).

RESULTS AND DISCUSSION

Part 1—Parental Religiosity and Adolescent Noncognitive Skills

Here, I present results for whether parental religiosity increases adolescents' noncognitive skills, as hypothesized. The answer is generally in the affirmative. Table 3.2, for instance, shows that children of religious parents report getting higher "residualized" GPAs, net of IQ, both in 8th Grade and in high school; remember, residualized GPAs here are proxies for effort, since raw intellectual ability has been netted out of these variables. Specifically, for every category more that parents attend religious services, their children's 8th grade GPAs, net of IQ, increase by 0.05 points, all else equal; for high school GPA, it is 0.04 points. Alternately, we can think that if parents increase their religious service attendance by 1 standard deviation, adolescent academic "effort" or success should increase by more than a twentieth of a standard deviation, both for 8th grade (Beta = 0.07) and for high school (Beta = 0.06), which puts it among the largest influences on adolescent academic achievement.[10] Table 3.2 also provides the results of analyses of more personality, or *habitus*-like, traits of youth. Highly religious parents seem to increase their children's effort, even on a test that does not affect their grades, like the ASVB test. For every category more that parents indicate they attend religious services, children increase their agreement by 0.024 points that they tried

TABLE 3.2 OLS Regressions Predicting Various Noncognitive Skills

	(1) GPA, net of IQ–8th Grade Coeff.	(2) GPA, net of IQ–High School Coeff.	(3) Tried Hardest on ASVB Test Coeff.	(4) Adolescent Cooperation Coeff.	(5) Adolescent Optimism Coeff.	(6) Noncognitive Skills Score Coeff.
Max. Parental Religious Attendance (1997)	0.052** [0.073]	0.043* [0.062]	0.024+ [0.044]	0.023* [0.049]	0.041+ [0.043]	0.06** [0.09]
Obs.	2,537	2,184	2,493	2,377	2,955	2,184
Adj. R²	0.086	0.088	0.017	0.032	0.072	0.117

Note: All models control for: Maximum Parental Educational Attainment; Log of Total Household Income; Log of Total Household Net Worth; Child Lived with Both Biological Parents until at least Age 12; Southern Residence; Rural Residence; Number of Siblings; Child's Race/Ethinicity; Female; Child's Age in 1997; Religious Affiliation; Parental School Involvement; Tidiness of Interior and Exterior of the Home; Parental Optimism; Parental Cooperativeness.

Beta coefficients in brackets

*** $p < 0.001$, ** $p < 0.01$, * $p < 0.05$, + $p < 0.10$

their hardest on the Armed Services test (and Beta = 0.044). A similar sized effect is found when a child's cooperativeness score is measured. NLSY97 interviewers find children of religious parents to be somewhat more cooperative (Beta = 0.05) compared to children of less religious parents. Lastly, highly religious parents also increase their children's sense of optimism, even net of the parents' own sense of optimism; the result is not terribly dramatic (Beta = 0.04) or at the highest levels of statistical significance ($p < .10$), however.

Lastly, Table 3.2 also shows the results for a model predicting a composite noncognitive skills score, which is the first factor score from a principal components analysis of all the previous noncognitive skills. There too, the more religious one's parents are, the higher the score on this composite measure (Beta = 0.09).

Part 2—Parental Religiosity, Parental Practices, Socialization and Noncognitive Skills

How do adolescents get their noncognitive skills? Let us start by entering adolescent religiosity into the model. Table 3.3 presents the results of an examination of whether the adolescent's own religiosity levels will partly explain the higher levels of noncognitive skills among adolescents of highly religious parents. The idea is that religious parents manage to inculcate and nurture a religious habitus in their children via socialization.

This hypothesis is very strongly supported. When children's religiosity is included alongside parental religiosity, it more than fully accounts for the parental religiosity effect on noncognitive skills noted earlier; this means that socialization is the *dominant* (if not exclusive) mechanism by which highly religious parents pass on noncognitive skills to their children, as long as the assumption is largely correct that children's religious attendance accurately captures children's religiosity levels.[11] Table 3.3 shows that the parental religiosity coefficient drops from (a statistically significant) 0.048 in Model 1 to (a statistically insignificant) –0.024 in Model 2, over a 150% drop and a change in the direction of the slope too. Actually, child religiosity is the single biggest predictor of higher noncognitive scores, with a Beta = 0.24, which is mammoth. Moreover, the adjusted R^2 increases 32% from 0.117 to 0.155 once adolescent religiosity is included, which means that our model can correctly predict the outcome with much better accuracy once adolescent religiosity is in the model.

Though it perhaps seems unnecessary given the above results, what happens if we also include parenting style and parenting behaviors in our model anyway? Two things happen. Firstly, we actually find that many parental behaviors strongly predict adolescent noncognitive skills, with a marked

TABLE 3.3   OLS Regressions Predicting Noncognitive Skills Score

	(1) Coeff.	(2) Coeff.	(3) Coeff.
Max. Parental Religious Attendance (1997)	0.048*	–0.024	–0.018
	[0.077]	[–0.039]	[–0.028]
Child's Religious Attendance (2000)		0.137***	0.099***
		[0.239]	[0.172]
Authoritative Parenting Style			0.351***
			[0.131]
Authoritarian Parenting Style			0.044
			[0.015]
Indulgent Parenting Style			0.333***
			[0.115]
Max-Know Child's School			0.085
			[0.054]
Max-Know Child's Close Friends			–0.068
			[–0.037]
Max-Know Child's Friends' Parents			0.117+
			[0.075]
Max-Know Who Child is With			0.139*
			[0.085]
Max-Child Wants to Be Like Parents			0.136**
			[0.090]
Max-Child Enjoys Being With Parents			–0.045
			[–0.022]
Child Always Turns to Parents			0.085
			[0.025]
Observations	1,580	1,580	1,580
Adj. R^2	0.117	0.155	0.215

Note: All models control for: Maximum Parental Educational Attainment; Log of Total Household Income; Log of Total Household Net Worth; Child Lived with Both Biological Parents until at least Age 12; Southern Residence; Rural Residence; Number of Siblings; Child's Race/Ethinicity; Female; Child's Age in 1997; Religious Affiliation; Parental School Involvement; Tidiness of Interior and Exterior of the Home; Parental Optimism; Parental Cooperativeness.
Beta coefficients in brackets
*** $p < 0.001$, ** $p < 0.01$, * $p < 0.05$, + $p < 0.10$

(38%) rise in adjusted R^2 from 0.155 (for Model 2) to 0.215 (in Model 3). The most important variable is that parents who display an authoritative parenting style (Beta = 0.13), relative to a neglectful parenting style—even being indulgent, which is being supportive without being particularly strict, enhance adolescent noncognitive scores (B = 0.11). Beyond those behaviors, it is important for parents to know the parents of their children' friends (Beta = 0.08, but $p < .10$), followed by parents knowing who their children are with at most times (Beta = 0.09), and lastly, children wanting to be like their parents (Beta = 0.09). This is an important finding in its own right, since to date, scholars have not linked parenting style and behaviors to adolescent noncognitive skills enhancement.

Secondly, however, even though they are important generally, superior parenting styles or behaviors account for virtually none of the noncognitive skills advantage that adolescents of religious parents have over ones with less religious parents. Even though adolescent religious service attendance is not a perfect measure because it probably captures some of the role of parental control too, the overwhelming size of the effect still implies that socialization is mainly driving this result.[12]

Part 3—Parental Religiosity, Noncognitive Skills and Educational Attainment

Table 3.4 shows the results for whether noncognitive skills can account for some of the positive effects that parental religiosity has on children's educational attainment. The evidence presented here suggests that noncognitive skills matter only slightly; they are surprisingly not the mechanisms by which religious parents advantage their children academically. Specifically, when all five noncognitive skills are included in the models, the coefficients on parental religiosity change very little.

For high school completion, as Model 1 indicates, for each category more of religious services parents attend, adolescents are 0.8% more likely to complete high school. Adding in noncognitive skills (in Model 2) decreased that probability to 0.7% and weakens its statistical significance to ($p < .10$). Despite only a small impact on the parental religiosity coefficient, noncognitive skills, however, do matter for high school completion, since the adjusted R^2 increases by more than 50% from 0.089 to 0.134, once noncognitive skills are added. The noncognitive skill that most predicts high school completion is (not surprisingly) residualized high school grades, purged of IQ (Beta = 0.16).

A similar pattern holds when the five noncognitive skills are included in the model predicting beginning any post-secondary schooling (in Models 3 and 4). Those noncognitive skills explain virtually none of the high parental religiosity advantage (going from a 2.4% probability down to a 2.1% probability, once noncognitive skills are added), but again, their addition to the education equation increases the variance explained. The adjusted R^2 increases from 0.175 to 0.225, which makes sense, since most of the noncognitive skills predict post-secondary schooling.

TABLE 3.4 OLS Regressions (Linear Probability Models) Predicting Education Attainment Outcomes

	(1)	(2)	(3)	(4)	(5)	(6)
	High School Completion		Starting any Post-Secondary Schooling		Completed BA in a Timely Manner	
	Coeff.	Coeff.	Coeff.	Coeff.	Coeff.	Coeff.
Max. Parental Religious Attendance (1997)	0.008* [0.059]	0.007+ [0.047]	0.024*** [0.107]	0.021** [0.092]	0.026** [0.159]	0.024* [0.146]
GPA, net of IQ–8th Grade		0.003 [0.015]		0.041*** [0.124]		0.016 [0.062]
GPA, net of IQ–High School		0.033*** [0.162]		0.042*** [0.124]		0.019 [0.071]
Adolescent Cooperation		0.033*** [0.105]		0.044** [0.083]		-0.008 [-0.021]
Tried Hardest on ASVB Test		0.012+ [0.044]		0.006 [0.013]		0.021 [0.068]
Adolescent Optimism		-0.003 [-0.017]		0.005 [0.021]		0.000 [0.002]
Observations	1,607	1,607	1,464	1,464	388	388
Adj. R²	0.089	0.134	0.175	0.228	0.043	0.047

Note: All models control for: Maximum Parental Educational Attainment; Log of Total Household Income; Log of Total Household Net Worth; Child Lived with Both Biological Parents until at least Age 12; Southern Residence; Rural Residence; Number of Siblings; Child's Race/Ethinicity; Female; Child's Age in 1997; Religious Affiliation; Parental School Involvement; Tidiness of Interior and Exterior of the Home; Parental Optimism; Parental Cooperativeness.

Beta coefficients in brackets

*** $p < 0.001$, ** $p < 0.01$, * $p < 0.05$, + $p < 0.10$

Lastly, when predicting completing college in a timely manner, the inclusion of the noncognitive skills explains virtually none of the parental religiosity advantage (2.6% before vs. 2.4% after), and that is not surprising, since none of the noncognitive skills variables predict college graduation by the age of 22. This shows that these noncognitive skills may be very time-sensitive and may not persist well into the future, as children's personalities and habits change.

Overall, these results indicate that noncognitive skills do affect educational attainment, but they are not a large mechanism by which religious parents specifically improve their children's chances of continuing for higher education.[13]

CONCLUSION

The goal of this chapter was to put a greater context around adolescent noncognitive skills by looking at where they come from, how they get utilized and if they produce positive consequences for young people. This was done through the prism of religion.

Religion does not sit easily within adolescent culture, especially not parents' religion (Pearce & Denton, 2012; Smith, 2005). That said, this chapter highlights that for those adolescents who have highly religious parents and then adopt their high religiosity for themselves, those adolescents can dramatically increase their noncognitive skills. Those skills do seem to make adolescents more conscientious, positive, and nice—and presumably have other benefits too—even if those skills do not translate into huge educational gains.

In general, the role of noncognitive skills in adolescents' lives needs vastly more study. After all, the measures I used to measure such skills are somewhat crude and only approximate, and so it is possible with a greater battery of questions that directly speaks to noncognitive skills (like those outlined in Farkas, 2003), we could learn even more about how they skills operate in adolescents' lives. Additionally, these models are strictly quantitative, and more light could be shed on these processes if researchers used other techniques, like interviews (as Smith, 2005, and Pearce & Denton, 2012 do) and ethnography as well.

Overall, this chapter highlights the critical role religion can play in altering adolescent behavior, failure and success, but also the difficulty in tracing the exact pathways by which religion comes to alter adolescent life chances.

In light of the above results, Farkas' (2003) omission of religion as a cultural resource (akin to racial/ethnic communities or high-culture activities) may be somewhat less critical. Clearly, noncognitive affect children's achievement to a degree, but the pathway from parental religiosity to increased noncognitive skills does not lead very powerfully to the ultimate goal of higher educational attainment. By tracing out all of these linkages, this chapter shows the value of this approach, however. Noncognitive skills, religion, and adolescent life chances do go together to some degree, but not quite in ways previously hypothesized.

NOTES

1. I will nonetheless include parental religious affiliation in my models as a control.
2. The sampling design is complex (for more on the design of the NLSY97, see Aughinbaugh & Gardecki, 2008). My sample (of approximately 2,850 children) differs from the initial sample (approx. $n = 9000$) because of attrition and missing data on key covariates. There are many ways of handling missing data (Allison 2001), but listwise deletion is the best in this case because it leads to conservative estimates of the effect of parental religiosity on education. Why? Firstly, if religion is associated with conscientiousness (McCullough & Willoughby, 2009) and if conscientiousness is also associated with completing a survey and staying in the sample (Floyd & Fowler, 2008), then the less religious people who *do* remain in the sample are likely to be the *most conscientiousness* of the less religious group. This ought to decrease any differences between highly religious and less religious parents, since their unmeasured characteristics should be more similar. Secondly, my listwise deletion strategy shrinks my sample size substantially, thus making it harder to detect small differences between groups; and so if I do find such differences, this suggests they are quite robust.
3. All of these transitions are based on educational attainment reported in 2004.
4. The original GPA measure is approximately 85th% correlated with the residualized GPA, but now residualized GPA is completely uncorrelated with ASVAB percentile, while initially GPA and ASVAB percentile were approximately 50% correlated.
5. For concision, I do not actually report these variables in the tables, but they are available upon request.
6. This includes Baptists, Holiness (Nazarene, Wesleyan, Free Methodist), Pentecostals (Assembly of God, Pentecostal Holiness), Nondenominational Christians (Bible Church), and other Protestants.
7. This includes Methodists, Lutherans, Presbyterians, Episcopalians/Anglicans, United Church of Christ (or Congregationalist or Evangelical Reformed), Disciples of Christ (or the Christian Church), and Reform (or Reformed Church in America or Christian Reformed Church).
8. I based the family's affiliation on the affiliation of whichever parent had the highest religious attendance, and I broke ties between parents at random.
9. The parents' level of supportiveness is derived from the variable, *Parents' Level of Supportiveness*. Children were asked to estimate, in general, how each parent acts toward them, in terms of being very supportive, somewhat supportive, or not very supportive. Four waves of data were averaged, and the maximum of either parent was taken. Then the data were split at the mean, and a "high

supportiveness" indicator was created for those above the mean. The parents' level of strictness was determined based on the variable, *Parental Strictness.* Children were asked to estimate, in general, how permissive or strict each parent was, about making sure they did what they were supposed to do. Four waves of data were averaged, and the maximum of either parent was taken. Then the data were split at the mean, and a "strict" indicator was created for those above the mean.

10. This effect is likely not because kids of highly religious parents go to schools that give higher average grades. We are capturing a real "effort" effect because (in results not shown) girls score much higher on this measure than boys; a large literature illustrates that girls are ranked higher on noncognitive skills (DiPrete & Jennings, 2012) and in this case, they get "residualized" GPAs that are almost a fifth of a standard deviation higher (Beta = 0.17 for 8th-grade GPA and Beta = 0.21 for high school GPA) than boys. Likewise, children whose parents score high on school involvement (Beta = 0.09) and keeping a tidy home (Beta = 0.11) also score higher on this measure, indicating that this proxy for "effort" is consistent with kids whose parents enhance their home environment or interaction with the school. Likewise, higher rates of parochial and private school attendance do not account for these higher grades either.

11. I also considered whether adolescents had even higher noncognitive skills scores if both they and their parents attended services frequently, but the interaction between those two variables was not statistically significant.

12. Even though this methodology probably undersells parenting behaviors a bit because they are implicated in adolescent religiosity, empirically, these parenting behaviors only explain about 5% of the relationship between parental religiosity and children's religiosity (in results not shown), though most of the parenting behaviors are statistically significant and positively related to adolescent religiosity.

13. Parental religiosity also affects educational attainment indirectly through increasing some of the noncognitive skills that then, in turn, increase schooling chances. But those indirect effects are minor as well. For instance, high school grades, net of IQ, have a Beta coefficient of 0.16 on predicting high school completion, and parental religiosity has a 0.06 Beta on the high school grades, net of IQ—and so, the additional indirect effect of parental religiosity on high school completion operating through high school grades, net of IQ is miniscule: $0.16 * 0.06 = 0.001$, meaning that this pathway increases the standardized linear probability of completing high school by only 0.001 of a standard deviation.

REFERENCES

Allison, P. D. (2001). *Missing data.* Thousand Oaks, CA: Sage Publications.

Aughinbaugh, A., & Gardecki, R. M. (2008). *Attrition in the National Longitudinal Survey of Youth 1997.* Washington, DC, Bureau of Labor Statistics Conference Center, NLSY97 Tenth Anniversary Conference, May 29–30, 2008.

Bartkowski, J. P., Xu, X., & Levin, M. L. (2008). Religion and child development: Evidence from the early childhood longitudinal study. *Social Science Research, 37*, 18–36.

Bowles, S., Gintis, H., & Osborne, M. (2001). The determinants of earnings: A behavioral approach. *Journal of Economic Literature, 39*(4), 1137–1176.

Coleman, J. S. (1988). Social capital in the creation of human capital. *American Journal of Sociology 94*, 95–120.

DiPrete, T. A., & Jennings, J. L. (2012). Social and behavioral skills and the gender gap in early educational achievement. *Social Science Research, 41*(1), 1–15.

Duckworth, A. L., & Seligman, M. E. P. (2005). Self-discipline outdoes IQ in predicting academic performance of adolescents. *Psychological Science 16*, 939–944.

Duncan, G. J., Dowsett, C. J., Claessens, A., Magnuson, K., Huston, A. C., Klebanov, P., . . . Japel, C. (2007). School readiness and later achievement. *Developmental Psychology, 43*(6), 428–446.

Eirich, G. M. (2012). Parental religiosity and children's educational attainment in the United States. *Research in the Sociology of Work, 23*, 153–181.

Ellison, C. G. (1992). Are religious people nice people? Evidence from the National Survey of Black Americans. *Social Forces, 71*(2), 339–363.

Ellison, C. G., & Sherkat, D. E. (1993). Obedience and autonomy: Religion and parental values reconsidered. *Journal for the Scientific Study of Religion 32*, 313–329.

Ellison, C. G., Bartkowski, J. P., & Segal, M. L. (1996). Conservative Protestantism and the parental use of corporal punishment. *Social Forces, 74*, 1003–1028.

Farkas, G. (2003). Cognitive skills and noncognitive traits and behaviors in stratification processes. *Annual Review of Sociology, 29*, 541–562.

Farrington, C. A., Roderick, M., Allensworth, E., Nagaoka, J., Keyes, T. S., Johnson, D. W., & Beechum, N. O. (2012). *Teaching adolescents to become learners: The role of noncognitive factors in shaping school performance: A critical literature review.* Chicago, IL: University of Chicago Consortium on Chicago School Research.

Fejgin, N. (1995). Factors contributing to the academic excellence of American Jewish and Asian students. *Sociology of Education, 68*, 18–30.

Floyd, J., & Fowler, J. (2008). *Survey research methods.* London, UK: Sage Publications.

Greeley, A. M., & Hout, M. (2006). *The truth about Conservative Christians: What they think and what they believe.* Chicago, IL: University of Chicago Press.

Gunnoe, M. L., & Moore, K. A. (2002). Predictors of religiosity among youth aged 17–22: A longitudinal study of the National Survey of Children. *Journal for the Scientific Study of Religion, 41*, 613–622.

Heckman, J., & Krueger, A. (Eds.). (2003). *Inequality in America: What role for human capital policy?* Cambridge, MA: MIT Press.

Hood Jr, R.W., Hill, P. C., & Spilka, B. (2009). *The psychology of religion: An empirical approach.* New York, NY: The Guilford Press.

Hsin, A., & Xie, Y. (2012, February). *Hard skills, soft skills: The relative roles of cognitive and noncognitive skills in intergenerational social mobility.* University of Michigan, Institute of Social Research: Population Studies Center Research Report.

Lareau, A. (2003). *Unequal childhoods: Class, race, and family life.* Berkeley, CA: University of California Press.

Lizardo, O. (Forthcoming). Habitus. In B. Kaldis (Ed.). *Encyclopedia of philosophy and the social sciences.* London, UK: Sage Publications

McCullough, M. E., & Willoughby, B. L. B. (2009). Religion, self-regulation, and self-control: Associations, explanations, and implications. *Psychological Bulletin, 135,* 69–93.

Muller, C., & Ellison, C. G. (2001). Religious involvement, social capital and academic achievement: Evidence from the National Education Longitudinal Study of 1988. *Sociological Focus, 34,* 155–183.

National Longitudinal Survey of Youth 1997 cohort, 1997–2004 (rounds 1–8) [computer file]. (2004). Bureau of Labor Statistics, U.S. Department of Labor. Produced by the National Opinion Research Center, the University of Chicago and distributed by the Center for Human Resource Research, The Ohio State University. Columbus, OH.

Nelsen, H. M., & Kroliczak, A. (1984). Parental use of the threat "God will punish": Replication and extension. *Journal for the Scientific Study of Religion, 23,* 267–277.

Nunn, C. Z. (1964). Child-control through a "coalition with God." *Child Development, 35,* 417–432.

Pearce, L. D., & Denton, M. L. (2012). *A faith of their own: Stability and change in the religiosity of America's adolescents.* New York, NY: Oxford University Press.

Regnerus, M. D. (2007). *Forbidden fruit? Sex and religion in American adolescence.* New York, NY: Oxford University Press.

Saroglou, V. (2002). Religion and the five factors of personality: a meta-analytic review. *Personality and Individual Differences, 32,* 15–25.

Smith, C. (2003a). Research note: Religious participation and parental moral expectations and supervision of American youth. *Review of Religious Research, 44,* 414–424.

Smith, C. (2003b). Theorizing religious effects among American adolescents. *Journal for the Scientific Study of Religion, 42,* 17–30.

Smith, C. (2005). *Soul searching: The religious and spiritual lives of American teenagers.* New York, NY: Oxford University Press.

Stokes, C. E. (2008). The role of parental religiosity in high school completion. *Sociological Spectrum, 28*(5), 531–555.

Swidler, A. (2001). *Talk of love: How culture matters.* Chicago, IL: University Of Chicago Press.

Tough, P. (2012). *How children succeed: Grit, curiosity, and the hidden power of character.* New York, NY: Houghton Mifflin/Harcourt.

Wilcox, W. B., Chaves, M., & Franz, D. (2004). Focused on the family? Religious traditions, family discourse, and pastoral practice. *Journal for the Scientific Study of Religion, 43,* 491–504.

Wolfe, R. N., & Johnson, S. D. (1995). Personality as a predictor of college performance. *Educational and Psychological Measurement 55,* 177–185.

Wong, M. G. (1990). The education of White, Chinese, Filipino, and Japanese students: A look at "High School and Beyond." *Sociological Perspectives, 33,* 355–374.

Yeung, W. J., Duncan, G. J., & Hill, M. S. (2000). Putting fathers back in the picture: Parental activities and children's adult outcomes. In G. W. Peterson, H. E. Peters, & R. D. Day (Eds.), *Fatherhood: research, interventions and policies* (pp. 97–114). New York, NY: Haworth Press.

CHAPTER 4

ADOLESCENT LITERACY DEVELOPMENT AND THE NEW LITERACIES

Challenges and Possibilities

J. David Gallagher

ABSTRACT

While it is being argued that adolescents will need to be the most literate workforce in history as they prepare for lives in the information society, the very definition of what it means to be literate is changing and evolving. For parents, teachers, coaches, organizations, and those tasked with guiding adolescent youth through the literacy demands of the changing world, the job can be equally unnerving. This chapter will present those challenges and possibilities for those educators supporting adolescents as they learn to use literacy to understand and make an impact upon their worlds. Research will be presented that examines the "new literacies," particularly those related to new technologies and adolescents' vernacular literacies, and the role they play in adolescent literacy development in new times. Implications for educators and other groups who have a vested interest in the literate lives of adolescent youth will be discussed.

Adolescence in the 21st Century, pages 63–85
63

INTRODUCTION

It is January and the ninth grade English class period is about to begin. Cadence,[1] a self-proclaimed "bookworm" and avid reader of fiction, informs her teacher, Mrs. Oakley, that she has accidently thrown away her vocabulary packet with the list of words and definitions for the week's vocabulary exam. Without the vocabulary packet, Cadence was going to have to look up each vocabulary word again to study for the end of the week exam. Marcus, one of Cadence's classmates, offered the suggestion of an online dictionary to help her quickly find the meaning of the words, and this suggestion set off a discussion about what counts as "real" texts and appropriate ways of engaging with these texts in the changing technology and literacy landscape.

Mrs. Oakley: Okay, [an online dictionary], or a real—you know, have you guys ever seen the old-fashioned, real dictionaries?
Student: Yeah.
Anthony: The *real* dictionaries? [with exaggerated emphasis on *real*]
Mrs. Oakley: [grabbing her dictionary off of her desk] They look like something like this.

. . .

Mrs. Oakley: How many of you have a really good dictionary at home, like this? (raising the dictionary up in the air)

[About 1/4 of the class raises their hands.]

Marcus: I have a question. //I have a question//.
Mrs. Oakley: //How many of you// use dictionaries online more nowadays?
Marcus: There is no need for [a traditional dictionary]. Why would you ever need that? (speaking quickly and with a bit of frustration) You have a computer that can go online.
Anthony: When you are playing Scrabble and you don't want to run to your computer all the time.
Marcus: It's way //faster than trying to figure it out//
Mrs. Oakley: //Well, this one// well it depends on what . . . I haven't used [online dictionary], but this one gives you word origins, there's several definitions—

[Several students begin talking loudly about online dictionaries.]

Marcus: You can get that online, everything.

What started off as a frustrating situation for Cadence turned into an active and meaningful discussion between the students and teacher, where they negotiated the appropriate/privileged texts and practices of the class-room. In the moment that Mrs. Oakley acknowledged the point of tension between traditional dictionaries and online dictionaries, the students pulled in their resources, being tech-savvy teenagers, disrupting what counts as of-ficial texts and literacy activities in the classroom during what is becoming an ever-changing literacy landscape. The construction of what counts as an English text occurs throughout the English class (as well as in a variety of contexts, in and out of the classroom) and is largely constructed in the as-signment and study of the selected texts of the classroom. I will argue that it is through a variety of processes throughout the year where the teacher and students work out what English is during this time of change.

Throughout the school year, I conducted an ethnographic case study where I explored how Mrs. Oakley, Cadence, Marcus, and the other stu-dents of the ninth-grade class handled the challenging tasks of learning to be literate and learning to use literacy to understand themselves, each other, and the world during these changing times. Together they explored traditional and contemporary literature and poetry, wrote lengthy respons-es to what they read, and conducted library research for evidence-based argumentative essays. As they engaged in these typical English classroom practices, they also explored the boundaries of what it meant to be literate, to read, to write, and to make meaning, within the current technological changes, growing cultural diversity, and increasing pressures for standards and high-stakes assessments (The New London Group, 1996).

ADOLESCENT LITERACY AND THE NEW LITERACIES

Adolescents are learning to be literate in exciting and turbulent times. While the expectations for the 21st-century literacy knowledge and skills are increasing and becoming more important, the very tools and practices associated with effective literacy competence and what counts as successful literacy are changing. At the turn of the 21st century, Moore, Bean, Bird-yshaw, and Rycik (1999) argued in their influential position statement on adolescent literacy that:

> Adolescents entering the adult world in the 21st century will read and write more than at any other time in human history. They will need advanced levels of literacy to perform their jobs, run their households, act as citizens, and conduct their personal lives. They will need literacy to cope with the flood of information they will find everywhere they turn. They will need literacy to feed their imaginations so they can create the world of the future. (p. 99)

Since Moore et al. (1999) wrote their position statement on adolescent literacy, many young people have done just that: used sophisticated and interconnected literacies to impact and change their worlds. The teenagers that Moore et al. (1999) were referring to ended up going on to develop new technologies and participate in the greatest technological and literacy revolution in modern times, changing the way many people communicate, share information, and live their lives (Grossman, 2010; Safian, 2012). While projects like Facebook, Box, and Summly were started and fueled by these students to whom Moore et al. (1999) were referring, over ten years later, young people are continuing to use their advanced levels of literacies to contribute to movements around issues important to them (Morrell, 2006; Meza, 2011), and fuel the increased production of multimodal content in the world each day (Nixon, 2009).

While we have seen evidence of youth using literacy to "feed their imaginations so they can create the world of the future," we are also aware that during this time when youth will need advanced levels of literacy, many adolescents are falling short in demonstrating their ability with academic literacies (National Center for Education Statistics, 2011). Likewise, alarming statistics continue to show adolescents less engaged and less motivated in areas of academic reading and writing (Iyengar, Ball, & National Endowment for the Arts, 2007). Therefore, on the one hand we have increasing expectations for the advanced levels of literacy expertise for effective public and work lives, and on the other hand, rapid change regarding the nature of literacies in and out of the classroom.

One powerful way in which researchers and educators have examined literacy development is by documenting the situated ways in which adolescent youth read and write in and out of school by documenting their everyday literacy experiences (Alvermann, Marshall, McLean, Huddleston, Joaquin, & Bishop, 2012; Gallagher, 2007; Moje, 2002). Following a theoretical perspective that sees literacy as a social practice, researchers examine the literacy texts and literacy practices (i.e., situated ways in which youth engage with texts), which are important in understanding "people's awareness of literacy, constructions of literacy and discourses of literacy, how people talk about and make sense of literacy" (Barton & Hamilton, 1998, p. 6). Those educators who have studied students' texts and literacy practices in and out of school argue that students, including students who struggle academically, engaged in sophisticated literacy activities in out-of-school contexts "to make sense of an take power in their worlds" (Moje, 2002, p. 217). Researchers have shown how these "new literacies" can be complex and purposeful and could be used as a scaffold to official literacy texts and practices, or even be included as valued texts in the official curriculum (Alvermann & Xu, 2003; Brass, 2008; Moje, 2002; O'Brien & Scharber, 2008; Sweeney, 2010).

Many of those researchers who view literacy as a social practice have been at the forefront of documenting the changing nature of literacies. Within their work on the new literacies, Lankshear and Knobel (2003, 2005) distinguish between two different conceptions of new literacies: the chronological and the ontological. The chronological refers to those literacy activities and practices that educators and literacy theorists have recently begun to recognize as valued literacies, which do not necessarily consist of new technical aspects, such as scrapbooking, collecting and sharing recipes, and reading and creating zines. These activities and practices are new in that they were previously not recognized as literacies. This becomes important for our work with adolescents as they historically have engaged in these sorts of activities that have not been understood nor valued as literacy practices within privileged or school related contexts.

The ontological sense of new refers to those literacies that are different from traditional literacies largely because of new technical resources available for the production and consumption of texts. Lankshear and Knobel (2005) refer to these ontologically new literacies as those that are mediated by "post-typographic forms of texts," such as "using and constructing hyperlinks between documents and/or images, sounds, movies, etc.; text messaging on a mobile phone" (p. 25) and

> reading file extensions and identifying what software will 'read' each file; navigating three-dimensional worlds online; uploading images from a camera or digital phone to a computer or to the Internet; inserting text into a digital image or animation, attaching sound to an image, or inserting sound into an image; building multimedia role play universes online; choosing, building or customizing a weblog template. (p. 25)

In recent years there has been an explosion in the amount of places that adolescents can turn to in order to access and produce texts through various media (most of which adolescents can access from their personal phones, tablets, or computers): books (both digital and in print), online websites, and online social networking spaces. What we have is a changing literacy landscape with an increasing need to prepare adolescent youth to meet the demands of these 21st-century literacies (Coiro, Knobel, Lankshear, & Leu, 2008). This leaves educators and those tasked with supporting adolescents during these turbulent times to be on the front lines for negotiating the texts and practices of the 21st century. In the following case study, the teacher and students were in the process of negotiating the boundaries of appropriate texts and practices for the English classroom. An integral part of "doing" English in "new times" involved the negotiation of what counted as "official" texts, which texts became selected for study, and which texts were valued as resources for meaning making. What follows in this chapter is a look into Mrs. Oakley's ninth-grade classroom as the teacher and students negotiate the boundaries of literacy practices, and an exploration of the possibilities and challenges for those educators involved in guiding adolescents to use literacy to understand and make an impact upon their worlds during these uncertain times.

POSSIBILITIES

Expanding What Counts as Texts and Literacies in the Classroom

At the heart of Mrs. Oakley's ninth-grade English class was the reading of a variety of literary texts—novels, plays, short stories, and a Greek tragedy (see Figure 4.1). These novels, plays, and short stories became much of the subject of English content (i.e., plot storylines, knowledge of characters), as well as the main vehicle in which literary analytic skills were learned (i.e., character development, symbolism). Therefore, these texts served as

---

*The Old Man and the Sea** (Ernest Hemingway)
A selection of short stories:
    "Scarlet Ibis" (James Hurst)
    "The Secret Life of Walter Mitty" (James Thurber)

Bean Trees (Barbara Kingsolver)

At Risk (Alice Hoffman)

Students chose to read one of the following books for a partner reading
    assignment:
    Bless the Beasts and the Children (Glendon Swarthout)
    So Far from the Bamboo Grove (Yoko Kawashawa Watkins)
    When the Legends Die (Hal Borland)
    Waiting for the Rain (Sheila Gordon)
    Children of the River (Linda Crew)
    Jemmy (Jon Hassler)

*To Kill a Mockingbird** (Harper Lee)

*Raisin in the Sun** (Lorraine Hansberry)

*Romeo & Juliet** (William Shakespeare)

The Odyssey^ (Homer)

---

* Selected by the English department as required texts of all English classes; the
  rest were part of a list of optional texts
^ Was not able to get to during the year

Figure 4.1 Assigned novels, plays, and short stories, in order in which they were studied.

the cornerstone for many of the pedagogical units and literacy practices that the class would engage in during the year, including teacher-led shared reading and literature discussions, quizzes and exams, individual written or artistic responses, take-home reading assignments, and from time to time, in-class silent reading. It was partly through the study of these official texts that the students and teacher came to negotiate which texts were valued, which were worth serious study, and which would become the "official" texts of the classroom.

All of the texts assigned to the students were fictional pieces of literature that had been approved by the English department. The curriculum was designed to include texts that would introduce students to classical and contemporary literature. Therefore, traditional texts of the English curriculum were included, such as Homer's *The Odyssey*, Shakespeare's *Romeo and Juliet*, Hemingway's *The Old Man and the Sea*, and a collection of short stories ("Scarlet Ibis," by James Hurst; "The Secret Life of Walter Mitty," by James Thurber). These texts have long been part of the high school English canon (Applebee, 1993) and reflect the school's curricular focus in the mythology of ancient Greece, Shakespearean plays, and American literature. The curriculum also included literature by contemporary authors (*Bean Trees* by Barbara Kingsolver; *At Risk* by Alice Hoffman) as well as texts that reflect multicultural and cross-cultural issues (*Raisin in the Sun* by Lorraine Hansberry; *To Kill a Mockingbird* by Harper Lee). Each of the texts fell into at least one of the three thematic categories (from innocence to experience, the heroic journey, and multiple perspectives), and many of the texts had topics that reflected contemporary issues in students' lives (AIDS, multiculturalism, poverty). Indeed, the curriculum was designed to introduce students to both traditional and contemporary literature, while also at times focusing on themes that reflected the age of the students ("from innocence to experience") and the current issues of the day (e.g., the increasing cultural diversity).

Although Mrs. Oakley had little choice in the texts that she selected for her class, she found curricular opportunities for her students to engage with texts that were outside of the standard curriculum. Many of the official texts offered were print-based texts, in the form of novels, plays, or short stories. In addition to these selections, Mrs. Oakley integrated a number of texts into the class that were not part of the standard texts designated by the English department, including more multimodal texts, like graphic texts, a combination of print and graphic, musical texts, film texts, and events and experiences that were quintessentially multimodal in nature (e.g., a celebration of Martin Luther King Jr. at the local university where the event included song, dance, poetry, and some of Dr. King's writings and speeches).

Mrs. Oakley frequently included texts in the classroom space that were a combination of graphics and print, usually in the form of traditional comic strips. Cartoons were given space in the classroom at different times during the year. Mrs. Oakley included cartoons that she cut out from the newspaper in assignments and quizzes that she gave to the students during the year. Usually the comic was just something that students would read on their own if they chose to do so. In a couple of instances, Mrs. Oakley used a cartoon to lead the class in a discussion of a particular topic. On one such occasion, late in the year, she distributed Gary Trudeau's cartoon *Doonesbury*, where he titled it "Operation Iraqi Freedom: In Memoriam," and listed the U.S. men and women who had died in the war since April 28, 2004, in a way that resembled the names on the Vietnam Memorial. Not having enough space in the cartoon for all the names of those U.S. soldiers who had died, Trudeau writes at the end, "CONTINUED NEXT WEEK" (capitalization in original). Mrs. Oakley introduces the cartoon by saying that Trudeau often comments on political topics, and in this cartoon he presents a perspective on the war, one that is different than just the normal "statistics on the front page, 12 people blown up today, or 12 people die in suicide bombings." She tells the class that she thinks they are in order of death dates.

> **Catherine:** That's depressing, why did he do that?
> **Mrs. Oakley:** Well, because this country has sort of forgotten in some ways
> that we are at war, and every single name on here represents
> a family and a group of friends that have lost this person.
> It is an extremely powerful statement that Gary Trudeau is
> making here.

Mrs. Oakley goes on to tell the class that it appears to her that there is a very different atmosphere now than there was during Vietnam, when they used to display the names of those killed each day on the evening news. She then asks the class if anyone has been to the memorial:

> **Student:** Last year, I went with the 8th grade trip to Washington, you
> got to go—I walked through, me and my friend walked
> through, we touched the whole wall, it was getting dark, it
> was the prettiest time, it wasn't pitch black but it was ____.
> **Mrs. Oakley:** A very moving experience. [The student then goes on to
> discuss other places she visited on that trip.]

Recognizing the important artistic decision, Mrs. Oakley pointed out the similarity between the way in which Trudeau listed the names on the cartoon and the Vietnam Memorial in Washington, DC. Asking students who had seen the memorial opened up opportunities for students' personal experiences and texts to enter the classroom. Mrs. Oakley's initial intention was for the students to quickly view the cartoon, its message, and then move on to the activities of the day. However, like other times in the year when powerful texts like this were provided, students asked questions and welcomed conversations on social and political issues, and Mrs. Oakley allowed them to go where it took them.

Mrs. Oakley: Well, we need to move on [She calls on Marcus who has had his hand up since Mrs. Oakley started talking about Vietnam.]

Marcus: I, I don't know, the Vietnam War, there was, if you think the—you don't want to compare deaths, but if you amount of deaths in the Vietnam War to the amount... It's not even close to being the amount. I think that is probably the reason why they are not it on the news because it is not 300 people a day that are dying, or 3,000 people a day that are dying.

Mrs. Oakley: But my point is, that to those families that //lose those//

Marcus: //I know, I know.//

. . .

Student: The wall was like that long. [motioning with her hands] The names were very small, and people had to look real close.

Allowing students to continue the discussion provided an additional opportunity for the student to utilize her experience with the Vietnam Memorial. This time, her experience becomes an important resource for conveying the number of people who died in the war, which was being disputed at the time. Although she could not give the number, the student was able to communicate the experience of seeing the entirety of the wall with the small printed names.

During the twenty minutes that they engaged with this unofficial text and the issues that arose as a result of it, they discussed important current social and political issues related to topics that were important to them and their families. The teacher and students were evidently moved by the cartoon and by what they had been watching and hearing in the media about the women and men in Iraq. Marcus was especially passionate about the importance of supporting the soldiers who were involved in the war, especially since his cousins were enlisting after they graduate from high school. The class was also moved by the questions and conversations raised in the discussion (e.g., what is meant by freedom? what is the role of government in "defending" freedom? when is war justified? what is the role of texts like the cartoon in raising important issues?). It was this reason that Mrs. Oakley, while recognizing the need to continue reading *Romeo & Juliet*, allowed the students to continue the dialogue. In instances like this one above, unofficial texts—the comic that started the discussion or the posters on the wall—become sites of entry into important discussion topics and meaningful learning opportunities for the students.

THE INCLUSION OF STUDENTS' LITERACY TEXTS: TEXTS AS RESOURCES FOR MEANING MAKING

One of the more robust conclusions from cognitive psychology and literacy research over the last half century is that students learn new information and ideas by connecting it with prior knowledge. One of the possibilities that arise when we value the rich literacy resources students bring to the classroom is that new opportunities for meaning making and effective processing of new knowledge and ideas are available. In Mrs. Oakley's classroom there were few texts that were out of bounds for students to integrate into classroom events as they made sense of new texts and ideas. As the year progressed, students learned that they could take advantage of this broad range of available texts and often were responsible for bringing in various texts and practices into the classroom. In any class period, students would include their own digital (video games, websites), musical (hip hop, jazz), and television/film texts (independent films, popular films, television series) as sources of meaningful connection with new classroom texts.

Of these various textual resources utilized in the classroom, television and film texts were most prevalent throughout the entire year. During just about every class meeting, a film text was referenced, quoted, and/or entered a conversation. Mrs. Oakley often included the description of scenes from a film to illustrate a theme or point she was making. She also welcomed film texts as important resources for students to contribute when discussing any other text or idea. Film texts, though often not included as part of the formal curriculum and official texts, were centrally positioned as a form of resource for students to make sense of the formal curriculum.

Since Mrs. Oakley wove these film and television texts throughout classroom activity, it was normal for students to do the same. While discussing the names that Harper Lee (1960) chose for her two protagonist characters—Scout and Jem—in *To Kill a Mockingbird*, Mrs. Oakley told the class that the names were androgynous, and asked them, "Do you know what androgynous means?"

Larissa: That means something that goes both ways.
Mrs. Oakley: Yeah, it can have characteristics of both, male and female, or not specifically male or specifically female.
Larissa: Like Pat, on SNL [Saturday Night Live]

Mrs. Oakley: Yes, okay, [laughing] how many of you have seen that, those skits with Pat, they are trying to desperately find out she/he is a boy or a girl, and every time they do something backfires, *very* funny scenes.

When Mrs. Oakley asked the class if they had seen the Saturday Night Live clips with Pat to which Larissa was referring, many of the students raised their hands. Seeing that this resource was an important one for the students, Mrs. Oakley suggested that they should watch one of the skits since it's "worth watching, and a great parody too."

It was evident from being in the classroom for any short amount of time that the students had a wealth of film and television knowledge that they could draw from during any of the class discussions. Often these texts were used to illustrate a concept, character, or theme that they were discussing in relation to one of the official texts of the classroom. Other times, film and television texts were offered when defining words (like "androgynous") and when discussing current issues that arose from these texts.

Drawing from these film and television texts became a valued way of participating in the classroom, as the students took the lead from Mrs. Oakley, who would often make text connections to film/television texts. Instances like the discussion of Pat from Saturday Night Live were common ways that the teacher and students expanded the boundaries of potential resources for making meaning of official texts (Fairclough, 2000). These film and television texts were mostly utilized as a scaffold for understanding, appreciating, and making sense of the formal, official texts of the classroom. In the "Pat" discussion above, although the possibility of bringing in the DVD of the scenes from the television program to study as text was mentioned, neither the teacher nor the students followed through with bringing in and incorporating the film clips as part of the texts of the classroom.

When students offered their own literacy texts, the classroom was transformed into a place of student participation and textual diversity. Students' outside texts and literacy practices became sites of resource and the classroom became one of sharing textual experiences and resources. During one of Mrs. Oakley's lessons centered on reading the newspaper (during this instance it was the school's newspaper), Marcus and Anthony claim classroom space and expand the discussion. Before going on to the activities of the day, Mrs. Oakley wanted the class to focus on a couple of things in the school's newspaper. Mrs. Oakley describes to the class the point-counterpoint feature of the opinion section of the paper, and tells them that it is similar to how it is done on a popular television news program.

Mrs. Oakley: They pick an issue, and I don't know how really they pick the issue, and they pick an issue and do a pro and a con, point and counterpoint. So they are always very interesting to read, and they have very, very different opinions and different references and people they are talking to and interviewing to support their particular ideas.

Mrs. Oakley begins talking about the newspaper, a text that is not part of the formal curriculum and often seen as the students' voice on the high school campus. Students are often flipping through the paper the day that it comes out, looking for the many stories about students (as Marcus points at), major news stories, and controversial issues. This begins as a quick discussion of a couple points from the newspaper and soon turns into a discussion of different sections of the paper. Mrs. Oakley has spoken during much of the discussion to this point, as it was supposed to be a quick deviation from the plan for the day. However, the discussion soon becomes a space for students to engage with their own texts and practices. Building off of the point/counterpoint discussion, Anthony turns to the class and asks: "Anyone read *The Onion* in here?"

Mrs. Oakley: *The Onion?* Is that the cartoon?
   Anthony: The fake newspaper.
    Marcus: My aunt was talking about that.
Mrs. Oakley: What is *The Onion,* I don't know what it is?
   Anthony: It is like a fake newspaper with all kinds of ridiculous articles with actual pictures and stuff. It's kind of like the *World Weekly News* and *The National Enquirer,* but it's more intelligent and not ridiculous humor, like they put out a parody of our terrorist colors, but the lowest one was like the lowest chance of seeing your children blown away in front of you, or something. [Mrs. Oakley and some students laugh] And the highest one is like, paradise is coming, or whatever.
Mrs. Oakley: Where do you get this, is this a printed thing, or on-line?
   Anthony: Yah, you can get it in Chicago, that's where //I got it.//
    Marcus: //They have// it in San Diego.
   Anthony: They have it all over the place. I'm trying to get the local 7/11 to start it but you know, it started in Madison, Wisconsin, but the point and counterpoint just reminded me of . . . the point was like Sudan: a developing nation with a lot many new cultures. And the counterpoint was get me out of this Hell-hole or something like that. Just //totally ridiculous.//
Mrs. Oakley: //It sounds like// those of you who like watching *The Daily Show* would like that paper, right.
   Anthony: Yah.

At the center of this discussion are Anthony's questions to the class about *The Onion,* and his willingness to connect *The Onion* to the point/counterpoint. While starting with the school's newspaper, a wide range of texts are included as part of the discussion: *The Onion, 60 Minutes, The Daily Show, The World Weekly News* and *The National Enquirer,* and the local newspaper created and distributed once a year. Anthony contributes *The Onion* as a text that might be meaningful if you like parody, and by the end of the discussion, Mrs. Oakley had made the suggestion that others might enjoy reading it. While Mrs. Oakley clearly has a set of texts that make up the official curriculum, both she and the students actively include a variety of texts and literacy practices that provide opportunities for students to make connections, use their textual resources, and ultimately play a role in bringing new literacies into the official space of the classroom.

CHALLENGES

What Counts as Texts?: "Touchstones" and the Authority of Official Texts

While Mrs. Oakley's classroom was often characterized by a fluid space of textual diversity, there were many instances where this fluidity was challenged and, at times, nonexistent due to various contextual influences at play. Mrs. Oakley had little space for making decisions to incorporate particular texts that fell outside of the official curriculum that she deemed important for students. This lack of choice (outside of the alternative list) in her curriculum was rarely something that was discussed by Mrs. Oakley or the students. On one occasion, Mrs. Oakley made her constraints transparent to her students, explaining that one of the reasons that they spend very little time in the class with creative writing is that "there is a certain canon of literature that we have to cover here at the high school, it's just part of the program." Making this departmental decision known to the students in these interactions contributed to establishing the fact that there are systematic forces outside of the classroom that contribute to the regulation of texts, and ultimately reinforced the importance and value of these texts for the students.

Mrs. Oakley rarely explained why they were reading the particular assigned text or piece of literature. At times, she would highlight an author's powerful use of description, saying that it is some of the best symbolism or character description she has ever read. However, the literary texts they spent weeks studying were just accepted as normal and appropriate for ninth-grade English students. Rarely did the students vocally question, resist, or express excitement over the text they were reading. Throughout the semester, the students accepted the selected official texts as routine, normal, and an aspect of the class that they had no real choice in changing.

While Mrs. Oakley did not individually select many of these assigned traditional texts, she did, though, believe that these texts provided "touchstones" for the students and were essential for the students in their preparation for future classes. Mrs. Oakley believed that ninth-grade English was responsible for informing students of specific influential characters and texts that were expected for first year students. This included knowing about the characters and storylines of texts that all classes were required to read during the year (e.g., *The Odyssey, Romeo & Juliet*). After not being able to read the abridged version of *The Odyssey* to fully read *Romeo and Juliet* due to a lack of time, Mrs. Oakley was upset at the possible ramifications for this lack of attention to these canonical texts:

> I'd like the 10th grade teachers to at least be able to say, "well you know this character from. . . . " They are supposed to have some touchstones and be able to talk about those characters like in Romeo and Juliet with some proficiency.

This desire for students to have "touchstones" was evident throughout the semester and was an important impetus for much of the decisions that Mrs. Oakley made for the students. At various times in the semester, she would highlight certain references that were common in particular literary works, with the hope that the students would have these "touchstones" to access in the future.

The "touchstones" that Mrs. Oakley wanted students to learn surpassed characters and storylines and focused on literary traditions. When reading *To Kill a Mockingbird*, Mrs. Oakley focused on the way in which Harper Lee created a sense of the history of the land and people, and how her techniques reflected what many other southern writers attempted to capture in their writing. She explained to the class:

> There is a whole southern tradition of writers, Carson McCullers, and there is Tennessee Williams, and William Faulkner. A lot of these writers you will be exposed to when you hit English 3 with American Literature. They have a deep sense to the longing to the place where they are. You will see this in *To Kill a Mockingbird* as [Harper Lee] talks about the family history, and how that evolves over time.

Presenting the literary elements in *To Kill a Mockingbird* as part of a larger tradition they will continue to explore as they take other English classes in future years, Mrs. Oakley creates opportunities for students to have these "touchstones" for which to read future texts. An integral part of the ninth grade English experience, Mrs. Oakley sees her task as preparing the students for future engagement in practices by creating a series of characters and texts that they may utilize in future courses and during future experiences with texts. The pressures for students to have these "touchstones" for later classes influenced the curricular decisions of the classroom and were integral to the pressures to teach and expect students to know these official texts.

Values and Beliefs Associated with Official Texts

> *The man who does not read good books has no advantage*
> *over the man who can't read them.*
>
> —Mark Twain

Written in bold across the top of the page, Mark Twain's quote headlines the recommended reading list of over 200 books Mrs. Oakley gave to the students for their summer break. Works by Emily Brontë, William Shakespeare, Daniel Defoe, Ralph Ellison, Sylvia Plath, and William Faulkner appeared on the "Recommended Reading List" list of good books recommended to the students. This document highlights two important beliefs that were integral to the construction of texts in the classroom, maintaining the authority of the traditional canon of literature and of literary studies in English education.

The first belief that this text suggests is that there is such a thing as a hierarchy of books, and texts that are not plays or novels that might not appear on the list are of little value. This belief is part of a long tradition of valuing select books over others (Bloome, 1994) and was integral to the construction of texts in the classroom. At times, students did not recognize other books (e.g., nonfiction, romance, mysteries) as "real" books. During a side conversation in one class period, one of the students told me "I have a book right now that I'm reading. Well not a book, a biography." While other forms of texts were integrated into the classroom (e.g., comic, film, music), they never received the formal attention that the fictional print-based texts received. This hierarchy was most prevalent when literature was placed in contrast to film texts. Although Mrs. Oakley and the students included film texts in discussions and curricular decisions, these texts rarely received the curricular space that would allow these texts the seriousness that fictional texts were afforded. Connected to this belief was the idea that print-based texts deserve serious study, whereas discussing and engaging with other forms of texts (e.g., film, music, cartoon) involved just playful activity. For this English class, fictional texts (classical and contemporary) were recognized as the privileged texts. These texts were the center of most of the activity in the classroom (i.e., writing and assessments in reaction to these texts, literature discussions) and were considered the serious texts of study, the official curriculum.

The second belief that this text suggests is that studying canonical texts will enhance one's privileged intellectual position, as well as one's general intellectual skills. Reading canonical books or traditional fiction associated with the English discipline revealed a person's intellectual rigor and sophistication. This was most articulated in the course when Mrs. Oakley was providing a rationale for reading *The Old Man and the Sea.*

Mrs. Oakley: You know you guys, when you are at a party someday, and you are sitting there and you could say, "Hey have you read any Hemingway?" You could talk about the fact that you read *The Old Man and the Sea*, you're going to impress the crap out of somebody. You will.

Impressing people at parties with their reading of Hemingway was not Mrs. Oakley's sole reason for teaching the students this particular text. She often would focus on the beauty of the language or the relationships you attain with characters as reasons for reading. However, the fact that impressing people was mentioned as an important rationale for reading *The Old Man and the Sea* reinforces the idea that certain books remain privileged and worth reading (even though most students struggled through it and disliked the experience), because it can provide you some sophistication and cultural capital in certain future situations. Additionally, Twain's quote above the summer reading document further reinforced the connection between canonical literature and one's intellectual abilities, as seen in Mrs. Oakley's rationale for taking advanced placement literature. Responding to a student's question of why she would want to take the advanced placement literature course as a senior, Mrs. Oakley explained, "An AP literature class will train you to be an absolute thinker, writer, analyzer of things." Therefore, not only do classical texts provide sophistication and "culture," studying official texts in an advanced placement setting will also make the student into a more sophisticated thinker. This connection between canonical literature and intellectual abilities is a belief that underlies the recommendation to read canonical fiction over the summer, so that the students may improve their "thinking" and "analysis" skills.

Valuing print-based texts over other multimodal texts has a long tradition in the English discipline (Luke, 2000; Scholes, 1998). This practice diminishes numerous other texts that fall outside the traditional print-based texts privileged in English classrooms. As many scholars have pointed out, these non-print-centered texts and multimodal texts, such as movies, music, weblogs, and online journals are valuable texts in sophisticated literacy practices (Alvermann, Hagood, & Williams, 2001; Knobel, 1999). Not only are these texts integral to the multifaceted lives of the students, but they are important for the changing literacy landscape the students must negotiate in the future (Cope & Kalantzis, 2000). However, this belief in the hierarchy of texts (canonical fiction and print over other forms of texts), which still underlies activity in English classrooms, continues to be an important belief that maintains the official texts of the ninth-grade English classroom.

Student Responses to Official Texts: Print/Visual Multimodal Responses within the Official Curriculum

Mrs. Oakley provided the students with many opportunities, in addition to the usual essay response tests, for responding to and demonstrating their knowledge of the class texts. For two of the novels during the year, students produced texts as part of a "culminating activity," where they combined print with visual design. The first assignment was a "reduction" of their first novel of the year, Ernest Hemingway's *The Old Man and the Sea*, into "essential happenings." Mrs. Oakley asked them to create a reduction of the novel, where she wrote in the assignment sheet that the purpose was to "crystallize the novel into its essential and significant parts ... and will also help you remember the storyline of the novel for the rest of your life." Each student represented the novel by selecting 12 significant events and illustrating them on large white poster board paper in graphic novel form, with quotes and plot lines beneath each picture. The students included three references to symbolism and some representation of the literary thematic elements of heroic code and grace under pressure, which they discussed in class when reading the novel. Many of the students produced extremely well-detailed and colorful texts. They were displayed during the class so others could look at the projects, and then a few particularly colorful and well-detailed projects were displayed on the wall of the room (see Figure 4.2).

In Mrs. Oakley's ninth grade classroom there was a deliberate focus on engaging the students in literary analysis, especially character development. Therefore, although Mrs. Oakley provided opportunities for expanding the privileged texts of the classroom, the central focus of *The Old Man and the Sea* "reduction" activity was to evaluate the students' understanding and analysis of the novel. The focus was on producing a representation of the novel in a "reduction" form, and as a result, much of the attention and assessment of the assignment remained on whether or not the student had an accurate and in-depth understanding of the official text based on the print-based part of the assignment.

The lack of emphasis on the visual design of the text was partly due to the fact that the assessments of visual and spatial aspects of texts were unclear, when compared to the print-based text. Mrs. Oakley made explicit on the assignment sheet for the reduction assignment for *The Old Man and the Sea* that the students were not assessed based on their "artistic talent,

Figure 4.2 Two frames of Stephen's *Old Man and the Sea* "Reduction" text.

per se," but on their "neatness and attention to detail." Discussions about expectations of what consisted a neat and detailed text were nonexistent. At times, Mrs. Oakley would hold up a project that was particularly careful in detail (and usually drawn fairly realistically), and say, "Isn't this wonderful." She would hang up certain projects on the classroom walls recognizing texts that she described as examples of being created with thought and meticulous detail. She often told the class that many of the projects looked beautiful and looked like they spent lots of time on them.

Mrs. Oakley and the students had not explicitly discussed what distinguished a "good" multimodal (especially visual and spatial) text from a "less good" text, although there were implicit standards that were followed having to do with details and neatness. There were no rubrics for evaluating the design of the scrapbooks, the way there were rubrics for the formal assignments. While there is a grammar being developed for visual representation (Kress, 2003), in Mrs. Oakley's English classroom this grammar was not established and conventionalized in the way that students' formal writing (e.g., 5 paragraph essays) was presented and evaluated. Therefore, in these practices, the print-based aspects of the texts were highlighted during the evaluation, privileging print-based text over the visual and spatial aspects of the texts.

The integration of graphic and other multimodal texts expanded the possibilities of the classroom, enabling space for other normally unsanctioned texts and practices to enter the official space of the classroom. While these practices were important in expanding writing texts in the classroom, they ultimately were unfulfilled in the possible ways they might have led to valuing the diverse textual practices available. Importantly, students did not receive explicit guidelines or have a comprehensive understanding of what distinguished a good design from a bad one, except for one's attention to detail and the appearance of the amount of time put into the project. Additionally, students were graded on the content they provided (although extra credit for especially detailed pieces like Stephen's) and the printed aspects of the text. Ultimately, the lack of attention provided to design in the construction and assessment of the texts worked to maintain the traditional aspects of the practice, privileging the print aspects of the text and purpose of recalling details from the text.

IMPLICATIONS

It is an exciting time to be a student learning to use literacy for social, personal, and academic purposes. Adolescents have more possibilities to access and create texts of all kinds than ever before. With this excitement and possibility comes the reality of learning how to make sense of the overwhelming amount of texts and the freedom provided by the increasing tools for textual production. The classroom (and most probably the English classroom) must become a place where students make sense of the textual possibilities available, explore ways of meaning making and meaning creation, and "feed their imaginations so they can create the world of the future" (Moore et al., 1999, p. 99). Using Mrs. Oakley's classroom as a case study, we see how the classroom can be a fluid space where texts and literacy practices flow, often included by Mrs. Oakley and brought in by the students. We also see how students and the teacher are in the middle of negotiating what counts as English and literacy, what counts as a text, and what should be included in the study of literacy during these times of change. This case study presents the following recommendations for educators and those tasked with supporting adolescents in learning to use literacy to make sense of the their lives and have an impact on their world.

- Educators and adolescents should explore the boundaries of what counts as literacy and as an official text in today's changing literacy landscape (Cope & Kalantzis, 2000). It is important to note that literacies are not equal (Gee, 1996, 1999), which is a reason why critical awareness as part of an English curriculum is essential for students of the 21st century. However, simply reproducing the canon, and delegitimizing sophisticated and impactful reading and writing practices because they are not traditional does little to critique the power relations that exist. As Scholes (1998) and Kress (2003) argue, it is important that we teach students ways of navigating across a wide variety of texts, as well as ways of critically examining the power relationships involved with different forms of texts and practices.

Educators must develop and promote the kind of instruction that allows for the expansion of 21st-century literacy skills.

- If students will need an awareness of literacy that extends beyond the study of literature and formal essay writing, educators must be prepared to teach these new literacies. While Mrs. Oakley provided opportunities for expansion to multimodal texts, she did not have the curricular preparation and the assessment rubrics in place to teach and assess for multimodality. To fully address the multimodal characteristics of texts in the rapidly changing literacy landscape, including the affordances and constraints that different texts provide, we must be knowledgeable about these features of texts and have familiarity with how to teach literacy in a world where it is becoming increasingly easier (and the expectation greater) to access and create multimodal texts.

- Rather than immediately condemning students' unofficial literacies, educators must consider the ways in which students' literacy resources can be recognized, valued, and integrated into the classroom. Considering the ways in which the students' literacy resources were integral to participation in the classroom and into meaning making, it is suggested that we not immediately condemn students' unsanctioned literacies, but consider what they might teach us about the students *and* the possibilities of the new literacies in public and professional spaces (Alvermann, 2001; Dyson, 2003; Moje, Ciechanowski, Kramer, & Ellis, 2004; Morrell & Duncan-Andrade, 2004). We should continue exploring ways of integrating students' literacies into classroom spaces, for scaffolding students to canonical texts and also for possibly expanding the official texts of the classroom.

We have seen rapid change over the last 20 years in the ways that we read, write, and communicate. By investigating the texts and literacy practices in Mrs. Oakley's ninth-grade English classroom, it has become clear in this moment of change that being more inclusive of textual difference in terms of texts allowed into the classroom, as well as those different experiences with texts, is incredibly valuable for both teachers and students, yet this inclusion also manifests uncertainty and the negotiation of official texts and practices in the classroom. While this change brings feelings of excitement, for many educators working with adolescents, the rapid change also brings feelings of fear of the new and unknown. As was seen in the case of the online dictionary that began this chapter, when the classroom becomes a space open to diverse texts and the negotiation of literacy practices (either included by Mrs. Oakley or offered by the students), the explicit discussion of the value and purpose of a text and literacy practice becomes central.

As in the online dictionary case, this discussion of texts/practices is ultimately important for students as they learn to become critically literate in exploring what texts and practices have to offer them as they use "literacy to perform their jobs, run their households, act as citizens, and conduct their personal lives . . . and feed their imaginations so they can create the world of the future" (Moore et al., 1999, p. 99).

NOTE

1. All of the names used for the people and places in this study are pseudonyms.

REFERENCES

Alvermann, D. E. (2001). *Effective literacy instruction for adolescents.* Executive Summary and Paper Commissioned by the National Reading Conference. Chicago, IL: National Reading Conference.

Alvermann, D., Marshall, J., McLean, C., Huddleston, A., Joaquin, J., & Bishop, J. (2012). Adolescents' web-based literacies, identity construction, and skill development. *Literacy Research and Instruction, 51*, 179–195.

Alvermann, D. E., Hagood, M. C., & Williams, K. B. (2001, June). Image, language, and sound: Making meaning with popular culture texts. *Reading Online, 4*(11). Available: http://www.readingonline.org/newliteracies/lit_index.asp?HREF =/newliteracies/action/alvermann/index.html

Alvermann, D., & Xu, S. H. (2003). Children's everyday literacies: Intersections of popular culture and language arts instruction. *Language Arts, 81*, 145–154.

Applebee, A. (1993). *Literature in the secondary school: Studies of curriculum and instruction in the United States.* Urbana, IL: National Council of Teachers of English.

Barton, D., & Hamilton, M. (1998). *Local literacies: Reading and writing in one community.* London: Routledge.

Bloome, H. (1994). *The western canon: The books and school of the ages.* New York, NY: Riverhead Books.

Brass, J. (2008). Local knowledge and digital movie composing in an after-school literacy program. *Journal of Adolescent & Adult Literacy, 51*, 464–478.

Cope, B., & Kalantzis, M. (Eds.). (2000). *Multiliteracies: Literacy learning and the design of social futures.* New York, NY: Routledge.

Coiro, J., Knobel, M., Lankshear, C., & Leu, D. J. (2008). Central issues in new literacies and new literacies research. In J. Coiro, M. Knobel, C. Lankshear, & D. J. Leu (Eds.), *Handbook of research on new literacies* (pp. 1–22). New York, NY: Routledge.

Dyson, A. H. (2003). *The brothers and sisters learn to write: Popular literacies in childhood and school cultures.* New York, NY: Teachers College Press.

Fairclough, N. (2000). Multiliteracies and language. In B. Cope & M. Kalantzis (Eds.), *Multiliteracies: Literacy learning and the design of social futures* (pp. 162–181). New York, NY: Routledge.

Gallagher, J. D. (2007). "You have to be bad or dumb to get in here": Reconsidering the in-school and out-of-school literacy practices of at-risk adolescents. In V. Purcell-Gates (Ed.), *Cultural practices of literacy: Case studies of language, literacy, social practice, and power.* Mahwah, NJ: Lawrence Erlbaum.

Gee, J. P. (1996). *Social linguistics and literacies.* Philadelphia, PA: Routledge/Falmer Press.

Gee, J. P. (1999). *An introduction to discourse analysis: Theory and method.* New York, NY: Routledge.

Grossman, L. (2010, December 15). Person of the year 2010: Mark Zuckerberg. *Time Magazine.* Retrieved from http://content.time.com/time/specials/packages/article/0,28804,2036683_2037183,00.html

Iyengar, S., Ball, D. & National Endowment for the Arts. Office of Research & Analysis. (2007). *To read or not to read a question of national consequence.* Washington, DC: National Endowment for the Arts.

Knobel, M. (1999). *Everyday literacies: Students, discourse, and social practice.* New York, NY: Peter Lang.

Kress, G. (2003). *Literacy in the new media age.* New York, NY: Routledge.

Lankshear, C., & Knobel, M. (2003). *New literacies: Changing knowledge and classroom learning.* Philadelphia, PA: Open University Press.

Lankshear, C., & Knobel, M. (2005). *New literacies: Everyday practices and classroom learning* (2nd ed.). New York, NY: Open University Press.

Lee, H. (1960). *To kill a mockingbird.* Philadelphia, PA: Lippincott.

Luke, C. (2000). Cyber-schooling and technological change: Multiliteracies for new times. In B. Cope & M. Kalantzis (Eds.), *Multiliteracies: Literacy learning and the design of social futures* (pp. 69–91). New York, NY: Routledge.

Meza, N. (2011). Creating effective social media campaigns—How #DREAMAct students built a movement. Retrieved from http://aquifermedia.com/2011/06/30/audio-creating-effective-social-media-campaigns-how-dreamact-students-built-a-movement/

Moje, E. (2002). Re-framing adolescent literacy research for the new times: Studying youth as a resource. *Reading Research and Instruction, 41*(3), 211–228.

Moje, E., Ciechanowski, K., Kramer, K., & Ellis, L. (2004). Working towards third space in content area literacy: An examination of everyday funds of knowledge and discourse. *Reading Research Quarterly, 39*(1), 38–71.

Moore, D., Bean, T., Birdyshaw, D., & Rycik, J. (1999). *Adolescent literacy: A position statement.* Newark, DE: International Reading Association.

Morrell, E. (2006). Critical participatory action research and the literacy achievement of ethnic minority groups. In J. V. Hoffman (Ed.), *55th Annual Yearbook of the National Reading Conference* (pp. 60–78). Oak Creek, WI: National Reading Conference.

Morrell, E., & Duncan-Andrade, J. (2004). What they do learn in school: Using hip-hop as a bridge between youth culture and canonical poetry texts. In J. Mahiri (Ed.), *What they don't learn in school* (pp. 247–268). New York, NY: Peter Lang.

National Center for Education Statistics (2011). *The nation's report card: Reading 2011*(NCES 2012–457). Washington, DC: Institute of Education Sciences, U.S. Department of Education.

Nixon, A. S. (2009). Mediating social thought through digital storytelling. *Pedagogies: An International Journal, 4*, 63–76. DOI: 10.1080/15544800802557169.

O'Brien, D., & Scharber, C. (2008). Digital literacies go to school: Potholes and possibilities. *Journal of Adolescent & Adult Literacy, 52*(1), 66–68.

Safian, R. (2012). Box founder Aaron Levie on the fears and realities of our chaotic times. Retrieved from http://www.fastcompany.com/3002519/box-founder-aaron-levie-fears-and-realities-our-chaotic-times

Scholes, R. (1998). *The rise and fall of English: Reconstructing English as a discipline.* New Haven, CT: Yale University Press.

Sweeney, S. (2010). Writing for the instant messaging and text messaging generation: Using new literacies to support writing instruction. *Journal of Adolescent & Adult Literacy, 54*(2), 121–130.

The New London Group. (1996). A pedagogy of multiliteracies: Designing social futures. *Harvard Educational Review, 66*(1), 60–92.

CHAPTER 5

SOCIOPSYCHOLOGICAL PROBLEMS AMONG YOUTH IN THE MODERN RUSSIAN FAMILY

Olga E. Lomakina and Tatiana I. Gustomyasova
Volgograd State University, Russia

INTRODUCTION

Modern Russian youth is characterized by a unique variety of psychological identities whose specific nature is determined by complicated combinations of external and internal factors: demographic, professional, ethnic, sociocultural, ecosocial and political. These are also associated with mental health, marital status, parenting, coping, and displays of emotion that lead to seeking purpose and meaning in life. Frequently, youth face the problem of discrepancy or social "alienation" when showing their personal views, values, and interests in public. The phenomenon of social alienation among Russian youth is a rather complicated and ambiguous issue today.

The rapidly changing sociocultural reality of Russian society and the related transformation of values, norms, and identity of both adults and adolescents explain the challenges of developing a mainstream sociocultural

Adolescence in the 21st Century, pages 87–99
Copyright © 2014 by Information Age Publishing

identity (Okunev, 2013). In the late perestroika era and the early years of post-communist Russia, many young people abandoned higher education as useless in Russia's emerging capitalist economy. By the late 1990s, young people were beginning to return to the university, most seeking degrees in economics, law, finance, and accounting, with a few pursuing language or environmental studies. However, the structure of Russian society is hardly a recipe for stability. Between 1 and 2 percent of the population constitute affluent people; 15–20% are middle class who are able to save and to contribute money to their children's education; 60–65% dwell in the "twilight zone" between the middle class and the poor; 15–20% are fighting for survival; and 5–7% have fallen to the social "bottom." Such a "pyramid" social structure is inherently prone to turmoil (Shevtsova, 2007). These changes have influenced the family institution and family morals. For example, at present, interaction and socialization among generations in Russia face difficulties because outdated values are becoming unacceptable and won't be adequately accepted by the younger generation.

SOCIOCULTURAL REALITY OF RUSSIAN SOCIETY

Social problems in contemporary Russian society are reactions to the process of its modernization. They reflect real contradictions in Russian society, because the society includes cultures at different stages of the historical process as a result of the process of social modernization. While some Russians have accepted modernization, others have failed to adapt. This has resulted in a country at varying stages of cultural development. Technological processes influence the process of social modernization. Cultural changes must follow technological ones, and human behavior must adapt to the new technical environment. Acceleration of technological and social changes has been appearing in Western European civilization for the last few centuries.

Most modern societies are not homogeneous. In the 21st century, societies are comprised of different sociocultural groups with unequal levels of modernization of culture. Some people may have adopted one kind of culture in their childhood, but after their environment was changed by the process of modernization, their culture did not correspond to the new environment. For example, in Russia a few generations ago, the majority of the population lived in a rural environment based on a natural, subsistence economy. Their culture corresponded to this level of environmental progress. The process of modernization has changed the economy and other aspects of the environment over the last two decades, but the culture was not able to change as fast. Some people take issue with the impacts and challenges of modernization (the market, the new division of labor, the new rights for women, etc.). There are a number of groups with different levels of cultural modernization and different reactions to the continuation of modernization.

The process of social modernization changes social relations as well. The processes of urbanization, industrialization, and division of labor often substitute personal, direct social relations of traditional society for impersonal, indirect relations. In turn, these changes are often mediated by economic concerns. Consequently, these changes in social conditions cause changes in human behavior and lifestyle, and cultural changes are inevitable. Different generations socialize in different social conditions, so they adapt different kinds of culture. A more modernized type of culture is adapted to more modernized type of social environment (Vasserman, 2009).

Modern Russian society is marked by the repositioning of three nested entities, namely, *the society, the family as a small group,* and *the individual.* In recent years, the phenomenon of an upturned pyramid has occurred. In the past, the individual was at its base and society was on the top. Now they have changed places, with society at the base, and the individual moved to the top.

The role of the male in Russian society has become more vulnerable, as social conditions changed and men lost status as the major breadwinner of the family and the man had to find something meaningful outside of his professional activity. Men run the risk of remaining without any social status and any emotional support. It happens that in conditions of societal transformation, the format of the "traditional" family helps both men and women to cope with difficult situations. Relatively speaking, this conclusion is supported by the situation of male and female mortality in the Russian Federation (ILO Subregional Office for Eastern Europe and Central Asia, 2009).

So, social problems in contemporary Russian society are reactions to the process of its modernization. They reflect real contradictions of the society: technological and cultural changes. There are a lot of different sociocultural groups with unequal levels of modernization of culture in Russia, as there are a lot of cultures with different levels of modernization in any country. In general, the Russian people have struggled with modernization. While the economy and other aspects of the social environment have changed over the last two decades, Russia's culture was unable to keep up.

RUSSIAN YOUTH: STATUS AND ROLE IN THE SOCIETY

The status of the young has been discussed in Russian society, mass media, and science. Although in the last few years interest has waned, the issue is still relevant it can be referred to as one of the key social and political problems of contemporary Russia. It is quite evident that modern young people vary both from each other and previous generations in their role in society, their educational and cultural levels, as well as in ideology, tastes, and opinions. Adolescent life nowadays is characterized by a complicated dynamic of change and transition in adolescence. Mass media enthusiastically creates the image of a guided flock, which prevents the society from gaining an objective perception of the phenomenon of adolescents and young adults in Russia today (Okunev, 2013).

Therefore, it is necessary to state that the portrait of Russian youth is full of contrasts. On the one hand, their economic status has improved somewhat in the past few years, which does not mean they are satisfied with it. However, on the other hand, a certain degree of frustration and disillusion becomes apparent when assessing the way Russian society functions. Several factors explain this complex phenomenon.

Confronted with the difficulties of everyday life, young Russians pay special attention to family, despite the breakdown of traditional family structures and the generation gap. Preserving good relations with parents and friends and maintaining links of solidarity are vital. The importance of interpersonal solidarity networks also explains why young Russians cite the "loss of relatives" as the event they are most afraid of, ranking higher than "terrorist attack threats," "poverty," "unemployment," or "national and ethnic conflicts" (Dafflon, 2009, p.32).

Moreover, dissatisfaction with the weakening of political rights in Russia is also an issue throughout the country. Young Russians do not expect much from the authorities or from society as a whole. Therefore, when it comes to assessing the future of the country, they are more pessimistic than they are about their own future. Discontent is evident in many aspects of social life, from career prospects in the workplace to environmental conditions in one's region, from the absence of leisure structures and opportunities to find a good job where one lives. This explains the large internal migration flows (Dafflon, 2009).

The social status of Russian youth has been considerably influenced by growing social differentiation, one of the negative results of Russian society's rapid development over the last two decades. Today the student body structure is impacted by numerous expressed social and, in particular, sociocultural differences in terms of value attitudes and ways of adaptation to present day life. Students are not content with the pace of social reforms. They face contradictions regarding the value of their youthful status and adolescence as a time for self-affirmation and self-realization. However, society, which still considers youth as being synonymous with immaturity, is also changing. The aspiration of students for independence and autonomy is growing as well as the significance of their reference groups, which often are at odds with each other. Many adolescents, who find themselves outside these groups, feel insecure and vulnerable. It is significant that such reference groups tend to form on the basis of monetary and ethnic characteristics, with the commonality of student interests moving to the background (Pazova, 2009).

In sum, status and role in the society of young Russians is considered to be one of the key social and political problems of modern Russia. Status depends on educational and cultural backgrounds, ideology, tastes, opinions, and a complicated dynamic of changes in social life. The portrait of Russian youth is full of contrasts: They pay special attention to family despite the breakdown of traditional family structures and the generation gap; they do not expect much from the authorities or from society as a whole, but they are more pessimistic about the future of the country than of their own futures.

PECULIARITIES AND FACTORS INFLUENCING MODERN RUSSIAN YOUTH

As we noted above, modern Russian youth are characterized by unique variety of "emotional worlds," and their specific nature is determined by complicated combinations of external and internal factors: demographic, professional, ethnic, sociocultural, ecosocial, and political (Babyntsev & Naberezhneva, 2009). These factors, in particular sociocultural ones, include such phenomena as social conflicts of youth evidenced in contradictory social decisions and actions; discontent with their unequal status in society; search for compatibility among friends; and protection of their own interests, values, needs, types of behavior and norms.

Two priority directions can explain the dynamics of managing youth conflicts. The vector of the first direction, connected with a constant attention to social problems of Russian youth in the basic life spheres, is assuring youth of the availability of education, employment, health protection, and assistance in the resolution of housing problems and recreation problems. Thus, the Russian governmental youth policy focuses on preventing the escalation of conflicts between youth and a society assigned to it, as well as providing optimum conditions for effective integration of youth into social structure.

The vector of the second direction is oriented toward the educational and social technologies aimed at developing decision-making skills so that Russian adolescents can make independent choices regarding conflict resolution, and more broadly, their life directions. Management of social conflicts among Russian youth is static. Social conflicts are solved with the help of educators, parents, and psychologists if adolescents show at least some willingness to make changes in their sometimes abnormal behavior.

We have noticed the significance of parental families and dependence of students upon them. However, the conflict between the concept and practice of paternalism is also evident. A cultural transformation has shattered the values of the older generation. In contrast, the young people's value and normative attitudes have been developing in the context of changes in Russia. This transformation of value attitudes among students is particularly difficult because the social attitudes of youth can be influenced by various types of crisis—crisis of self-realization, of socialization, and of trust in sociopolitical institutions of the society. The established core of Russians' values includes order, family, and communication. Order is regarded as stability of life and equality of rights, as guaranteed by the law. Since the population has been experiencing a significant lack of such order over the last two decades, it has assumed a value of utmost importance in the mentality of the Russians.

Our observations indicate that for the majority of the Russians, family and communication remain a safe harbor, protecting adolescents from social upheavals. Value orientation both on federal and regional levels can clearly be seen. The first and second places are occupied by health and family (Vishnevski & Shapko, 2006).

Therefore, peculiarities of modern Russian youth are characterized by complicated combinations of external and internal factors: demographic, professional, ethnic, sociocultural, eco-social and political. For example, sociocultural factors include such phenomena as social conflicts among the youth. We define social conflicts of Russian youth as permanent public relations among actively adapting and self-developed young subjects, participants who occupy unequal status in social structure of the society. Two priority directions for managing youth conflicts were analyzed: the vector of the first is connected with a constant decision regarding social problems of youth in the basic life spheres (availability of education, self-realization, youth employment, health protection, assistance solving housing and recreation problems); the vector of the second direction is oriented on nonviolent and constructive realization of current and perspective life plans and solving social problems by means of social technologies.

PROBLEM OF YOUTH DISCREPANCY AND SOCIAL OUTSIDERISM

It is evident that modern Russian youth has its own status, role in the society, and peculiarities of social consciousness. Today the emotional life of Russian youth is characterized by rather a complicated dynamic of changes. Feeling like a social outsider is common for a considerable number of young people in Russia. Moreover, the phenomenon of adolescent social outsiderism is a complicated and ambiguous issue nowadays. In our view, there are at least 2 dimensions to this phenomenon.

The first dimension—*socioeconomical*—is related to the living conditions of young people who are ascribed a number of destructive tendencies. The regional development of Russia is characterized by an increase of social differentiation in society, which is particularly evident in the increase of the number of young people who are not involved in vital social processes. These young people have lost perspectives for social leadership and have no access to resources that are indispensable for successful adaptation and self-development into adulthood (property, qualitative education, full and reliable information, professional development, power). Many young people encounter the problem of employment. They either cannot find a job, or they work in a field having no relation to their qualifications. These tendencies will undoubtedly increase under the conditions of economic crisis. However, socioeconomical outsiderism of young people should not be exaggerated. "At present, there are a number of the teenagers who suffer from the outsiderism in regions but it is not considered by them as something fatal for their future" (Babyntsev & Naberezhneva, 2009, p. 295).

Youth employment issues get a rather low profile role in public politics. As younger generations don't have high work qualifications, sometimes they are rejected by employers. However, it should be noted that special youth employment programs exist in many regions of Russia and that the existence of young people in the labor market draws attention of the authorities at a local level.

Young people in the Russian labor market appear to be, generally speaking, the most mobile part of the population. This group is characterized by a faster speed of adapting to the needs of the market. One could tentatively conclude that Russian employers give a certain preference to people of younger age when considering their new potential hires. More so, under open-hire conditions (when using advertisement for existing vacancies or relying on placement agencies), many employers in Russia specify that they accept applications only from people under a certain age (as a rule, those under 30). As a result, young people in Russia today have much better prospects for finding jobs than those of middle or older age, despite the fact that young people usually do not have work experience.

The youth employment level is defined by several specific factors. First, there are those that vary depending upon age. For young people aged 15–24 years, there is a maximum opportunity for migration and relocation, which will considerably influence the demographics of the job markets in certain regions. Furthermore, this group is largely participatory in various forms of education and training. The next group, 25–29 years, exhibits a drastic drop in educational activities as compared to younger ages. Second, indicators of the youth job market are influenced by gender-related factors: for men, it is military service; for women, it is birth of children. The birthrate indicator is highest for women in the age group 20–24 years.

Theoretically, the level of employment among young people is inversely related to the scope of participation of young people in education. To a certain degree, education and work could be regarded as alternative types of activities. In real life, however, this relationship is not seen very easily. Across the regions of Russia there is an incredibly large variation in the percentage of the employed as well as in the percentage of students. In reality, the number of the employed and the number of students within age groups of the young people are connected not by an inverse, but by a direct relationship. In other words, in regions with low levels of employment, a low percentage of the young people go study at university (Agranovich, Korolyova, Poletaev, Sundiev, Seliverstova, & Fateeva, 2013).

However, the majority of Russian young people believe in success. For them, success is, first of all, welfare, achieved through having a career and obtaining a high social status. Young people become frustrated by their diminished position in the society, the low estimation of their opinions and positions by the general public, and by the small number of chances for their self-expression. At present, the link between money and employment is ambiguous for adolescents. For a certain percentage of young people, having an income becomes a value in itself. Therefore, they often are ready to do any job to earn even a very small sum of money.

More significant is the second dimension of the problem of social out-siderism, which we describe as *dispositional*. In this case, the issue is that outsiderism has turned into a phenomenon of youth consciousness and is revealed in a number of value- and purpose-specific attitudes and motiva-tions. The following are the major indicators of dispositional outsiderism:

1. Inability to realistically and reflexively evaluate life conditions and the chances for success in the selected life strategy.
2. Instability of ideas, opinions, views, which are subject to change daily. The youth are not careful to keep to their own minds; they easily take risks in their actions and display irresponsibility in words and promises. This leads to adults' reluctance to trust adolescents and involve them in serious matters.

    However, young people, especially those living in big cities and who are getting or have already gotten a good education, are charac-terized by active and rational approach to reality.
3. Contradictory inner world. Having a number of inner disputes, adolescents often are unable to develop their own interpretation of social norms, rules, and regulations. Their inner psychological fight between society and themselves can be very difficult and sometimes unbearable.
4. Alienation from state and society. This is revealed in, first of all, the growth of distrust in major state and public institutions. The most urgent and difficult tasks addressed in the process of development and implementation of modern management strategy are recovery

of trust in social institutions and intense stimulation of people's willingness to get involved in addressing the problems of state and society (Babyntsev & Naberezhneva, 2009). The young people live in their own worlds; they often avoid being connected with the state and society.

THE ROLE OF YOUTH IN FAMILY RELATIONS IN RUSSIA

Changes in Russian society at the end of the 20th and beginning of the 21st century have affected the family significantly. Essentially, it can be characterized as loss of previously held formal institutions and strengthening of informal positions (Kartseva, Soetendal, Gordijn, Akkermans, & Schildwacht, 2003).

The concept of family has garnered a great deal of attention, and not only by experts. Family has become part and parcel of the political and authoritative discourse, which proves that a public and multiprofessional debate about modern Russian family, its structure, and its prospects is long overdue.

The developments of the late 20th and early 21st century demonstrated to the world that the institution of family emerged as one of the most stable social formations in the course of centuries-long history. However, it is important to define what the modern Russian family represents. This would require the exploration and research of various social and family situations, as well recommendations on the direction and shape of future relations between the family and the state. Specifically the character of these interrelations will predetermine to a large extent the general trend of the nation's development.

Therefore, the research of the strategies of the family behavior of youth in general and student youth in particular is of high priority given the deterioration of the demographic situation in the country and the role of youth, not only as the replacement of older generation, but also in the social structure of the society on the whole.

As we noticed, individualistic values are steadily growing in Russia, but they are still not as widespread as in Western European countries. Therefore, it is thus quite uncommon for young Russians to live on their own in a separate apartment. Similarly, it is very uncommon for young Russians to share an apartment with friends. It is also very hard for young Russians to afford to live on their own; there are many housing possibilities available, but the rents are extremely high. Whereas this situation may, on the one hand, strengthen interfamily solidarity, it may, on the other hand, create intergenerational tensions and give rise to frustration, especially since many young Russians enter the labor market at an early age and should therefore theoretically be financially independent. In comparison to their

Western European counterparts, young Russians indeed join the labor market rather early. Dafflon claims that at age 24, 65% of young Russians are working, 11% work and study simultaneously, and 4% study only (Dafflon, 2009, p. 11).

Let's consider *three models* of the modern Russian family. *First, the theoretical model* in modern Russian society is not well defined and varies according to the source. This reflects the situation when there are multiple marriages. The children from previous marriages essentially become members of two families. As a result, no clear theoretical model of the modern Russian family has been currently shaped.

Morals are stereotyped, especially family morals. Family concerns were not openly discussed in the past because people were ashamed of public condemnation. Many families believed that "one should wash dirty linen at home." In the event of a very serious family conflict, there remained only one means of resolution—that is, litigation.

Second, the empirical model of the modern Russian family is, in some ways, simpler. Studies of modern families have been conducted both at the federal and regional (local) levels. There have been also many individual research projects, the materials of which are used for dissertations; these research projects can be conducted in the framework of certain projects or be part of more comprehensive studies. However, this model is more complicated than the theoretical model, in the sense that these research projects are numerous, but they do not provide a unified picture of family relations in the Russian Federation.

The third and final model of familial relations is the *egalitarian model*. However, this model is rarely credited as being representative of everyday life. The new phenomenon more actively involves women in business life than men in housekeeping. Women began to question traditional role distribution in the family and tried to achieve gender alignment based on equal opportunities in all areas of activity (ILO Subregional Office for Eastern Europe and Central Asia, 2009).

So, the three models, theoretical, empirical, and egalitarian, suggest collectively and individually that there is no unanimity in the definition of the notion, even though many studies of modern families have been conducted both at the federal and regional (local) levels.

INTERACTION AND SOCIALIZATION OF GENERATIONS IN SOCIETY AND IN A FAMILY

In the years following the breakdown of the Soviet Union, Russia has experienced profound changes both on a political and on a socioeconomic level. Each generation experienced this process differently.

For obvious reasons, Russians under 30 years old are less affected by these changes, and one can say that there is a generation gap in terms of mentality between young Russians and the generation of their parents.

Many young Russians have the feeling that their parents do not understand them and that they do not know what life is like for young people. Social codes have evolved; the ideological framework has disappeared, and this has led to new practices to which the young have adapted more easily. The older generations may tend to keep ideological frameworks from the past in the back of their minds and are scared of thinking and talking freely. They are conservative in their thoughts and actions (Dafflon, 2009).

Various problems become aggravated in the relations between generations in society as a whole and in a family. The family is the most important institution of society's reproduction and the socialization of young people, but at present interaction and socialization between generations is difficult. The elders are at a loss for how to transfer their experiences to the youth. However, young people do not adopt the elders' experience easily. Therefore, distinctions among age groups become deeper, contradictions between generations emerge, and domestic disputes accelerate.

The problem of intergenerational conflict often characterizes the Russian family. This conflict expresses itself in hard, tense interaction between parents and their children (especially grown-up sons or daughters), between grandparents and grandchildren, and among other family members. Meanwhile, the impact of change's processes on the generational interaction in Russian family has not been studied enough. The role of social conflict is discussed in contemporary pedagogical science. Any disagreement has a lot of negative and positive outcomes. This clash exerts ambiguous influence on a family, the generations, and society. At the same time as it has extremely destructive consequences, it can be a stimulus for the development of some social processes.

We can allocate two main functions of the conflict between generations: institutionalization and socialization. The former is that the conflict can encourage a creation and a development of some social institutions, which have orientation to communication and translation of culture for generations, such as a family, school, science, social work, law, economy and other social institutions (Vdovina, 2009). And the latter means that the conflict can encourage socialization of the individual, the passing and acquisition of social norms and values of the younger members of the family that sometimes are hard to acquire.

The conflict between generations influences the society as well. The consequences sometimes become dramatic as teenagers commit suicide. While this doesn't happen often, researchers and many pedagogical institutions seek newer approaches and methods to handle generations' tension and gap.

The expectation to build strong relations between generations in Russian families is becoming vital for those parents who are realistic, not indifferent, and not lenient. Of course we have noticed there is a generation gap between them, but it is easily navigated. As we also noticed, there are many qualities in adolescents' upbringing that are positive—a happy family, well-bred children, willingness to get high-quality education, and further, an interesting and well-paid job, the latter being foremost in most Russian families.

CONCLUSION

The rapidly changing sociocultural reality of Russian society in transition that results in the transformation of values, norms, and identity explains the challenges of the developing mainstream sociocultural identity of the society in our country at the present time. Modern Russian youth are responding to complicated combinations of external and internal factors: demographic, professional, ethnic, ecosocial, political, and sociocultural.

One of the most important challenges facing Russian youth as they progress through adolescence is defense of their own interests, values, needs, types of behavior, and norms. The challenge leads to social conflicts that can be solved with the help of educators, parents, and psychologists, along with problems of discrepancy or social "alienation" in their personal views, values, and interests with the surrounding. There are at least two dimensions that help explain this problem: (1) *socioeconomical*, which is related to the real living conditions of young people, and (2) *dispositional*—there are major indicators of dispositional outsiderism, such as inability to realistically and reflexively evaluate life conditions and the chances for success in the selected life strategy; instability of ideas, opinions, views which are subject to change daily; contradictory inner world; alienation from state and society.

The expectation to build strong relations between the generations is becoming vital for those parents who are realistic, who are not indifferent, and who are not absorbed in their own work. It happens that it is becoming very difficult for teenagers to overcome the generation gap because older generations are reluctant to think and talk freely, and because they are conservative in their thoughts and actions. However, the conflict between generations can encourage the socialization of the individual, the passing and acquisition of social norms and values of the younger members of the family that sometimes are hard to acquire.

So, family has evolved and plays a crucial role in the upbringing of younger generations in Russia. The majority of Russian youth experience challenges while trying to maintain good relationships with their parents and grandparents, develop excellent social skills, fighting with their superego and inadequate ambitions on the one hand and timidity on the other hand. Becoming a good citizen of society is a hard but worthwhile. Many in Russia realize this already at the age of 13–15 and present a wonderful paragon of proper upbringing and respect of the older people.

REFERENCES

Agranovich, M., Korolyova, N., Poletaev, A., Sundiev, I., Seliverstova, I., & Fateeva, A. (2013). Youth development report: Condition of Russian Youth. In *Unescodoc.* Retrieved from unesdoc.unesco.org/images/0014/001431/143147e.pdf

Babyntsev, V. P., & Naberezhneva, M. A. (2009). *Problem of social outsiderism of youth in Russian regions.* In V. A. Mansurov (Ed.), *European society or European societies: A view from Russia* (pp. 295–297). Moscow: Maska.

Dafflon, D. (Ed.). (2009). *Youth in Russia: The portrait of a generation in transition. A research report by the Swiss Academy for Development (SAD).* Bern, Switzerland: Coloroffset AG.

ILO Subregional Office for Eastern Europe and Central Asia. (2009). *Family strategies of modern Russian student youth. Work–family conflict resolution.* Retrieved from http://www.ilo.org/public/english/region/eurpro/moscow/info/publ/fam_strategy.pdf

Kartseva, V., Soetendal, J., Gordijn, J., Akkermans, H., & Schildwacht, J. (2003). *Distributed generation business modelling.* Project Deliverable BUSMOD EU project.

Okunev, I. (2013). The problem of youth leadership in Russia. In *Paperroom.* Retrieved from http://paperroom.ipsa.org/papers/paper_2367.pdf

Pazova, L. L. (2009). Some aspects of formation of civil culture of present-day students. In V. A.

Mansurov (Ed.), *European society or European societies: A view from Russia* (pp. 329–331). Moscow: Maska.

Shevtsova, L. (2007). Post-communist Russia: a historic opportunity missed. *Journal Compilation.* Blackwell Publishing Ltd. / The Royal Institute of International Affairs. Retrieved from http://iis-db.stanford.edu/evnts/5027/Shevtsova.pdf.PDF

Vasserman, Y. (2009). *Sociocultural consequences of modernization.* In V. A. Mansurov (Ed.), *European society or European societies: A view from Russia* (pp. 402–404). Moscow: Maska.

Vdovina, M. V. (2009). Conflict between generations in a family: Its functions. In V. A. Mansurov (Ed.), *European society or European societies: A view from Russia* (pp. 301–303). Moscow: Maska.

Vishnevski, Y. R., & Shapko, V. T. (2006). Paradoxical young man. *Sotsiologicheskie Issledovaniya, 6,* 26–36.

PART II

CONSTANTS

Purpose, Agency, Motivation

Frances Spielhagen

One constant force in adolescent development is the search for identity. Adolescents strive to carve out a place in the world that is unique, or at least feels unique. The adolescent struggle for individuation offers many challenges, but the struggle is a constant in human development. From the "Greatest Generation" of World War II to the "emerging adult" generation of the 21st century, the essential identifier of adolescence is the drive to determine how one fits in the society at large. Societal forces, like World War II, shape and buffet the struggle, but the search for identity remains essential to human endeavor.

This quest involves three key concepts: purpose, agency, and motivation. How successfully the individual navigates adolescent years will be manifest in the degree to which he or she defines a purpose in life. The degree to which the individual develops the capacity, or agency, to pursue that purpose is another important component of the process. Finally, the motivation to progress positively toward those personal goals emerges as perhaps the most critical component of all.

The second annual conference sponsored by the Center for Adolescent Research and Development of Mount Saint Mary College in 2011focused on the ways in which adolescents pursued these three key components of the path to adulthood. Keynote speaker William Damon captured the critical connection between the quest for purpose and civic engagement for the good of society. Professor Damon is the director of the Center on Adolescence at Stanford University. His book, *The Path to Purpose: Helping Our Children Find Their Purpose in Life* (Free Press, 2008), was based on the findings of the Youth Purpose Project, conducted by Damon and his center. This four-year nationwide study of young people, ages of 12–26, suggests that adolescents in the 21st century are struggling to find their purpose in life because our society has focused on superficial, short-term success. At the 2011 CARD conference, Damon pointed out that shallow goal-setting has diminished the natural optimism of adolescents and has led to increasing numbers of young people lacking confidence, direction, and idealism. As a result, civic engagement among young adults appears to be declining.

In the following chapters, various scholars have explored the ways in which adults can help adolescents find their purpose in life, for the good of themselves and for society as a whole. Tolan, in Chapter 6, provides a comprehensive synthesis of service learning as a way to foster civic engagement and build on the inherent idealism of youth. This scholarly chapter focuses on the behaviors that lead to civic responsibility and offers insights into how educators can create situations that support civic involvement. It is particularly interesting that the author of this chapter is a professor of business administration. Certainly, employers have a vested interest in the purposeful and engaged behaviors of their employees.

In a similar vein, Caporimmo and Kerner, in Chapter 7, describe a very successful social justice project among inner-city high school students. Despite the prevailing wisdom that paints this population as disengaged, this chapter offers a vivid firsthand account of the powerful interactions between the teacher and the students. It explains how these adolescents demonstrated growth in their approach to their own education and learning, critical thinking, and social/emotional development. In essence, they were on the path to finding purpose in the lives.

In Chapter 8, Van Riper takes the reader to a group of adolescents who are challenging to many working with adolescents—that is, students with Autism Spectrum Disorder (ASD). She offers a clear explanation of the factors affecting the development of these youngsters as they journey through adolescence. The major concern of adults interacting with these adolescents is whether and how they will "fit" into society. Van Riper explains ways in which these students can be encouraged to grow. She also provides clear explanation of the challenges facing them in the ways they differ from "typically developing" adolescents.

The final chapter of this section focuses on the development of adolescents as peacemakers. In Chapter 9, Murphy and Bliss describe their own experiences in bringing older adolescents to an awareness of their own prejudices regarding those they perceive as different from themselves. In light of historic and recent events of mass violence, including genocide, school shootings, and bullying, these two college professors describe the various approaches they take to teaching a world religions course. One focuses on the impact of language and the second focuses on experiential encounters as ways of promoting increased and respectful understanding of the "other" in today's college students.

The following four chapters examine the concept of *purpose* through the lenses of four separate disciplines: business, psychology, education, and theology. However, they all point to the need for understanding and clear goal-setting among adults who wish to foster purpose in adolescents. These chapters offer ways in which a reasoned, research-based approach to adolescent development can help young people in their own path to purpose.

CHAPTER 6

SERVICE LEARNING AS A TOOL FOR DEVELOPING EMERGING ADULTS INTO PRODUCTIVE EMPLOYEES AND CITIZENS

Moira Tolan

ABSTRACT

To what extent can service learning provide for developing students who will be productive workers and citizens? A research study that investigated the relationship between college student participation in service learning projects and their future participation in organizational citizenship behaviors (OCBs) will be discussed. Organizational citizenship behaviors are those discretionary individual behaviors that are not part of the job description but can have a significant impact on the effective functioning of an organization. Partaking in OCBs resembles volunteerism because it involves engaging in task-related behaviors at a level so far beyond required or generally expected duties. Some of the most common OCBs in the workplace include helping others who have been absent, giving advance notice when unable to come to work, exhibiting a willingness to tolerate the inevitable inconveniences and impositions of work without complaining, and being concerned about the company's life (Organ, 1988, 1990).

Adolescence in the 21st Century, pages 105–124
Copyright © 2014 by Information Age Publishing
All rights of reproduction in any form reserved.

Previous researchers have shown that service learning offers a way of informing students that they can play an integral role in affecting the lives of many people outside of their college campus. This is especially true for those entering adulthood (Astin & Sax, 1998; Astin, Sax, & Avalos, 1999; Batchelder & Root, 1994; Boss, 1994; Dunlap, 1998; Eyler & Giles, 1999; Kenny, Simon, Kiley-Brabeck, & Lerner, 2002). The current study's results indicate that service learning projects can prepare students for future participation in OCBs. This is the first study to associate service learning with OCBs in a formal manner.

This study highlights the important role that service learning can play in both undergraduate and graduate student development. It also displays this methodology's teaching potential. It can assist in the development of individuals who will participate as responsible members of their organizations and in the society at large.

INTRODUCTION

In recent years, colleges and universities have faced criticism from multiple stakeholders for providing students with traditional, static approaches to learning in a time of rapidly changing societal needs. As students prepare to enter the workplace and a world that is more diverse, competitive, and technological than in the past, educators have been criticized for what is viewed by many as their inadequate response in training students to meet some of the challenges they will face. Employers, both in the for-profit and not-for-profit sectors, are concerned about the breadth of skills and ethical values that potential hires possess. In addition, educational researchers, cognitive scientists, and academic accrediting bodies have all begun to speak out against the way that American schools are preparing students for their future lives. Many of these critics argue that students will not be technically able to perform and, in addition, will not function well in a world that is quite different from that which they have been exposed to in their academic lives. Nahser and Ruhe (2001) assert that the challenge to educators will be to "help students and practitioners make sense of an environment generating massive fragmentation of knowledge with facts and trends that present choices, options, problems, situations, and issues; both good and bad" (p. 317). The study under discussion highlights the important role that service learning may play in student development.

IMPORTANCE OF STUDY

Human resource professionals seek to recruit and retain personnel who will most effectively contribute to their organization. Educators should work to prepare students for careers by providing training that will allow them to perform necessary technical skills while enhancing the social framework of the enterprise. The study described links service learning to an inclination toward future participation in OCBs. These findings build on the literature that supports service learning as an effective pedagogy for developing engaged, productive citizens.

OCBs have been classified as being directed toward other individuals (OCBI), toward the organization (OCBO), or as general civic gestures. The distinction between them is important because prior work suggests that the forms of OCB activities can have different antecedents and because some research has not included multiple dimensions.

Although many organizational theorists have knowledge about the importance of the OCB contribution and what it consists of, not much attention has been paid to the development and maintenance of these OCBs (Allison, Voss, & Dryer, 2001). Behavioral patterns embedded in ideas about contextual performance and OCB have many important implications. The implications, both theoretical and practical, apply to virtually all kinds of human resource practices including job analysis, recruitment, selection, training, development, performance appraisal, compensation, and even labor and employee relations (Werner, 2000). If service learning can be shown to be empirically related to OCB performance, educators will have another supportive reason to apply this teaching pedagogy in their programs.

WEAKNESSES IN UNDERGRADUATE EDUCATION

A gap exists between traditional curricular content and society's needs for new competencies in its workers and citizens (Boyer, 1987). In 1991, the Association of American Colleges observed that there was a lack of connectedness in higher education and a related lack of application of what is learned (Jeavons, 1991). Many employers have become more selective about the individuals they hire (Ettore, 1992; Mason, 1992). They have become more concerned about individuals in technical and managerial positions meeting job-specific knowledge, skills, and capabilities. "These include the people skills, the creativity, the negotiation skills, an aptitude for teamwork and the ability to speak and write with clarity—the skills required of a good manager" (Dumas, 2002, p. 255).

The deficiency in the delivery of educational content is twofold. The first issue is that knowledge is compartmentalized by discipline. This prevents students from experiencing the relationships among various modes of knowledge. The second concern is that the relationships between specific subject matter and societal issues often go unexamined. Weaknesses with the traditional methods of classroom learning and schisms between the learned and applied have been discussed since the early 20th century by prominent educational researchers (Boyer, 1987; Dewey, 1938; Jeavons, 1991; Whitehead, 1929).

In their book, *Management Education and Development: Drift or Thrust Into the 21st Century*, Porter and McKibbin (1988) provided a comprehensive critique of American business schools. They wrote that the need for breadth, interaction, and engagement with the external environment is a pressing need within management education. They also discovered a concern among business executives that college business students were being too narrowly educated. Porter and McKibbin reported that the students they studied often understood the concepts they had been taught. Most, however, had little or no opportunity in the educational experience to apply newly acquired knowledge and skills to a real work setting (Madsen, 2004).

WHAT IS SERVICE LEARNING?

Service learning is one pedagogical tool that attempts to address the complementary nature of multiple learning strategies. It provides students with structured opportunities designed to promote their learning and development. The practice holds promise in preparing students who will function as productive and socially involved members of the organizational world and the society in which they live.

The National and Community Service Act of 1990 defined four specific criteria for service learning:

1. "Students learn and develop through active participation in thoughtfully organized service experiences that meet actual community need and that are coordinated in collaboration with the school and community;
2. The experience is integrated into the students' academic curriculum or provides structured time for a student to think, talk, or write about what the student did and saw during the actual service activity;
3. The experience provides students with opportunities to use newly acquired skills and knowledge in real-life situations in their own communities; and
4. The experience enhances what is taught in school by extending student learning beyond the classroom and into the community and helps to foster the development of a sense of a caring for others." (cited in Weber & Sleeper, 2002, p. 418)

At its core, service learning is about creating opportunities for students to apply theory they learn in the classroom to real-world problems and real-world needs (O'Neill, 1990). Service learning has been described as a "tool for reawakening civic learning and a programmatic educational response to the atrophy of public life and civic judgment" (O'Neill, 1990, p. 199).

A major strength of service learning projects is that they contain both concrete experiences and reflective opportunities (Billig & Eyler, 2003). Reflection involves discussing and writing about one's experiences in order to enhance the impact of the projects. Empirical studies show that a reflective component must be present for the service learning experience to have a developmental impact. This reflection requires participants to think about the meaning of their service experiences and connect them with broader social issues and personal values (Eyler & Giles, 1999).

Service learning attempts to move students from charity to justice (Eyler & Giles, 1999). A critical distinction must be made between service learning and volunteerism. A reciprocal benefit is an integral concept of the practice, and the service recipients should be aware of the important role that they are playing in the students' development. Service learning, in this regard, relates to James McGregor Burns' theory of transformational leadership. Burns suggests that both the served and the server teach each other and grow from the relationship (DiPadova, 2000). The student is serving in order to learn, and those who accept the service are doing so in order to teach the student (Stanton, 1994).

Eyler and Giles (1999), in the most comprehensive study of service learning to date, found that the opportunity to interact in meaningful ways with people from diverse backgrounds is among the most frequently reported values of service learning. Students also reported that service learning contributed to greater self-knowledge, spiritual growth, and finding reward in helping others. Academic results included an increased understanding of course material and application of knowledge, increased engagement with and curiosity about course material, stronger reflective practice, increased critical thinking and problem solving skills, and perspective transformation.

The work of Astin and Sax (1998) came to many of the same conclusions as the work of Eyler and Giles (1999). The 35 student outcomes that were measured were all favorably influenced by service participation. These included academic outcomes, civic responsibility, and life skills.

Service learning has been found to be effective in providing learning opportunities for students to develop the additional competencies that Porter and McKibbin (1988) discussed and that, according to the International Association for Management Education (formerly the American Association of Collegiate Schools of Business), all business graduates should embody. These include skills related to citizenship (Godfrey, 1999); leadership and conflict resolution (Thomas & Landau, 2002); teamwork, interaction, time management and networking (Tucker, McCarthy, Hoxmeier & Lenk, 1998); cultural awareness and diversity (Vernon & Foster, 2002); and written and verbal communication (Tucker et al., 1998). The development of these skills, especially if they are transferable into cooperation through OCBs, might prove to be advantageous to American businesses that seek to prosper in the modern economy.

ORGANIZATIONAL CITIZENSHIP BEHAVIORS (OCBS)

Employees contribute to the social and psychological context of the workplace through their participation in organizational citizenship behaviors (OCBs) (Williams & Anderson, 1991). By definition, these behaviors are discretionary, not directly or explicitly recognized by the formal reward system, and in the aggregate promote the efficient and effective functioning of the organization (Organ, 1988, 1990; Organ, Podsakoff, & MacKenzie, 2006). Although organizational citizenship behaviors are not part of the job description, they can have a significant impact on the effective functioning of an organization (Organ, 1988, 1990). Partaking in OCBs involves engagement that is so far beyond minimally required or generally expected levels that it resembles volunteerism. Some of the most common OCBs in the workplace include helping others who have been absent, giving advance notice when unable to come to work, exhibiting a willingness to tolerate the inevitable inconveniences and impositions of work without complaining, and being concerned about the company's life.

Positive changes in organizations may result from the many small adjustments people make in their behavior, including the suggestions they offer for how best to implement new strategies. Grooming students to perform through OCBs may present a remedy for some of what ails contemporary organizations and society. Service learning is a teaching approach that alerts students that to the integral role they can play in affecting lives outside of their college campus. Through the correct application of service learning, it may be possible to sharpen students' understanding of their roles as citizens of a college, a particular organization, their country, and the society at large.

Existing literature on organizational citizenship behavior reveals that it may be critical to effective organizational functioning. Although OCBs have been acknowledged for many years under many different labels, formal efforts to elicit their occurrence on the part of organizational members appear to be limited.

Previous research indicates that OCB antecedents are, in many cases, conceptually related to service learning outcomes. Students who participate in service learning projects appear to develop those qualities that may lead to increased performance of OCBs. Because of the many benefits that OCBs have been found to provide to both individuals and organizations, it appears that educators should work to prepare students to perform them in their futures. If service learning is found to be empirically related to increased levels of both "historical OCB" (established or learned patterns of OCB) and "OCB intentions" (Williams & Wong, 1999) or to specific components of "historical OCB" and "OCB intentions," its applicability and potential to education should be explored.

MAKING THE CONNECTION BETWEEN SERVICE LEARNING PARTICIPATION AND OCB PERFORMANCE

Despite the focus on what is now termed "OCB" throughout the writings of prominent organizational theorists, Allison et al. (2001) acknowledge that the OCB concept has largely been ignored in management education. Allison et al. (2001) present a case for the development of OCBs as part of the educational process and suggest that business educators should (1) encourage students who do not engage in these critical behaviors to do so and (2) hone the OCB skills of students currently practicing them. The results of their study showed that students do indeed engage in OCB, with a sizable number of students regularly practicing OCB in an academic setting. The authors recognize that attention should be paid to that percentage of students engaged in relatively low levels of OCB and suggest that the low OCB scores demonstrate a substantial unmet need for instilling in students an understanding of the value of OCBs. As Wagner and Rush (2000) point out, a review of the OCB literature reveals that the rendering or withholding of OCB represents a deliberate, controlled, and instrumental act rather than a type of expressive or emotional act (Organ, 1990; Organ & Konovsky, 1989; Wagner & Rush, 2000). This would appear to support the Allison, et al. (2001) contention that OCB can be aroused or enhanced (Allison et al., 2001).

Those four attitudinal measures that Organ (1997) has identified as comprising a general morale factor and that are diagrammed in Figure 6.1 appear as though they might be closely related to dispositions that could be developed through service learning experiences. Satisfaction, fairness, affective commitment, and leader consideration are the four dispositional antecedents to OCB that Organ (1997) considered. Because service learning has been found to improve student satisfaction with college (Astin & Sax, 1998; Eyler & Giles, 1999), a service learning experience may be associated with future job satisfaction. Satisfaction, in the Organ (1997) study, is an overall measure of job satisfaction. Fairness was measured by Organ (1997) as overall fairness, which measures distributive, procedural, and interactional fairness. In the Organ (1997) study, affective commitment represents an individual's desire to remain in an organization and leader consideration is a measure of leader supportiveness.

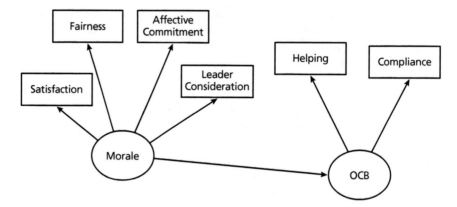

Figure 6.1 Attitudinal and dispositional antecedents of OCB (Organ, 1997).

The benefits of service learning are potentially far-reaching. Students engaged in service learning report stronger faculty relationships than those who are not involved in service learning (Astin & Sax, 1998; Eyler & Giles, 1999; Gray et al., 1998) and are also more likely to graduate (Astin & Sax, 1998; Roose et al., 1997). There may also be a potential connection between these outcomes and future dispositions toward affective commitment and leader consideration. Service learning has been shown to have an impact on self-reflection (Friedus, 1997; Schmiede, 1995) as well as views of institutional support and cohesion (Ward, 1996). It is therefore possible that service learning might influence some or all of the "morale" components (Organ, 1997). The possibility exists that the enhanced satisfaction with college that the students in Eyler and Giles (1999) study experienced is related to future job satisfaction.

Repeated evidence shows the relation between the integration of service learning into a curriculum and student awareness about their societal responsibilities (Dalton & Petrie, 1997; Eyler & Giles, 1999; Graham, 1991; Smith, 1994). The participation of students who recognize their role as citizens in a democracy, with certain responsibilities and obligations to others, would appear to continue into the student's future employment. Ehrlich (1997) notes that problem-based learning, linked with service learning and cooperative learning, forms an effective set of methods to educate for civic responsibility.

Eyler, Root, and Giles (1998) use the term "expert citizens" to link the problem-solving literature on novices and experts in cognitive science and the problem-solving demands of citizenship. They see citizens in a democracy as having the role of solver of open-ended societal problems and have worked to see if service learning might provide a way to move students toward taking a larger role in the meeting of civic needs. In fact, Eyler and

Giles (1999) found many outcomes that would suggest that students have a greater inclination toward participation in civic affairs after their participation in service learning. Some of the findings indicate that service learning enhances students' awareness about their responsibilities to the society in which they live. In particular, they found that service learning impacted a student's view that it is important to change policy, that social justice is important, and that they have an important influence on political structures. Godfrey (1999) also found improved tendencies toward citizenship on behalf of service learning participants.

Personal attitudes, beliefs and life experiences are likely to influence individual member-citizens' propensity to form strong relational ties with an organization (Graham, 1991). Service learning may in fact be a tool to provide those life experiences that would strengthen this propensity, possibly through the impact that it has on attitudes and beliefs.

In the Eyler and Giles (1999) study, 85% of the students studied indicated that finding reward in helping others was the most important or a very important thing they had learned from their service learning experiences; 81% reported that learning to work with others was the most important or a very important thing they had realized from the experience. The study also indicated that many students also underwent transformation of perspective after participating in service learning. For example, service learning impacted the students' openness to new views. Openness to new views is potentially related to those qualities that one who participated in OCBs toward individuals (OCBI) would possess.

The Eyler and Giles (1999) study indicated improvements in personal and interpersonal development following service learning experiences that also appear to be related to performance of OCBs toward others (OCBO). Personal efficacy, leadership skills, and career skills were all significantly impacted by service learning experiences. Some of the personal and interpersonal development items related to citizenship include a sense of personal efficacy in affecting community issues, a belief that the community itself can be effective in solving its problems, and feeling connected to the community. Batchelder and Root (1994) found that service learning increased students' perceptions of the multidimensionality of social problems as well as influenced their prosocial decision making and prosocial reasoning and identity processing. Again, one sees the possibility of a connection between the outcomes of service learning and the antecedents to contextual performance in which all OCBs are performed. That is, the personal development concepts that service learning researchers find are enhanced through service learning appear to be related to those that have been shown to be antecedents (predictors) of organizational citizenship behavior.

Much OCB research has determined that task productivity is determined largely by technology and job design, with variations dependent on an individual's cognitive ability, while the more discretionary contributions that go beyond narrowly defined task productivity are more likely to involve personality factors or beliefs and attitudes (Motowidlo & Van Scotter, 1994; Organ et al., 2006). Research in social psychology also supports the idea that altruism (or helping behaviors) may be predicted by personality or dispositional variables as well as by early learning experiences and social considerations (Eisenberg, 1991; Krebs, 1970; Rushton, 1980; Vitz, 1990). These findings indicate that service learning experiences might help to develop individuals who are more likely to perform OCBs. More specifically, the constructs that Motowidlo and Van Scotter (1994) have shown to be antecedents to OCB appear to be related to many of the individual outcomes of service learning. They are work orientation, dominance, dependability, adjustment, cooperativeness, internal control, and experience.

THE STUDY

The research study being discussed investigated the relationship between college student participation in service learning projects and their future participation in organizational citizenship behaviors (OCBs). Service learning has been found to be a teaching pedagogy that offers a way in which to inform students entering adulthood that they can play an integral role in affecting the lives of many people outside of their college campus (Astin & Sax, 1998; Astin et al., 1999; Batchelder & Root, 1994; Boss, 1994; Dunlap, 1998; Eyler & Giles, 1999; Kenny et al., 2002). The current study's results indicate that service learning projects can prepare students for future participation in OCBs.

This study's results highlight the important role that service learning can play in student development. It also displays the potential of this teaching methodology to assist in the development of individuals who will participate as responsible members of their organizations and the society at large. Morton (1995) writes that the idea that service learning moves students from charity to justice is a pervasive one, although little is known about how it occurs or what programmatic elements facilitate it. This study attempted to determine if changes that occur in an individual during a service learning experience are related to increased propensity toward OCB. The research also attempted to ascertain the process through which the changes in an individual occur during the experience.

The research project had three phases. The first phase was a quasi-experimental field study conducted at a small liberal arts college. One introductory marketing class was taught utilizing traditional teaching methods. The second used a service learning approach. Both classes took pre- and post-tests that assessed their levels of organizational citizenship behavior (OCB).

Qualitative data were also utilized to assess the impact of service learning on a student's inclination to perform OCBs immediately and their intent to perform them in the future. These data came from student reflections that took place at various times during the semester and from student evaluations of the courses.

The second phase of the research was conducted at the conclusion of an accelerated, six-week graduate course in marketing management. In-depth interviews were conducted with the students after they participated in a service learning experience. Changes in the individual as a result of the service learning course were assessed through these interviews. The impact of service learning on undergraduate students in a traditional format was compared to the impact on graduate students in an accelerated program.

A third phase of the research involved the analysis of archival records, including the qualitative comments on course evaluation forms that have been collected in three previous classes. Reflective comments about the service learning experience and its influence on the students were collected at multiple times during a semester. The notebooks from two of the service learning classes that contain these reflections were analyzed.

The study's results have implications for education as well as organizational recruitment, selection, and training. If educators can see the benefits of utilizing service learning as a teaching pedagogy, it may be employed as a strategy to prepare students for participation in the workplace. Human resource professionals may benefit through the recruitment and selection of those students who have participated in service learning projects. Corporate training may be enhanced if students have already been exposed to new ideas and multiple ways of thinking through their service learning experiences. They may, for example, have gained the ability to empathize, to appreciate diversity, and to recognize their responsibilities as a member of an organization.

OVERVIEW OF FINDINGS

This study examined the relationship between the service learning experience and students' immediate propensity to perform OCBs (historical OCB) as well as their intentions to perform OCBs at future points in time (OCB intentions). Specifically, it was hypothesized that a service learning experience would impact student levels of historical OCB and OCB intentions, as well as several dimensions of each, including historical OCBI (organizational citizenship behaviors directed toward individuals), OCBI intentions, historical civic virtue, civic virtue intentions, historical OCBO (organizational citizenship behaviors directed toward an organization), and OCBO intentions. The study also hypothesized that there would be a relationship between historical OCB and OCB intentions. The analysis of quantitative data from the quasi-experiment conducted in Phase 1 of the study provided only partial support for the proposed hypotheses. These results were complemented by the results of the analysis of qualitative data collected in all three phases of the project. Results of the data analyses from the quasi-experiment, the qualitative interviews and the archival materials all supported the hypothesis that service learning is related to enhanced levels of both "historical OCB" and "OCB intentions" and their various dimensions, although it may not have the same impact on all students.

IMPLICATIONS OF STUDY

Relationship of Findings to Current Research on Service Learning

The research done in all three phases of this project supports the potential benefits of service learning as a teaching pedagogy in addition to being a possible precursor to the performance of OCBs. In addition, linkages have been proposed regarding the possibility of future participation by students in organizational citizenship behaviors (OCBs) in their work environments. Service learning was specifically related to an aroused interest on the part of students to help others and a desire to become more engaged in the society in which they live. Much evidence was also provided to support the notion that students who were enlightened and aroused by their experience were interested in pursuing OCB-type activities in the future. For example, the themes of helping others in their future appeared repeatedly in student reflections at all phases of this research as did their intentions to respond to others' needs and to actively participate and fulfill their responsibilities to their communities.

The findings indicate that academic benefits, when measured by the course grades, were similar among students in both sections of the marketing classes in Phase 1 of the research. Many of the service learning students in all three phases of the research expressed, however, that they had learned more in this class than in others they had taken. The qualitative reflections in all phases of the study indicated that students grow from this experiential activity with regard to their knowledge of the world, other people, organizational life, and societal obligations. A study by Boss (1994) revealed that students in an experimental (service learning) group used principled moral reasoning after the experience at a much higher level than the control group. In Phases 2 and 3 of this study, students in service learning classes spoke frequently about duties to society and civic responsibility, as well as helping others.

Kendrick (1996) found that students in an experimental service learning section showed greater improvements in measures of social responsibility, personal efficacy, and the ability to apply course concepts to new situations. Compared to the control group, service learning students in that study indicated that it was more important to work toward equal opportunity and to volunteer time to help others. There was no significant difference, however, between the service learning and the control group in grades. Astin and Sax (1998), in contrast, found that service participation did positively influence GPA, retention, degree completion, amount of interaction with faculty, and increase in knowledge.

In Phase 1 of the research, service learning on its own had a negative coefficient in each regression analysis except with historical OCBO as the dependent variable. This finding suggests that, overall, the students in the service learning section of the marketing class reported significantly lower scores for overall historical OCB, overall OCB intentions, civic virtue intentions, and OCBO intentions after completing the assignment than those in the regular section. The older students, however, do have higher levels of overall historical OCB, overall OCB intentions, and all other dimensions except historical civic virtue and civic virtue intentions than do younger students. After completing the service assignment, the better students (as measured by higher GPAs) display scores for historical OCB, civic virtue intentions and OCBO intentions scores that are significantly higher than those of students with lower GPAs. Students with higher GPAs also score higher on the OCB dimensions of historical OCBI, OCBI intentions, and historical OCBO after the course regardless of whether they participate in the service learning experience. This is probably due to the intellectual maturity of these college students and their recognition of the importance of displaying citizenship behaviors in organizations.

It may be hypothesized that the younger undergraduate students in the service learning experimental class experienced anxiety as a result of the project. In the student reflections, some expressed concerns about their discomfort with this type of nontraditional academic activity. Some students reveal that the service learning assignment was not what they expected when they registered for the marketing course. The activity may represent a learning technique that is very unlike any they have previously experienced. It can also be hypothesized that, in many cases, students with higher GPAs are able to adapt better to diverse learning modes such as those required in service learning. These students may also adapt faster to the project because they understand the value that their participation may have on society.

Service learning has been shown in this study and in others to enhance a student's academic and life experiences. Duration and intensity of service in service learning assignments have previously been found to have an impact on student outcomes (Astin & Sax, 1998; Astin et al., 1999). However, McCarthy (1996), in writing about one-time and short-term service learning experiences, notes:

> [E]xposure to some form of service learning may assist students to begin making connections between knowing about and doing something about a community issue or problem. Experiences that require students to associate a name and a face with the lives of homeless or mentally ill persons or to shadow a health care professional in an inner-city hospital or hospice can open students' eyes to ethical and moral issues, racism, and economic class differences and motivate them to take further action. To be effective, course assignments should be tied to the goals of the class; include adequate preparation and reflection opportunities; engage students in service activities that are meaningful to the students and the community members toward which their efforts are directed; and be evaluated by faculty, students, and community representatives.

The service experiences studied in the three phases of this project are not part of an overall curriculum that is dedicated to service, nor are they particularly intense. The results then would appear to show support for the impact of even a short (6 weeks) exposure to a service project or limited work at an organization (10½ hours).

One of the most frequently mentioned negative concerns raised by service learning participants focused on the time pressures for completing the necessary work, especially during the six-week accelerated session. Burr (1997) reported this problem, as well as the problem of traveling to service sites, in a case study that highlighted both the problems with and the possibilities of a progressive approach to service learning. Responses in this study indicated that careful attention should be paid early in a semester to the students' concerns about their grades and to how the nontraditional format meets their needs. Instructors should allay student concerns with careful grading policies and careful integration of the service activities into their required coursework. The requirements of the course should be repeatedly discussed as well as the positive, reciprocal benefits.

Cram (1998) conducted a quasi-experimental study examining three sections of a community college course on ethics, with one section engaging in service learning. He did not find any significant differences between service learning and non-service learning students on either moral development or increased self-esteem (Cram, 1998). The results of the study under discussion appear to contradict these findings. While quantitative data in Phase 1 does not indicate significant differences between the service learning and non-service learning students at the end of the semester, as measured by the OCB scale, qualitative data often revealed that progress was made by the student toward taking a more considerate view of others and toward recognizing the important role that an individual can play in societal affairs. It may be that, by the end of one semester, the students are only beginning to change their attitudes with regard to these values and they are not yet apparent in the quantitative measures used.

In the first phase of a two-phased study by Fenzel and Leary (1997), students enrolled in an introductory philosophy service learning class were compared with students who were enrolled in the same course without service learning. Students in the service learning class did not show greater gains in attitudes toward personal and social responsibility or in moral judgment. The second phase of that study involved 134 students in six service learning philosophy classes at different course levels (84 in 100-and 200-level courses, and 50 students in a 300-level course). Those enrolled in upper-level courses reported integrating experience and philosophy through application of theory to real-life situations significantly more often than did students in lower-level courses. The results of both phases of that study appear to be consistent with the findings of this research. The interaction of the service experience with age was consistently related to improvements in OCB scores. This interaction variable was significantly related to all of the OCB measures, indicating that the age of the student plays a role in the response that they have to the service learning experience. It is important to note that the effect of the interaction between age and service was present even when service alone had an overall negative or non-significant impact on scores. Qualitative comments also reflect that the upper-class and graduate students who participate in service learning may be more profoundly impacted by their experiences than freshmen and sophomores.

Astin et al. (1999) found that students who spent six or more hours a week performing volunteer work during their last year of college were almost twice as likely to perform volunteer work after college. They also found that nine years after graduating from high school, the frequency of volunteering still correlated with the amount of volunteering during high school. Volunteering was also associated with attending graduate school, donating money to the undergraduate college, socializing with diverse people, helping others in difficulty, developing a meaningful life philosophy, promoting racial understanding, participating in community action programs, participating in environmental cleanup, developing a sense of efficacy, earning higher degree levels, spending more hours volunteering, preparing well for careers, and developing degree aspirations. The analysis of qualitative and quantitative data in all three phases of the current study indicates that many students intend to continue with the types of activities that they partake in during the service learning course.

Relationship of Results to Undergraduate and Graduate Education

This study confirms some desirable outcomes of a service learning experience that should strengthen support for its application in both undergraduate and graduate academic settings. In recent years, many arguments for this experiential and reflective pedagogy have been provided in an effort to develop greater interpersonal, intercultural, and ethical sensitivity (Zlotkowski, 1996) in students. None of the arguments for service learning in management education, however, have specifically addressed the outcomes in terms of future productivity in the workplace. As Porter and McKibbin wrote in 1988, "business schools seem to be turning out focused analysts, albeit highly sophisticated ones, adept at measuring and calculating the probabilities of certain outcomes, but at the same time, graduates who often are unwittingly insensitive to the impacts of these outcomes on factors other than the 'bottom line'" (p. 316). These authors recommended that business schools concern themselves with the education of the whole student. If OCBs, do, in fact, contribute to productivity in the ways that have been proposed, the results of this study would provide further support for service learning in that, in addition to providing students with a holistic education, it can also develop more productive workers.

With regard to the general finding that age may be a determining factor in the impact of the service learning experience, some recent literature has argued for younger participation in experiential academic activities (Steffe, 2004). The results of this study offer support for saving experiential activities until later in an academic career as has historically been the case. In line with this study's results, Henry, Razzouk & Hoverland (1988) reported that internships have the most advantageous outcomes when taken during the junior year of college. Further research should attempt to determine optimum timing for service learning as well as other experiential activities, including internships and supported research.

Higher education is currently under much external scrutiny to produce research that is relevant to problems of the real world and to add value to the community (Kenny et al., 2002), at the same time as producing high quality scholarship that contributes to the knowledge base in the field and is published in leading journals (Lerner & Simon, 1998). Educators must also prepare undergraduates and graduates for careers while pursuing programs that are consistent with institutional missions, which almost universally include the holistic education of the student along with advancing teaching and research (Kenny et al., 2002). As Kenny et al. note, "We believe that the cutting-edge of the successful synthesis of teaching, research, and service is outreach scholarship coupled with service learning that imbues undergraduates with the sense of the need, and provides them with the opportunity, to participate in the community-based outreach scholarship of faculty and graduate students" (2002, p. 6).

The results of this research indicated that students engaged in service learning do, in fact, begin to experience an education such as that which was recommended by Boyer (1990), which includes being able to translate one's academic knowledge (including technical knowledge) into information of value to one's life and to those of one's family, community, and society.

REFERENCES

Allison, G., Voss, R. S., Dryer, S. (2001). Student classroom and career success: The role of OCB. *Journal of Education for Business, 76*(5), 282–289.

Astin, A. W., & Sax, L. J. (1998). How undergraduates are affected by service participation. *Journal of College Student Development, 39*(3), 251–263.

Astin, A. W., Sax, L. J., & Avalos, J. (1999). Long term effects of volunteerism during the undergraduate years. *Review of Higher Education, 22*(2), 187–202.

Batchelder, T. H., & Root, S. (1994). Effects of an undergraduate program to integrate academic learning and service: cognitive, prosocial cognitive, and identity outcomes. *Journal of Adolescence, 17*, 341–355.

Billig, S. H., & Eyler, J. (2003). The state of service learning and service learning research. In S. H. Billig & J. Eyler (Eds.), *Deconstructing service learning: Research exploring context, participation, and impacts* (pp. 253–264). Greenwich, CT: Information Age Publishing.

Boss, J. A. (1994). The effect of community service on the moral development of college ethics students. *Journal of Moral Development, 23*(2), 183–198.

Boyer, E. (1987). *The undergraduate experience in America.* New York, NY: Harper Collins.

Boyer, E. (1990). *Scholarship reconsidered.* Princeton, NJ: Carnegie Foundation for the Advancement of Teaching.

Burr, K. L. (1997). *Problems, politics, and possibilities of a progressive approach to service learning in a community college: A case study.* Unpublished Dissertation, Oklahoma State University, Stillwater, OK.

Cram, S. B. (1998). The Impact of service learning on moral development and self esteem of community college ethics students. Unpublished Dissertation, University of Iowa, Iowa City, IA.

Dalton, J. C., & Petrie, A. M. (1997). The power of peer culture. *Educational Record, 78*(3–4), 18–4.

Dewey, J. (1938). *Experience and education.* New York, NY: Collier Books.

DiPadova, L. (2000). *Service learning initiative.* Academy of Management. Retrieved from www.aom.pace.org

Dumas, C. (2002). Community-based service learning: Does it have a role in management education? *International Journal of Value-Based Management, 15*, 249–264.

Dunlap, M. R. (1998). Adjustment and developmental outcomes of students engaged in service learning. *Journal of Experiential Education, 21*(3), 147–153.

Eisenberg, N. (1991). Meta-analytic contributions to the literature on prosocial behavior. *Personality and Social Psychology Bulletin, 17,* 273–383.

Ehrlich, T. (1997). Dewey versus Hutchins: The next round. In R. Orrill (Ed.), *Education and democracy: Re-imagining liberal learning in America* (pp. 225–262). New York, NY: College Entrance Examination Board.

Ettore, B. (1992). Executives debate new competitive strategies. *Management Review, 81*(7), 42–47.

Eyler, J. S., & Giles, D. E. Jr. (1999). *Where's the learning in service learning?* San Francisco, CA: Jossey-Bass.

Eyler, J., Root, S., & Giles, D. E., Jr. (1998). Service learning and the development of expert citizens: service learning and cognitive science. In R. Bringle & D. Duffey (Eds.), *With service in mind* (pp. 85–100). Washington, DC: American Association for Higher Education.

Fenzel. L. M., & Leary, T. P. (1997, March). *Evaluating outcomes of service learning courses at a parochial college.* Paper presented at the Annual Meeting of the American Educational Research Association, Chicago, IL.

Friedus, H. (1997, March). *Reflection in teaching: Development plus.* Paper presented at the Annual Meeting of the American Educational Research Association, Chicago, IL.

Godfrey, P. C. (1999). Service learning and management education: A call to action. *Journal of Management Inquiry, 8*(4). 363–379.

Graham, J. W. (1991). An essay on organizational citizenship behavior. *Employee Responsibilities and Rights Journal, 4,* 249–270.

Gray, M., Ondaatje, E., Fricker, R., Geschwind, S., Goldman, C., Kaganoff, T., ... Klein, S. (1998). *Coupling service and learning in higher education: The final report of the evaluation of the Learn and Serve America, higher education program.* Santa Monica, CA: The RAND Corporation.

Henry, L. G., Razzouk, N. Y., & Hoverland, H. (1988). Accounting internships: A practical framework. *Journal of Education for Business, 64*(1), 28–31.

Jeavons, T. (1991). *Learning for the common good: Liberal education, civic education, and teaching philanthropy.* Washington, DC: Association of American Colleges.

Kendrick, J. R. (1996). Outcomes of service learning in an introduction to sociology course. *Journal of Community Service Learning, 2,* 71–81.

Kenny, M., Simon, L., Kiley-Brabeck, K, & Lerner, R. (2002). *Learning to serve: Promoting civil society through service learning.* Norwell, MA: Kluwer Academic.

Krebs, D. L. (1970). Altruism: An examination of the concept and a review of the literature. *Psychological Bulletin, 73,* 258–302.

Lerner, R. M., & Simon, L. A. K. (Eds) (1998). *University-community collaborations for the twenty-first century: Outreach scholarship for youth and families.* New York, NY: Garland.

Madsen, S. (2004). Academic service learning in human resource education. *Journal of Education for Business, 79*(6), 328–332.

Mason, J. C. (1992). Business schools: Striving to meet customer demands. *Management Review,* September, 10–14.

McCarthy, M. (1996). One-time and short-term service learning experiences. In B. Jacoby (Ed.), *Service learning in higher education: Concepts and practices* (pp. 113–134). San Francisco, CA: Jossey-Bass.

Morton, K. (1995). The irony of service: Charity, project and social change in service learning. *Michigan Journal of Community Service Learning, 2*(1), 19–32.

Motowidlo, S. J., & Van Scotter, J. R. (1994). Evidence that task-performance should be distinguished from contextual performance. *Journal of Applied Psychology, 79*(4), 272–280.

Nahser, F. B., & Ruhe, J. (2001). Putting American pragmatism to work in the classroom. *Journal of Business Ethics, 34*, 317–330.

O'Neill, E. H. (1990). *The liberal tradition of civic education.* In J. C. Kendall & Associates (Eds.), *Combining service and learning: A resource book for community and public service* (Vol. 1, pp. 190–200). Raleigh, NC: National Society for Internships and Experiential Education.

Organ, D. W. (1988). *Organizational citizenship behavior: The good soldier syndrome,* Lexington, MA: D.C. Heath.

Organ, D. W. (1990). *The motivational basis of organizational citizenship behavior.* In B. W. Staw & L. L. Cummings (Eds.), *Research in organizational behavior* (Vol. 12, pp. 43–72). Greenwich, CT: JAI Press.

Organ, D. W. (1997). Toward an explication of "morale": In search of the m factor. In C. I. Cooper & S. E. Jackson (Eds.), *Creating tomorrow's organizations* (pp. 493–503). London, UK: John Wiley & Sons.

Organ, D. W., & Konovsky, M. (1989). Cognitive versus affective determinants of organizational citizenship behavior. *Journal of Applied Psychology, 74*(1), 157–164.

Organ, D. W., Podsakoff, P. M., & MacKenzie, S. B. (2006). *Organizational citizenship behavior: Its nature, antecedents, and consequences.* Thousand Oaks, CA: Sage.

Porter, L. W., & McKibbon, L. E. (1988). *Management education and development: Drift or thrust into the 21st century?* New York, NY: McGraw-Hill.

Roose, D., Daphne, J., Miller, A. J., Norris, W., Peacock, R., White, C., & White, G. (1997). *Black student retention study.* Oberlin, OH: Oberlin College.

Rushton, J. P. (1980). *Altruism, socialization, and society.* Englewood Cliffs, NJ: Prentice-Hall.

Schmiede, A. (1995). Using focus groups in service learning: Implications for practice and research. *Michigan Journal of Community Service Learning, 2*, 63–71.

Smith, M. (1994). Community service learning: striking the chord of citizenship. *Michigan Journal of Community Service Learning, 1*, 37–43.

Stanton, T. (1994). The critical incident journal. In A. A Watters & M. Ford (Eds.), *A guide for change: Resources for implementing community service writing* (pp. 58–60). New York, NY: McGraw-Hill.

Steffe, J. (2004). Creating powerful learning environments beyond the classroom. *Change, 36,* 46–50.

Thomas, K. M., & Landau, H. (2002). Organizational development students as engaged learners and reflective practitioners: The role of service learning in teaching OD. *Organization Development Journal, 20*(3), 88–100.

Tucker, M. L., McCarthy A. M., Hoxmeier, J. C., & Lenk, M. M. (1998). Community service learning increases communication skills across the business curriculum. *Business Communication Quarterly, 61*(2), 88–99.

Vernon, A., & Foster, L. (2002). Nonprofit agency perspectives of higher education service learning and volunteerism. *Journal of Nonprofit & Public Sector Marketing, 10*(2), 207–230.

Vitz, P. C. (1990). The use of stories in moral development: new psychological reasons for an old education method. *American Psychologist, 45,* 709–720.

Wagner, S. L., & Rush, M. C. (2000). Altruistic organizational citizenship behavior: Context, disposition and age. *The Journal of Social Psychology, 140*(3), 379–391.

Ward, K. (1996). Service learning and student volunteerism: reflections on institutional commitment. *Michigan Journal of Community Service learning, 3,* 55–65.

Weber, P., & Sleeper, B. (2002). Enriching student experiences: Multi-disciplinary exercises in service learning. *Teaching Business Ethics, 7,* 417–435

Werner, J. M., (2000). Implications of OCB and contextual performance for human resource management. *Human Resource Management Review, 10*(1), 3–24.

Whitehead, A. N. (1929). *The aims of education and other essays.* New York, NY: Macmillan.

Williams, L. J., & Anderson, S. W. (1991). Job satisfaction and organizational commitment as predictors of organizational citizenship and in-role behaviors. *Journal of Management, 17,* 601–617.

Williams, S., & Wong, W. T. (1999). Mood and organizational citizenship behavior: The effects of positive affect on employee organizational citizenship behavior intentions. *Journal of Psychology, 133*(6), 656–668.

Zlotowski, E. (1996). Opportunity for all: Linking service learning and business education. *Journal of Business Ethics, 15*(1), 5–20.

CHAPTER 7

DOING SOCIAL JUSTICE

The MYTI Program and Inner City Students

Rosaria Caporrimo and David Kerner
Montclair State University

ABSTRACT

This chapter describes a small program initially developed to interest and recruit "minority" high school students into the education professions. The MYTI Program (Minority Youth Teaching Initiative) began with a small internal grant when participating students were freshmen at a New York City high school. A variety of activities included directly addressing racism and stereotypes in education and community through guest speakers, group discussions on timely topics, critical thinking activities, receiving tutoring, tutoring younger students, and preparing for college. While only a few students planned to enter education, results did reveal growth in students' approach to their own education and learning, critical thinking, and social/emotional development.

It began innocently enough. I received a small grant from my institution; the goal was to work with inner-city, low-SES high school students to interest,

Adolescence in the 21st Century, pages 125–139
125

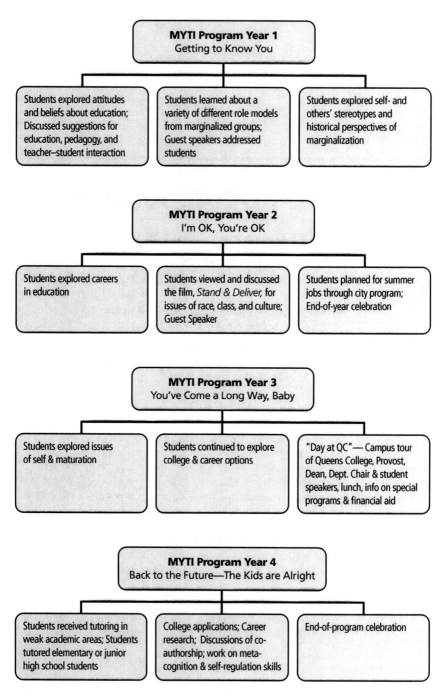

Figure 7.1 MYTI program developmental model.

and possibly recruit them into the field of teaching or into education in general. Historically, there has been a shortage in the number of minority group teachers in the U.S. (Ancarrow, 1991; Goodwin, 1991; Polansky, 1999). Over the past two decades, various recruitment programs have addressed this paucity, resulting in more than double the number of minority teachers in U.S. classrooms, as the number of majority teachers decreased (Ingersoll & May, 2011). More recent research has found a more troubling pattern—that is, although more individuals from minority groups are entering the teaching profession, they are far more likely to leave teaching, due to a variety of problems. These problems include a lack of autonomy and support in the low-income schools in which they were motivated to teach (Ingersoll, 2007; Ingersoll & May, 2011).

At the time, I was a faculty member in a college within a city university system, one that prides itself on having the most diverse population of students in America's most ethnically diverse county. As an educational psychologist in a teacher education program that prepared students to work in inner-city schools, I was always surprised at the small number of minority students in our various programs. Thus began my search for an inner-city high school that would accept me to run a small, intimate program to inform students about the rewards of a career in education. I contacted two institutions and was granted permission by one, a low-income, inner-city high school in New York City. From the onset, the administration was welcoming and supportive of the project and assisted in recruiting the group of students with whom I would work for four years, from their freshman year through graduation.

I thought carefully about the program goals and was certain there was a need to empower the students and discuss issues of social justice with them before even beginning to address the concept of careers. As a total stranger from a different culture and background, I also understood that in order for me to be credible, I needed to be accepted by these adolescents. This is elaborated upon in the section on the first year of the program.

Reflections on this unique situation allowed me to formulate goals I saw as much more realistic in terms of providing the scaffolding that would allow them to share their own challenges as minority adolescents attempting to navigate the waters of high school and to begin thinking beyond those somewhat sheltered years. Thus, my goals for the program were fairly simple: (1) empower traditionally marginalized adolescent students in the context of social justice issues and academic achievement, (2) introduce program participants to the issues facing education in the 21st century, (3) motivate students to consider entering teaching or another education profession, (4) develop an ease of transition between high school and entry into college, and (5) become a mentor to participating students. What transpired was a life-changing experience for me—hopefully, for all of us. I have always enjoyed working directly with adolescents, but these students were special. They knew so much more than schools and society can appreciate, and were able to clearly articulate their concerns. For example, they spoke about being treated poorly and how teachers would get much more cooperation and success from their students if they treated them more respectfully. In this chapter, the journey is shared with you; it is no less a journey than any that allows us to grow as individuals, to develop our hearts, souls, and intellects.

CO-AUTHORSHIP, RECIPROCITY, PERSISTENCE

I begin by focusing on the concept of co-authorship, as described by Nakkula and Toshalis (2006). Co-authorship recognizes that development is a reciprocal process. Not only do we influence the development of the adolescents with whom we work; they also impact our development—as professionals, as part of our continuing social and cognitive development, and as human beings. According both to the students and their guidance counselor, the issues we discussed and the perspectives gained have been invaluable to this group of adolescents. From the perspective of the program director, I have learned so much more than I had anticipated. Actually, I had anticipated changing their lives, which, I suppose, is the usual perspective we take when we attempt to impact the lives of others whom we see as less fortunate in a variety of ways. Their optimism and naiveté allowed me to reexamine not only my perspective but the concepts of teacher, student, learner, and learned. I am aware of co-authorship as it occurs throughout my teaching experiences with pre- and in-service teachers as I prepare them to work with this type of population; however, the co-authorship I experienced with these young people was much more powerful, and empowering, as we sought to understand and negotiate our relationship. It is this concept of co-authorship that I encourage all educators to examine and acknowledge in working with adolescents; there is no doubt that the process has always occurred, but it is in its recognition and acknowledgment that we become enlightened to its power and seek to enhance the co-authorship experience on an ongoing basis. One must be open to total honesty, to be able to express deep thoughts and feelings in a "safe space" (Nakkula & Toshalis, 2006), one in which the facilitator becomes the student, and the students become the facilitators. Traditional barriers between the teacher, the adult, and the "children," the students, must be dissolved as discussions focus on perceptions and experiences, both common and novel. It requires all members to think and function outside of their comfort zones, yet within their zone of proximal development (see, for example, Vygotsky, 1978). True growth and development cannot occur if the parties involved are unwilling to be vulnerable—and true teaching requires individuals to allow themselves to be vulnerable; it opens minds to possibilities rather than only to "what is" or "what has been experienced." In one of our fourth-year meetings, the discussion focused on the recognition and value of the co-authorship experience both from my perspective and those of the students. The conversation elucidated, for all of us, the power of truly working collaboratively toward the goal of social justice. This type of discussion involves metacognitive processes and interpersonal skills that most high school teachers, particularly those in low-SES schools, fail to recognize and honor.

Although I have dedicated most of my professional life to social justice issues, I was not prepared for how deeply these students would touch my heart. From our first meetings and the connection that was made, our journey together was productive in ways that go beyond "measurement." Our co-authorship began on an autumn day in 2007 when I met with all the freshman students, split into several groups by lunch period, in the library of their high school. My purpose was to discuss the dearth of minority representation in the education fields and to find out which students were interested in becoming part of a program I was commencing at their high school. They were to be part of the MYTI Program—Minority Youth Teaching Initiative. At first, many students signed on, but as the weeks went on and they realized there would be an actual commitment, I was left with a core group of 25–30 students initially. Over the course of the next three years, the attrition rate resulted in a core group of 20–25 students, with approximately 8–15 students per meeting, depending on student availability. Because of schedule restrictions, we were only able to meet for short intervals—during lunch sessions. What we accomplished during those short meetings is testimony to the power of commitment, persistence, honesty, challenge, and the vibrancy and resiliency of youth!

FIRST YEAR

The first year was about building trust, though with this particular group of students it was not a difficult task. Once they saw that I was "on their side" and that I would engage them in conversations regarding whatever was on their mind related to the program goals, they opened up. I told them that behind the closed doors of the library they could share with me anything that was transpiring in their classes, with various teachers, though I told them never to use teachers' actual names. However, I knew that I had to share with them first, so during the first meeting I told them about me, why I did this type of work, and my experiences as the daughter of Sicilian immigrants; I told them about my experiences with stereotypes and discrimination. To them, I was a "white teacher" from Queens College; by appearance there was no way for them to know about who I really was. I also shared with them my admiration for the social justice work and music of Bob Marley—little by little they began to see me as someone beyond the professor who visited them from the college. This allowed them to see me not just as a professor but also as a human, as someone on their side willing to work with them and advocate for them.

One of the first goals was to allow them to freely express their experiences, likes, and dislikes of their academic experiences in high school. I asked them to share their thoughts on the following: "How do you know that a teacher respects you?" "How do you know when a teacher doesn't respect you?" "How are your classes run?" "How would you like to see them run?" While I did not conduct a full qualitative study on this program, it is important for readers to experience some of the feedback these students shared. The following quotes will give the reader an idea of these students' perceptions at the age of fourteen and fifteen, when they were just freshman and new to high school. I share these with the reader to give insight into the thoughts and situations of these adolescent students.

What Teachers Do:

- When kids scream, some teachers scream back at them. That's wrong.
- I like it when a teacher stays on my case; it means they care.
- I don't like it when teachers yell at us. Sometimes when kids are yelling, teachers yell back. That's wrong. If a teacher respects me I'll work more and listen more.
- I like it when teachers stop and explain things—it helped me understand Shakespeare.
- Some teachers just write work on the board—they don't help us and we don't even know what's on the test.
- Last week a teacher said to me, "Are you dumb or stupid?
- A teachers said, "I'm not repeating myself—if you can't see the board, that's tough!"
- A teacher told me," I want you to fail—you won't go anywhere anyway."
- The teacher talked bad about my family and picks on everyone.
- One teacher made racist comments.

What Teachers and Staff Don't Do:

- When we do seatwork, it's noisy and the teacher does nothing. I was once told to keep quiet and "be a man."
- Lots of teachers don't do their job—they should be fired.
- The counselors and administrators seem helpless to change things.
- I think teachers are just in it for the money.
- Teachers should make stuff interesting; classes are boring because of the way teachers teach. They don't make it interesting.

- If I ask a teacher to please slow down they just ignore me. It's not right to ignore a kid who has a question. It happens to lots of kids in different classes.
- When kids raise their hands, teachers don't call on them.
- Teachers just don't pay attention. They don't know our problems, what's going on in our lives.

Further, the challenges in their lives were many, from absent parents who had stayed in their home country and sent their child to New York City to be educated in this country, to the student who lived with a brother because the parents were nowhere to be found, and another brother was in prison. Many students dealt with personal issues, many related to being in a minority status or living in low-income areas.

The first year was, indeed, an eye-opening experience for me because so many students "bought into" the stereotypes that are so prevalent for minority students from low-SES levels or schools with reputations less than stellar. During the first few meetings of that first year, chaos abounded because these students were fourteen and fifteen years old and undergoing so many of the changes related to adolescence. They were negotiating their psychosocial development (Erikson, 1968; Marcia, 1991), dealing with changes and growth in the adolescent brain (Price, 2005), learning to live in new bodies due to adolescent maturity and, in addition to these common adolescent experiences, many of them lived in less than ideal situations. These early meetings were challenging to me as a psychologist who truly believes in empowering students and using Vygotskian and Freirian techniques toward that end. There was much talking both while other students were speaking and while I was speaking; there was a fair amount of flirting, pinching, sitting on one another's laps, and general early adolescent behavior. At one point, in a session when only about 12 students attended, all boys as it turned out that day, I was feeling rather frustrated and remarked that I was not surprised that some teachers lost their patience if this was how they behaved in class. One of the boys, who turned out to be a genuinely polite, ambitious, lovely young man, said, "What do you expect, Miss, we're a bunch of black kids all together in a room." Horrified, I used his comment as a teachable moment, telling him and the rest of the group that they should just keep on thinking like that. If they wanted those "in charge," those in power, to continue viewing them through a stereotypical lens, then it would be fine to think of themselves like that. In fact, I remarked that the "haves" in society would prefer they think of themselves like this because the balance of power would remain as it always had, because those "in charge" need people who view themselves as inherently "less than" in order for others to remain in charge and in power. It did turn out to be that teachable moment.

We had a discussion about "haves" and "have-nots" and the meaning of hegemony and power differentials and how we can change society by working as "radicals"—that is, by working from the root of the problem. I reminded them that change has never occurred because those in power were magnanimous in "giving" rights and privileges to others, but because those who had been historically disenfranchised fought for change and their voices to be heard. In subsequent meetings, we discussed "minority" role models who fought from the roots without expecting those in power to hand things to them. Role models like Gandhi, Martin Luther King, Jr., Malcolm X, Mother Theresa, and others. As the students opened up and realized they had to become an active part in their own empowerment, the discussion became more focused with students using metacognitive skills and interacting in ways they had not previously.

SECOND YEAR

One of the highlights of the second year was the students' viewing of the film, *Stand and Deliver*. I felt this was appropriate for this group of students, many of whom were considered the same type of "throw-away kids" featured in the movie and so lovingly nurtured to success by Jaime Escalante. The true story engaged the students more than a discussion of the story would have. After they viewed the film, a guest speaker, a colleague of one author, engaged the students in a discussion regarding their futures and how their present behavior, studies, and demeanor related to that future. He was able to reach out to them and challenge them to think more deeply about their behaviors and responses. Whether this was related to the fact that he was a Black professional who had emigrated from an African nation is not clear. However, the students responded quite positively, and the event appeared to highlight for them the possibilities in their own lives.

Together we discussed how the situations of the students in the film were similar to theirs and how those students had experienced failure and low expectations—situations with which the students in the program could identify. Since the film is based on a true story, I was able to share some of the actual successes of the students portrayed in the film, who eventually became successful in their chosen fields. They were amazed at the respect and love that Escalante showed his students and were impressed at the power of a teacher to motivate, encourage, and teach for real success. For these adolescents, this might have been a rare glimpse into the possibilities that life held for them as well.

Toward the end of the school year, we worked on getting summer jobs for the students. Several had already made arrangements, and others used the resources available through a New York City program, yet there were a number who planned to do nothing other than "party," although we discussed the importance of employment on college applications and the need to network in order to get references for college applications. At the end of the second year, as with the first, an end-of-year party allowed students to relax with some typical teenage fare, reggae and hip hop music, and the promise of continued work with them in their next year. It was particularly satisfying to learn from their guidance counselor that students regularly went to her to find out when our next meeting would be. If schedules permitted we would have met weekly; still, it was motivating to know these students were committed to the program and were willing to attend more meetings than could realistically be provided.

THIRD YEAR

The third year revealed some interesting developmental changes in these students. Because I had the opportunity of interacting with them throughout their high school years, I was able to see these changes and was willing to share my observations with them. During one of our first meetings of the third year, I noted how much they had matured; I reminded them how during our first few meetings when they were freshman there had been so much talking at the same time with little listening, and how they had attempted to use much of the time for socializing rather than focusing on the discussion or task at hand. They were able to reflect on this and discuss their own development as teenagers. Most of them were amused when they reflected on some of those initial behaviors, and discussed why they had changed. For some it was an opportunity to share difficult moments in their lives that had forced them to mature but for most it was a discussion of the normal developmental processes of adolescence, with an acknowledgment of the necessity to assume more responsibility both in their personal and academic lives. I asked them to write a few sentences on how they had changed from Year 1 of the program to Year 3. Some of their responses appear below.

Academic and Behavioral Changes:
- I changed—academically because I got new classes and new teachers. Well, I think that from 14 to 17 I've matured in a sense that I take more responsibilities in the importance of work and anything important. I am a little bit more in tuned to taking care of my responsibilities. I'm applying for college soon, therefore, I feel it's best if I'm more responsible.
- I have changed a lot since my freshman year. . . . The way I act, think, and respond to things is more mature. I plan on getting good

grades unlike in the beginning when I really didn't care. I am proud of myself and I have achieved. I am a DJ and get paid.

- I know more subjects. I'm a little better in math, I read a little more than I did. I also study. I stopped playing a lot in classes and now I meet new people faster.
- In my grades I didn't really grow. I stayed the same getting a good average, but now I am more focused because in a year and a couple of months I am going to college. I'll have to focus very hard.

Social/Emotional Changes:

- . . . I also changed socially because I became more mature and listened more to other people.
- From freshman year till now I changed a lot. I got taller and I got smarter. I understand things better and I got my permit so I could drive now. My personality has changed—I was the shy type but now my confidence has grown off the chart.
- Over the years I changed in a couple of ways. I stopped playing around a lot with my friends and people who I was making friends with who weren't good for me. I've also calmed down on my talkative ways and I also expand on my thoughts more.
- . . . I'm also into cars, so I want to get my own car since I drive a lot. The people I hang out with changed a little bit. Now I hang more with the good kids, the ones I know will be successful in their lives.
- I have changed a lot from age 14 to 17. I have made a lot more friends. I tried different programs in school and I have matured a lot. I have become a lot stronger of a person.
- I changed tremendously. I have grown to understand a lot of things. I have learned that you can't judge people. The changes I have made have been for the better and I am glad I made them. I also changed in class. I pay more attention and study more.

The students' recognition of their own development of identity and their experiences and, sometimes, struggles, to be better individuals, is quite remarkable. For example,

I've changed since freshman year, like I used to love to fight and now ever since I've grown up I became a big person, I started to learn that life is not a joke. In order to become someone you have to fight for what you want to achieve—to achieve your goals. I also learned that in life you're not always going to find that friend to help you through life. There is always going to be someone to put you down. But if you're a strong person you would let it pass you by.

Another student asserted:

> Over the past couple years I feel as though I have changed in many ways. Socially, mentally, physically, in many ways. . . . I slowly took the time and broke away from my friends and asked myself, "What am I doing? How can this affect my future? What do I want to be?" Very soon my grades went way up and I set my goals for myself and 2 years later I have hope, a future, and love from many. Yes, I am beautiful, unique, and have a busy life but it's my life and I LOVE IT!

For some, recognition that a change in social habits and friends was needed was apparent—for others, there was a recognition that changes needed to be made in academics in order to be successful. Clearly, these students were struggling with issues of identity during their high school years, as described by Erikson's stage of *identity vs. confusion*. Marcia (1991) further elaborated on this stage by noting that the process of identity development is flexible, with students experiencing the various statuses therein, including *identity achievement, moratorium,* and *diffusion.* Reading these statements regarding student identity development and discussing them was an informative experience. This process allowed students to reflect on their experiences and choices as adolescents. Each time I met with "my kids" I felt we bonded more and more and I won more of their trust, often simply by allowing them to be themselves and share their thoughts freely.

What we all considered to be the highlight of the third year was the capstone event in June. Students participated in a Day at the College. I decorated the room with the colors of the college and was able to purchase a "goody bag" for each student that included items from the college bookstore and bearing the name and/or insignia of the college. The day was scheduled in various sessions with guest speakers. Students were fortunate to hear brief presentations by the Provost, Dean of Education, representatives of each department within the education division, and representatives of the admissions and financial aid departments. Moreover, one session included current graduate and undergraduate students who related their experiences at the college and responded to questions from the MYTI students. Lunch in the college cafeteria and a tour of the campus, including the new dormitory, completed their day. The feedback from university professionals who participated was very gratifying; they were impressed with the students' behavior and the quality of their questions. The feedback from the students, relayed to me by their guidance counselor, was also gratifying; students thoroughly enjoyed the day and felt very "grown up" regarding their participation and ability to interact with college professionals as well as graduate and undergraduate students. According to the guidance counselor, this was the topic of much conversation for these students, further allowing them to feel "special" as participants in the program.

FOURTH YEAR

The fourth year revealed amazing changes in this group of dedicated students. They researched and applied to colleges and received tutoring in weak areas to boost their GPAs. This was not an easy process since all tutors were providing this service on a volunteer basis. Although the school itself did provide tutoring, the scheduled times did not necessarily fit in with my students' schedules of classes. Thus, I recruited students from my classes and, although many were interested, the number of students with availability was limited. What I had thought would be a relatively easy process turned out to be yet another challenge.

The other commitment required of program participants was to tutor younger students, those in elementary or middle schools. This would provide them with experience not only in working in a "teaching–learning" situation, but also with community service hours for college applications. Several students were already involved in tutoring experiences they found on their own. Other experiences were coordinated through the office of one of the assistant principals at the school. These experiences further provided these students with experiences outside their daily school and work routines, allowing them to explore their role as teachers and learners, discussions that continued throughout the last year.

Also, in this fourth year we continued discussions of self-regulation and metacognition to prepare students for the rigors of college study. Moreover, discussions of co-authorship permitted students to view the teacher–student relationship through a different lens that would soon evolve into the professor–student relationship. Understanding that one's behavior and thoughts affect and are affected by others' behavior and thoughts is crucial to negotiating the subtle social contracts of college life and adult life in general. Thus, these discussions further allowed students to more fully develop into adults who will better function in academic and social contexts.

The students were able to self-regulate at this point, sharing thoughts and experiences and truly listening when other group members spoke. They articulated concerns over attending college and the responsibilities and expectations of studying at that level. They shared anxieties about becoming adults and how that would impact their lives; they even discussed getting married and having children and how life would go on beyond the safe walls of their high school. At this point, I merely facilitated the discussions, since they were able to organize their thoughts much more clearly and share in reciprocal conversations.

DISCUSSION AND REFLECTION

This was a small group of students, and this work was in no way a program from whose results we expected to generalize. However, when one engages in this type of work, one must bear witness and share the experience, since social justice often involves the "small works" of kindness and joy that do make a difference in the lives of all participants, even in small numbers. Even to call it social justice somehow diminishes the spirit in which the work was done, even if that work is characterized by variables and activities that qualify it as social justice work. From my perspective, social justice was experienced by all who participated. What I am able to bring from this experience, sharing in the lives and development of "my kids," has been priceless. According to their counselor, their lives have changed because of this experience. Thus, true co-authorship occurred.

Although we are unable to generalize and give advice regarding this type of limited program, some personal experiences have been shared with the reader. We recommend that faculty and graduate students attempt a similar type of program, suited to their needs and the needs of students in their community. The size of the MYTI program, due to restricted resources, allowed the program director to be involved in all aspects of the program, as limited as it may have been. Each encounter allowed us to build our relationship. However, the relationships and trust that were built were not only between the students and me; these shared times allowed the students to become a cohesive group, even if they were not good friends outside the context of our program meetings.

GOALS OF THE PROGRAM—RESULTS

The first goal, to empower traditionally marginalized adolescent students in the context of social justice issues and academic achievement, was certainly realized. The program, no doubt in concert with normal adolescent development, resulted in students beginning to understand and negotiate issues of social justice in their lives. Further, the number of students planning to attend college indicated cognitive growth and comprehension of what would be necessary to support oneself or one's family in the future. The first author was thrilled when both the students' guidance counselor and assistant principal acknowledged their belief that much of the change in these students was a direct result of the program.

The goal to introduce program participants to the issues facing education in the 21st century was successful in that over the four years students were able to discuss current challenges in education, particularly those that impacted them directly. These included standardized testing, teacher accountability, and issues related to classroom teaching and learning. By the end of their senior year, students were able to address these various issues more deeply, reflecting both cognitive development and the experience of being exposed to these issues in the program.

The third goal, to motivate students to consider entering teaching or another education profession was only mildly realized. One student definitely planned to become a secondary education history teacher and another expressed a strong desire to become a high school counselor. Other students planned to enter the business field and others were not sure exactly in what field they would major. Two students planned to enter the military, mostly because they felt college would only be affordable with the use of the GI bill.

In terms of the goal to develop an ease of transition between high school and entry into college, both the guidance counselor and I felt that these students were better prepared to make that transition considering the support they received not just from the program director, but from one another as they progressed over their high school years. Finally, clearly I had become not just a mentor, but a friend and supporter of these students. During our last meeting, there were many hugs, some tears, and much appreciation. I will never forget the statement one young man made as he gave me a farewell hug, "You're alright, Dr. C, you're alright. Thank you."

In the end, it does not matter that only a handful of students intended to enter the education professions. What seemed to be most important was that these students intended to pursue college careers and had goals they might have imagined but may not have had the support to pursue. This support had various layers—from the program itself, from each other, from the guidance counselor who lovingly gave her time and commitment to assist in the program and, for some, from family members who wanted a better life for them. Perhaps, then, we do have some advice for those who have yet to experience this type of personal involvement with adolescents. Yes, go "do" social justice, not only for those young people whose lives you will touch, but for yourself, your spirit, and for the ability to know, truly know, you have made a small difference for yourself and others.

For the first author and program director, "doing social justice" with these students was both humbling and empowering. I remain humbled by their persistence and courage in the face of some very difficult personal situations. I am humbled that they allowed me into their lives with open arms and made me feel welcomed and appreciated. I am empowered by knowing that I was able to effect change in the lives of adolescents directly, in a setting that may not necessarily have provided that level of support, understanding, and love. One thing remains sure—I will never forget this group of adolescents. I hope they never forget one another and their times together in that library, in that old building where they spent their adolescent years. And perhaps they will remember one of the people who believed in them, who listened to their worries and their dreams, and who believed they could succeed when so many others did not. Perhaps. . . .

REFERENCES

Ancarrow, J. S. (1991). *Teacher shortages: Results of the teacher demand and shortage survey for public schools, 1987–1988.* Washington, DC:Office of Special Education and Rehabilitative Services.

Erikson, E. H. (1968). *Identity, youth, and crisis.* New York, NY: Norton.

Goodwin, A. L. (1991). Problems, process, and promise: Reflections on a collaborative approach to the solution of the minority teacher shortage. *Journal of Teacher Education, 42*(1), 28–36.

Ingersoll, R. M. (2007). Short on power, long on responsibility. *Educational Leadership, 65*(1), 20–25.

Ingersoll, R. M., & May, H. (2011). The minority teacher shortage: Fact or fable. *Phi Delta Kappan, 93*(1), 62–65.

Marcia, J. E. (1991). Identity and self-development. In R. Lerner, A. Peterson, & J. Brooks-Gunn (Eds.), *Encyclopedia of adolescence* (Vol. 1), New York, NY: Garland.

Nakkula, M. J., & Toshalis, E. (2006). *Understanding youth: Adolescent development for educators.* Cambridge, MA: Harvard Education Press.

Polansky, H. B. (1999). Combating teacher shortages: Frameworks for minority recruitment. *School Business Affairs, 65*(5), 43–44.

Price, L. F. (2005). The biology of risk taking. *Educational Leadership, 62*(7), 22–26.

Vygotsky, L. S. (1978). *Mind in society: The development of higher mental processes.* Cambridge, MA: Harvard University Press.

CHAPTER 8

AUTISM IN ADOLESCENCE

Facing the Challenges

Irene Van Riper

INTRODUCTION

The incidence of students with autism spectrum disorder (ASD) has been increasing in the past 40 years, as has the importance of communication and personal interaction in our evolving society. ASD is a neurobiological disorder that affects individuals in varying degrees with a heterogeneous array of characteristics. It is a spectrum disorder, as the name states, and usually presents itself by the age of three years. The DSM-IV-TR (American Psychiatric Association, 2000) lists the five categories of ASD: autistic disorder, Asperger's disorder, pervasive developmental disorder not otherwise specified, Rett's disorder, and childhood disintegrative disorder.

Under the autistic disorder umbrella, characteristics include a deficit in social interaction, inability to develop peer relationships, and a deficit in sharing emotion. These individuals often do not understand another person's perspective. The regression of language and awkward body posture may not be present until the age of three.

Adolescence in the 21st Century, pages 141–154
Copyright © 2014 by Information Age Publishing
All rights of reproduction in any form reserved.

Asperger's disorder has parallel characteristics; however, language development usually develops typically and is not lost. Individuals with Asperger's disorder also have deficits in maintaining and initiating social interactions and may demonstrate a higher cognitive level than others diagnosed with ASD.

Individuals with pervasive developmental disorder not otherwise specified (PPD-NOS) usually have impairments similar to autistic disorder, but the timeline of the onset of their deficits not be typical. These individuals may demonstrate a few of the characteristics of ASD, but may be typically developing in other ways.

Rett's disorder is typically found only in females; it is a mutation of the x-chromosome. Females possess two x-chromosomes, but males have only one. Because of this difference, male embryos with Rett's generally do not survive. Girls who have Rett's usually develop normally until they reach between five and 30 months. At this time, signs of degenerative physical and language development are typically observed. These characteristics, as well the constant wringing of hands, are accompanied by a regression in language and social interaction. Childhood disintegrative disorder is also a disability that affects language and social interaction. Typical development occurs until the age of two. Loss of motor and language skills begins around this time, including a degeneration of bodily functions control.

According to the Centers for Disease Control and Prevention (2012), an average of one out of every 88 individuals has been diagnosed with ASD. Such statistics underscore the increasingly urgent need to address deficits in social skills among adolescents with ASD through explicit training and research-based intervention. One such intervention (Van Riper, 2010) used instruction and training from an evidence-based program that targeted reading skills. This structured program, adapted for adolescents with ASD, caused a positive change in their social skills. It explicitly taught them a systematic plan for discussing their thoughts and gave them the confidence to enter into social interaction with their peers. The procedures that were implemented and the ways in which the students responded to those intentional strategies will be discussed later in this chapter.

HISTORICAL OUTLOOK

It will be easier to follow the discussion with a bit of background information. Understanding autism spectrum disorders (ASD) means understanding their many and varied characteristics. Youngsters with ASD cannot perceive another person's point of view—a condition that marks the struggles faced by adolescents with ASD. This concept was coined *theory of mind*, which refers to a social system through which typically developing individuals relate to one another. Baron-Cohen, Leslie, and Frith (1985) explained that individuals with ASD have an inability to understand another's perspective. While each student with ASD has unique instructional needs, their primary deficits are in language and communication. Adolescents with ASD are usually lacking in social skills and pragmatics, the tacit rules governing conversation. But there is no "one-size-fits-all" remediation. They possess heterogeneous traits, characteristics, and learning styles as individual as their fingerprints.

The broad areas within the autism spectrum led to an equally diverse array of theories. In 1943, the seminal research in this disability studied children who demonstrated "a disturbance of affective content" (Kanner, 1943). This research study did not explain the seemingly antisocial behavior of these individuals, but implied that they shut other people out of their lives. Kanner's resulting conclusion was that these individuals could not bond with their parents. According to Bishop (2008), in the 1960s the origin of ASD was viewed as being environmental. Since there was no indication of neurobiological damage, and individuals with ASD appeared normal in physical appearance (Bishop, 2008), the cause of ASD was not obvious. Frith (1972) reported that youngsters with ASD lacked the cognitive ability to generate ideas. In 1988, Attwood, Frith, and Hermelin reported that expressive gesturing was not evident when they observed individuals with ASD. Frith (1989) deduced from her studies that ASD was a neurobiological disorder.

Lorna Wing (1981) explained the research of Hans Asperger, and coined the term "Asperger syndrome." Asperger discussed his study of children who had deficits in social interaction. These individuals seemed to withdraw from interpersonal connections. According to Asperger, they did not understand the rules of pragmatics, and they appeared "naïve and peculiar" in their social behavior. When they spoke, their conversations consisted of repetitive language. The content of their discourse generally revolved around a fixation on a particular subject, while they remained unaware of the needs of their partner in conversation. Asperger explained that school-based experiences in social settings are impaired, and most youngsters experience bullying and become over-sensitive to criticism. They seem to "give the impression of fragile vulnerability and a pathetic childishness" (Wing, 1981, p. 117).

Individuals with Asperger's syndrome typically possess a level of cognitive functioning within the normal to high-normal range and develop language skills that are equivalent to their nondisabled peers. They are, however, considered to be odd (Wing & Gould, 1979) due to their choice of words when responding to others. Competence in conversation demands astute interaction and understanding: being able to view another's perspective, awareness of facial expressions and verbal nuances, as well as a demonstration of the tacit rules of appropriate social behavior. This is a huge challenge for any youngster. Imagine the obstacles facing a student with Asperger's syndrome, who is also struggling with adolescence! Autism spectrum disorders are indeed a broad spectrum of heterogeneous characteristics. Autism and Asperger's syndrome are just two components of that spectrum.

SOCIAL INTERACTION

Social interaction is an essential element in the life of normally developing adolescents. Most of these individuals know what they can say and when they can say it. They understand that they speak in one jargon to their parents, another way to their teachers, and have the flexibility to use slang with their peers.

Appropriate social interaction presents a real problem for students with ASD, who do not have the ability to recognize or understand the subtle nuances of discourse so essential to the development of appropriate social skills. In the world of the typically developing adolescent, spoken communication becomes peppered with quirky statements and is supported by expressive body language. These embellishments require rapid acquisition and understanding of popular trends and interests among these young individuals as they discover and begin to assert their personalities while developing into young adults. This presents the adolescent with ASD even greater potential for distancing themselves socially from others their nondisabled peers.

Most of the slang phrases adopted at this stage come from sarcastic twists on familiar phrases. The nuances and inferences will almost certainly be missed by the youth with autism, unless they are carefully explained. Even then, many idioms will be too complex for them to follow. Something as simple as, "Wow, she's hot!" could have a teenager on the spectrum thinking the girl in question is uncomfortable in the heat.

Street slang can be even more difficult. Consider a phase such as: "That new CD is totally phatt!!" The disc would, obviously, be the same thickness as any other CD, leaving our adolescent with ASD confused and disconnected.

The prevalence of body language and gestures, accepted as typical behavior and very popular with this age group, presents still more problems for the adolescent with ASD. A thumb and forefinger, placed on the forehead to form the letter L has been recognized for generations as the universal symbol for "loser." It is a referential symbol, and therefore a problem for a youngster with ASD. Symbols require interpretation and an understanding of figurative communication. Youngsters on the spectrum see the world in only quite literal terms. They may often observe people twirling their finger around an ear, or passing a hand over their head, and not realize that these are unkind symbols used to comment on the lack of social skills.

A student with ASD cannot distinguish which jargon to use with whom. They may speak very formally to their friends, and ask inappropriate questions of their teachers. For example, a middle school youngster may ask the principal how old she is, or how much she weighs. The ability to identify and establish socially appropriate communication, such as initiating a meaningful conversation and generating an interesting response, may present a challenge for most adolescents with ASD. Youngsters with ASD may not be able to articulate what they are conceptualizing. When, in fact, they do make an attempt to understand the demands of discourse, the difficulties and frustrations they are likely to encounter may cause embarrassment. Frustration can lead to inappropriate behavior, deepening the rift between themselves and their nondisabled peers. However, despite their deficits in social functioning, adolescents with ASD have been found to be eager to collaborate with peers in the academic arena (Van Riper, 2010).

Deficits in social skills may manifest themselves in unacceptable actions. One teacher from a middle school tells of an adolescent with ASD in a self-contained classroom who was fixated on women wearing skirts. If he saw a teacher attired in a dress or skirt, he would fly down the hallway and attempt to engage her in inappropriate conversation, winking at her and flirting with her. This young man did not understand that his behavior was inappropriate. Students displaying such inappropriate actions must be taught explicitly how to behave properly. If this student had acted on his fixation while in a public setting, he might have been forcibly restrained or arrested by police.

ANXIETY AND ASD

Adolescents with ASD generally exhibit higher levels of anxiety than their nondisabled peers (Bellini, 2004). This may lead them to become even more frustrated in and out of the school environment. For example, an adolescent with ASD who is having trouble transitioning from elementary school to middle school will need a systematic routine with reinforcements to help ease the way for assimilation into a new environment. While the challenges for these students may seem severe, research indicates that there is hope. With structured support and intervention, communication and social skills can increase in both quality and quantity (White, Keonig, & Scahill, 2007).

An example of this was observed recently. A young man entering middle school did not understand the new schedule to which he would have to adhere. He had to get to know his new teachers and was in an unfamiliar classroom with new peers. He could not articulate his fears and frustrations, so he threw chairs and books when the anxiety became overwhelming. He acted in an aggressive manner, hitting his head against the wall when his needs were not understood.

A plan was developed to alleviate his anxiety and frustration. It included a written schedule that he and his teacher completed each day. He had to finish the tasks and attend the classes indicated on his schedule for the morning. If he was able to articulate his feelings, and his behavior was not aggressive, he earned a reward at lunchtime. His teacher began to understand his needs because he was encouraged to talk about them. From this understanding, his teacher was able to develop effective reinforcements for his good behavior.

One of his reinforcements was to be given permission to use the classroom computer. This young man liked to print out intricate pictures that he could take home to color. His behavior also became more composed at home because his reward system was consistent both at home and in school. He and his teacher decided on the quantity of pictures he would be allowed to print each day, determined by his behavior. Good behavior depended on his ability to talk about his feelings.

After just one school year of explicit and systematic social skills instruction, this young man became well liked by his peers as well as school staff members. He would carry out simple chores for the school secretaries. He was given responsibilities such as doing some of the school laundry, using the washing machine that was provided in his self-contained classroom. When the items were dried, he would fold them and deliver them where needed. At the end of the school year, this young man, who entered middle school feeling misunderstood and angry, was spending his days learning academic and social skills while enthusiastically helping others.

PRAGMATICS AND ASD

It is very difficult for an adolescent with ASD to make friends. By definition, these individuals find it very hard to initiate and maintain peer relationships. A low level of shared experiences and poor focus of attention, plus a lack of facial expressions and gestures, are common traits found with ASD. Wing and Gould (1979) reported that individuals with ASD might appear aloof or passive in social situations. This does not mean they are disinterested in socialization. Some may try to build social relationships. However, they do not have the skills needed to recognize the clues that could help them understand the dynamics of their social environment.

The way people communicate involves the use of pragmatics, the tacit rules governing discourse. Deficits in social skills, including the interpretation of the perspectives of others and the ability to make inferences regarding that interpretation, impede peer relationships. As a child with ASD develops into an adolescent, the social environment expands and becomes more anxiety provoking. They may feel frustrated, rejected, and isolated from their nondisabled peers (Bauminger & Kasari, 2000). A lack of acuity in expressive language may also limit success in an academic environment, leading to increased behavioral problems and anxiety (Bellini, 2004; Howlin & Goode, 1998).

BEHAVIOR AND ASD

Impairments in social skills for adolescents with ASD are demonstrated in a number of ways. It was reported (Van Riper, 2010) that students in a middle school setting did not acknowledge their peers or teachers when they passed in the hallway. When these students were greeted by nondisabled peers in the hallway or in the cafeteria, they did not look at those who were speaking, nor did they respond without prompting. One such young man, who was nonverbal for 12 years, was encouraged by his teacher to say "Hi" to the principal every morning when he saw her. The teacher would explicitly model how to greet the principal and where to stand when speaking to someone. After a year of modeling the appropriate behavior for greeting someone, the young man was successful! One morning, while walking down the hallway to the classroom, he saw the principal, walked toward her, looked at her, and said, "Hi!"

This same young man had idiosyncratic behavior called "stims." After completing an academic task, he would stand in the middle of the classroom, and maneuver his fingers in an intricate, interwoven pattern. He manipulated this pattern the identical way each time. "Stims" are a common trait of ASD, but they differ greatly in their presentation; some with the disorder many constantly jingle change in their pocket, while others may twist strands of hair, pull on their ear, or clear their throat over and over. The variety is endless. These patterns of behavior are thought to decrease stress and anxiety; however, they must not detract from time spent on task in the classroom (Grandin, 2006). A teacher might allow for time for a student with ASD to decompress, using a timer as a reminder, but should always guide the student back to re-engage in classroom activities.

A language deficit that many individuals with ASD demonstrate is the inability to comprehend abstract or figurative language. In a phase of life such as adolescence, when understanding the perspective of others and catching on to humor is socially demanding, it is frustrating to not understand your peers' laughter and innuendo. On entering middle school, one student having an identification of ASD was placed in a self-contained classroom with other low-functioning students. On his first day in school, his new teacher ate lunch with him in the cafeteria. After they ate, his teacher asked if he enjoyed his lunch. He replied, "It hit the spot!"

His teacher, aware of the deficits of understanding idioms and metaphors in individuals with ASD, became suspicious of the validity of this young man's established diagnosis. With further evaluation, the teacher reported (Van Riper, 2010) that this student indeed had some characteristics of ASD, but his cognitive level was higher than previously observed in elementary school. This student was moved to a prevocational classroom with other students who were higher functioning, after which his behavior and his skills for social interaction improved.

Youngsters with ASD may exhibit inappropriate or unconventional behavior. They lack the knowledge needed to initiate free-time activities, have only a limited understanding of body language, and often misinterpret nonliteral information. Adolescents with Asperger's syndrome who possess the degree of intellect needed for adapting to social-relational approaches (Hall, 2013) may still not be able to achieve the level of social development found in nondisabled students of the same age. This is due to the neurobiological nature of their disability. They may be very smart, but still behave like much younger, less mature children.

TEACHING SOCIAL SKILLS THROUGH DISCUSSION

The research supporting the value of reading strategies such as the Directed Reading-Thinking Activity (Stauffer, 1969) for scaffolding the skills needed for social interaction is evident. Palmen, Didden, and Arts (2008) conducted a study of nine adolescents with ASD. The participants in this study were explicitly taught the skills they needed for the DRTA using questioning, visual cues, and graphic organizers. In small groups, the students were encouraged to use these skills to engage in social discourse. The results of this study describe a successful intervention for understanding.

In the intervention mentioned at the beginning of this chapter, students with ASD in middle school were explicitly taught the strategies they needed for discussion of a story they were studying in a reading comprehension class (Van Riper, 2010). First, their teacher read the story aloud to them, simultaneously expressing her thoughts as she was reading. She gave explicit examples for retrieving ideas from past experiences for the purpose of making connections with the story. They were instructed to visualize what the text described, then draw a picture of what they had envisioned. Although these were adolescents, their disabilities caused them to give unsophisticated and below grade level examples while making connections. When a student read that a character in the story had blonde hair, the student explained that it must have looked like butter.

Deficits in figurative language were apparent when the students tried to make an inference while reading this story (Van Riper, 2010). It was difficult for the students with ASD to gain the perspective of characters in the story. One such example taken from this study (Van Riper, 2010) was of a student who could not interpret the feelings of two characters from the story he was reading. The nature of the concept being portrayed was abstract; the author's message was about feeling trustworthy.

This middle school student with ASD could not fully grasp the language or draw conclusions from the inferences. Instead of interpreting the character as trustworthy, the student thought the character was unfriendly. The level of comprehension was not grade appropriate, but the discussion continued as the teacher explained the difference between trust and friendship. As these students discussed their understanding of the story, the teacher intervened with clarifying examples.

The implementation of explicit social skills instruction for the adolescent with ASD is demonstrated (Bellini, Peters, Benner, & Hopf, 2007). Social skills intervention should be based on the theoretical approaches of social development. Identified goals and objectives should target the strengths as well as the deficits of individuals while supporting their interests and schemas. There is also evidence that the importance of physical orientation, eye contact, and facial expressions must be addressed in social skills instruction (Tara, Matson, & Leary, 1988).

Although there are a wide variety of methods for targeting deficits in social skills for this heterogeneous population, not all are successful (White et al., 2007). Due to the complexity of social skills needed for successful interaction, students with ASD may not have learned these strategies or guidelines to help them retrieve the words or reactions needed. It is a struggle for these students to engage in peer interactions because they do not have the ability to spontaneously respond to or initiate a conversation (National Research Council, 2001).

Explicit strategies presented to these students may prove to be meaningful and helpful. For instance, Sartini, Knight, and Collins (2013) reported on ten guidelines for facilitating social groups for students with difficulty in maintaining eye gaze and demonstrating appropriate body language. Using visual supports, reinforcers, and confederate peers, they are taught social skills through rehearsal and practice trials. Skills such as these might be learned, but not generalized to alternate settings and conditions. In this study, the students were taught how to utilize these strategies with other peers, in different settings, and with various materials. Ongoing investigation should demonstrate that these specific skills are being used as the student continues on in school and community.

GENERALIZING SOCIAL SKILLS THROUGH DISCUSSION

Van Riper (2010) derived that, despite their idiosyncratic behavior and deficits in social skills, adolescents with ASD are able to enjoy social interaction with their peers. A middle school girl with ASD was enrolled in a small reading class that was comprised specifically of students with moderate ASD. She was extremely shy at first and very rarely participated in class discussion about the text.

After several weeks of modeling and using a think-aloud technique, the teacher reported that this student offered many good and even innovative ideas. She made connections with the text, saying: "The snow covering the ground seemed like cotton candy." This youngster even got up in front of the class and taught the students a math lesson that she had made up. She imagined that there was new number between one and ten that she called "dirt." She taught the class how to add and subtract using that number. She even called on some of her classmates to ask and answer questions!

In this ten-week study, a reading program was designed and adapted for students in a middle school prevocational course in preparation for transition to high school. These students moved as a unit in a special education program dedicated to targeting their specific needs as adolescents with ASD. In the reading program, they were taught explicit comprehension strategies taken from the Report of the National Reading Panel (National Institute of Child Health and Human Department, 2000).

Language and social processing are essential for reading comprehension (Steele, Joseph & Tager-Flusberg, 2003). Nonlinguistic representations were used as one type of instructional strategy, tailoring the lessons to the visual strengths of students with ASD. Charts, tables, and graphic organizers are examples of nonlinguistic representations of what students might conceptualize. In this study (Van Riper, 2010), the teacher modeled several strategies using visuals to underscore the components of the story. After modeling each strategy, the students would practice until they were proficient at using that chart or graphic organizer. For instance, to learn a main idea, the students brainstormed and agreed upon five main points of a particular chapter of the novel they were reading. The main ideas were written on sentence strips, and the strips were put in order of their occurrences.

The next time the group met, the teacher mixed up the order of the main idea sentences, and the students worked together to figure out the correct sequencing of the ideas. They discussed which sentence belonged where in the story with prompting words written on the board, like "beginning," "then," "after that," and "finally." They collaborated on the sequencing using the transition words as a guide. These students were more likely to learn through images and tactile methods than through abstract concepts.

The main idea sentence strips also became the prompts for topic sentences for a writing activity of a summary of the chapter. After considerable time spent on the main ideas, the students were able to write a summary narrative using visual and tactile aids.

Multisensory instruction was instituted for instruction of summarization. Kinesthetic and tactile-driven activities, using sentence strips and graphic organizers, were manipulated to improve proficiency in the mastery of summarization skills. After each 50-minute lesson, the students were asked a prompting question and then encouraged to discuss the readings by making personal connections and visualizing what they had read. When asked to make predictions regarding what might happen in a chapter, the students would scan the selection after reading the title of the chapter. They would study the pictures and look for any vocabulary words that they deemed important.

One young man in this reading class answered the prediction question of a chapter entitled "Getting Ready" by standing up and singing the song "Get Ready" by The Temptations. In this small arena, he felt comfortable interacting with his peers and was able to share his ideas. He answered the question in a means of representation that was appropriate for him, and it was well received by the class. Within this systematic and intentional educational approach, sensory learning matched the social development of the student with ASD in a meaningful way (Mirenda, 2003).

BRAIN STUDIES

Activation of background knowledge and prior experiences helps students with ASD to develop mental pictures (Gately, 2008). Visual prompts, picture walks, and graphic organizers support students with ASD, helping them to understand a narrative written in figurative language. Using tools and techniques to turn the abstract concept into concrete images levels the playing field for the individual with ASD.

It is important to remember that the ability to extract nuances must be taught explicitly. In brain studies (Kana et al., 2006), individuals with ASD demonstrated that they were reliant on the visual areas of the brain when reading and thinking. Access to cues, such as icons and objects, may give supportive prompting to students with ASD and help facilitate their language-processing skills. Using graphics, such as thought bubbles, pictorial scripts, sentence strips, and concept organizers, may help develop a deeper understanding of innuendo and the tacit rules of social interaction.

AFTERTHOUGHTS

Public schools and teachers are now charged with the responsibility of not only teaching typically developing generations of students, but also educating a whole new, rapidly increasing population of youngsters with ASD. With the new DSM-V (American Psychiatric Association, 2013), the educational support for these individuals is unknown. The DSM-V has consolidated the subsets on the spectrum and eliminated Rett's disorder from the ASD umbrella. Individuals with Asperger's disorder may no longer be considered for special services if they don't meet the very narrow view of this diagnosing system. However, as educators, we still must meet the needs of these students.

This new challenge is daunting in the complexity presented by a lack of similarity in these disabilities. Social and communication skills deficits are the main threads that run through the fabric of ASD. Interventions for successful social interaction should be taught explicitly to these students, providing them with the supports needed to coexist with their nondisabled peers as productive citizens. Students on the spectrum can learn social skills and communication strategies if an educational system is designed with their unique needs in mind.

REFERENCES

American Psychiatric Association. (2000). *Diagnostic and statistical manual of mental disorders* (4th ed., text. Rev.). Washington, DC: Author.

American Psychiatric Association. (2013). *Diagnostic and statistical manual of mental disorders* (5th ed.). Washington, DC: Author.

Attwood, A., Frith, U., & Hermelin, B. (1988). The understanding and use of personal gestures by autistic and Down's syndrome children. *Journal of Autism and Developmental Disorders, 18*, 241–257.

Baron-Cohen, S., Leslie, A. M., & Frith, U. (1985). Does the autistic child have a "theory of mind"? *Cognition, 21*, 37–46.

Bauminger, N., & Kasari, C. (2000). Loneliness and friendship in high functioning children with autism. *Child Development, 71*(2), 447–456.

Bellini, S. (2004). Social skills deficits and anxiety in high-functioning adolescents with autism spectrum disorders. *Focus on Autism and Other Developmental Disabilities, 19*(2), 78–86.

Bellini, S., Peters, J. K., Benner, L., & Hopf, A. (2007). A meta-analysis of school-based social skills interventions for children with autism spectrum disorders. *Remedial and Special Education, 28*(3), 153–162.

Bishop, D. (2008). Forty years on: Uta Frith's contribution on autism and dyslexia, 1996–2006. *The Quarterly Journal of Experimental Psychology, 61*(1), 16–26.

Centers for Disease Control and Prevention (CDC). (2012, March 30). Prevalence of autism spectrum disorders—Autism and developmental disabilities monitoring network, 14 sites, United States, 2008. MMWR. Morbidity and Mortality Weekly Reports. Retrieved from http://www.cdc.gov/mmwr/pdf/ss/ss6103.pdf

Frith, U. (1972). Cognitive mechanisms in autism: Experiments with color and tone sequence production. *Journal of Autism and Childhood Schizophrenia, 2*(2), 160–173.

Frith, U. (1989). Autism and "theory of mind". In C. Gillberg (Ed.), *Diagnosis and treatment of autism* (pp. 33–52). New York, NY: Plenum Press.

Gately S. E. (2008). Facilitating reading comprehension for students on the autism spectrum. *Teaching Exceptional Children 40*(3), 40–45.

Grandin, T. (2006). *Thinking in pictures: My life with autism.* New York, NY: Random House.

Hall, L. J. (2013). *Autism spectrum disorders: From theory to practice.* (2nd ed.). Boston, MA: Pearson Publishing.

Howlin, P., & Goode, S. (1998). Outcome in adult life for people with autism, asperger syndrome. In F. R Volkmar (Eds.), *Autism and pervasive developmental disorders* (pp. 209–241). New York, NY: Cambridge University Press.

Kana, R. J., Keller, T. A., Cherkassy, V. L., Minshew, N. J., & Just, M. A. (2006). Sentence comprehension in autism: Thinking in pictures with decreased functional connectivity. *Brain, 129*(9), 2482–2493.

Kanner, L. (1943). Autistic disturbances of affective contact. *Nervous Child, 2,* 217–250.

Mirenda, P. (2003). "He's not really a reader..." Perspectives on supporting literacy development in individuals with autism. *Topics in language disorders, 23*(4), 271–282.

National Institute of Child Health and Human Department (NICHD). (2000). *Report of the national reading panel. Teaching children to read: An evidence-based assessment of the scientific research literature on reading and its implications for reading instruction* (NIH Publication No. 00-4769). Washington, DC: U.S. Government Printing Office.

National Research Council. (2001). *Educating children with autism.* Washington, DC: National Academy Press.

Palmen, A., Didden, R., & Arts, M. (2008). Improving question asking in high-functioning adolescents with autism spectrum disorders: Effectiveness of small group training. *Autism, 12*(1), 83–98.

Sartini, E. C., Knight, V. F., & Collins, B. C. (2013). Ten guidelines to facilitate social groups for students with complex special needs. *Teaching Exceptional Children, 45*(3), 54–62.

Stauffer, R. G. (1969). *Directing reading maturity as a cognitive process.* New York, NY: Harper and Row.

Steele, S., Joseph, R. M., & Tager-Flusberg, H. (2003). Brief report: Developmental change in theory of mind abilities in children with autism. *Journal of Autism and Developmental Disorders, 33*(4), 461–467.

Tara, M. E., Matson, J. L., & Leary, C. (1988). Training social interpersonal skills in two autistic children. *Journal of Behavior Therapy and Experimental Psychiatry, 19,* 275–280.

Van Riper, I. (2010). *The effects of the directed reading-thinking activity on reading comprehension skills of middle school students with autism.* Unpublished doctoral dissertation, Widener University, Chester, PA.

White, S. W., Keonig, K., & Scahill, L. (2007). Social skills development in children with autism spectrum disorders: A review of intervention research. *Journal of Autism and Developmental Disorders, 37,* 1858–1868.

Wing, L. (1981). Asperger's syndrome: A clinical account. *Psychological Medicine, 11*(1), 115–129.

Wing, L., & Gould, J. (1979). Severe impairments of social interaction and associated abnormalities in children: epidemiology and classification. *Journal of Autism and Developmental Disorders, 9,* 11–29.

CHAPTER 9

EDUCATION OF PEACEMAKERS

Raising College Students' Awareness of and Respect for the "Other"

Margaret Murphy, O.P. and Diane Bliss

ABSTRACT

In light of historic and recent events of mass violence, including genocide, school shootings, and bullying, educators should look for ways to cultivate a culture of peace and respect rather than a culture of violence, particularly against the "Other." Two college professors, one from a public community college and one from a private four-year college, describe the various approaches they take to teaching a world religions course in these two institutions. One focuses on the impact of language and the second focuses on experiential encounters as ways of promoting increased and respectful understanding of the Other in today's college students.

The headlines are telling, and the mere mention of places like Columbine, Aurora, Newtown, Virginia Tech, and now even the University of Central

Adolescence in the 21st Century, pages 155–165
Copyright © 2014 by Information Age Publishing
All rights of reproduction in any form reserved.

Florida evokes responses of sorrow, shock, and horror at the real and potential violence within our society and schools today. Each of these resulted, or had the potential to result, in mass deaths at the hands of individuals who variously were bullied or suffered some mental state that had pushed them to the edge of "Other-ness." Even the recent Steubenville, Ohio incident involving the rape of a 16-year-old girl at the hands of student athletes bespeaks the violence that grows out of an objectification of another human and that may illustrate the hostility in our schools for those not of "our group"—in this case, a young female that the male athletes "treated like a toy" (Pearson 2013). As Olson (2007) notes, the dehumanization of the Other often arises from ignorance and can manifest itself in "hate speech" or bullying first that eventually "incites or encourages physical violence toward minorities" or the Other. In some cases, such as Columbine, the Other strikes back violently. Place that ignorance and the associated fears in the adolescent population seeking to establish both individual and group identity, and the result can be volatile. Stephen Wessler, founder of the Center for Prevention for Hate Violence, says, "The place where tension over changing demographics," resulting in the influx of more Other-ness, "is most likely to erupt into open discord and violence is school" (2011, p. 36). Wessler also explains that dialog is key to addressing student fears and anxieties about the Other or about "tensions" arising from those demographics and resulting incidents of hate or violence. To that end, he observes, "Educators not only reinforce the values of respect on which our school communities are built, but also help youth develop the skills, confidence, and courage to be the leaders we need" (Wessler, 2011, p. 39), especially to face the challenge of promoting understanding in order to effectively defuse violence against the Other.

Initially this paper was developed as a presentation for the Ethel LeFrak Conference on Holocaust Education at Seton Hill University in Pennsylvania (see Murphy & Bliss, 2010). However, its connection to adolescent education and the issue of violence against the Other has become more evident with each incident of school violence, bullying, or violence against the Other that appears in the news.

When the causes of such horrific events as the Holocaust, genocide, and other forms of mass violence against the Other are examined, one comes to the realization that our attitudes towards the Other are often born out of ignorance as well as fear. As noted in a recent *U.S. News & World Report* interview with Stephen Prothero, while "roughly 9 in 10 of [United States] citizens [claim] to believe in God or a Supreme Being . . . it ranks among the most ill-informed" about religion (Tolson, 2007, p. 1). In fact, "in a land of growing religious diversity, only 10 percent of U.S. teenagers can name the world's five major religions" (Tolson, 2007, p. 1). What our students lack is both appropriate language for, as well as experiential exposure to, the

Other in order to broaden their understanding and respect for the Other, in a way that promotes tolerance and peace over the ignorance, fear, and violence that can lead to bullying, school violence, or even genocide. College courses teaching the basics of world religions are one way of providing our students with that language and experience. Two teaching approaches to these courses are described here.

In the case of the public community college course described below, the emphasis of the teaching method is on providing students with the appropriate language by first making students aware of how they currently describe or discuss the Other and then moving students towards more open-minded inquiry and understanding. In the case of the private four-year college, the emphasis is on providing students with an awareness of the need for better knowledge and with experiential learning opportunities geared towards promoting greater understanding and tolerance of the Other. Both approaches are geared towards the education of peace-makers who will counter the ignorance that leads to disrespect, bullying, and violence and, on a more regional or global scale, may set the stage for genocide.

A COMMUNITY COLLEGE EXPERIENCE— SUNY ORANGE PROFESSOR DIANE BLISS

As a public community college English professor who also teaches our world religions course, Religious Concepts, I see language as key to my pedagogical approach to world religions, with its emphasis on philosophical concepts and modes of expression. Indeed, Schwartzman (2009) confirms the importance of language particularly as a major factor leading up to the conditions conducive to the Holocaust. He claims, "The perceived Jewish menace was not merely a postulate; it was actively built and reinforced through language" (p. 899). Schwartzman posits that the Nazis engaged in a conscious use of language, particularly derogatory towards Jews, through concerted propaganda campaigns and the supposed objectivity of the language of science and logic, to build a cultural mindset conducive to violence towards the Other. Looking at "key metaphors—in this case biological and medical—can reveal how linguistic resources that foster bigotry and genocide persist *before* becoming manifest in overt violence" (Schwartzman, 2009, pp. 897–898). In other words, Schwartzman suggests that "language paves a path to genocide." Anne Bartlett (2008) concurs, noting in her article, "The Power to Name in Darfur," that "Labels . . . are not an afterthought: they define and make real a situation and its consequences" (p. 155).

For the Religious Concepts course I teach, then, one of my goals is to impress upon students the power of language in coloring our perceptions of others. Their understanding of this is important because students are often lacking in the language and knowledge of cultures or traditions other than their own, and in some cases even of their own. Our community college students are overwhelmingly "local," and the vast majority remain in the area after graduating. They come mainly from lower to middle socio-economic ranges, and the average age is declining to the mid-lower 20s as the college draws in more traditional age students in hard economic times. The diversity of students is fairly reflective of the Hudson Valley area; of our student population who self-identify, approximately 67% identify themselves as White, approximately 11% as Black, approximately 16% Hispanic, approximately 2.6% Asian/Pacific Islander, and .5% Native American. At the beginning of the course, when asked where they have gained their "knowledge" of other religions or religious traditions, many admit that it is primarily from the media, especially television. An additional factor for our students is the proximity of the county and college to New York City and the impact of September 11, 2001, since many of our students' parents, relatives, neighbors, or friends work in New York City, and many lost family members or people they knew during that terrorist attack. The religious traditions of the students vary but are for the most part Christian, perhaps evenly divided between Roman Catholics and non-Catholic Christians; other major religious traditions have included Jewish, Buddhist, and Muslim, as well as others. However, since the course is taught in a public community college, I do not ask students specifically to identify their religion, nor do I ever reveal mine.

That students are in need of such a course and a basic understanding of other religions and cultures becomes evident in the first exercise I ask the students to do: an initial perceptions survey. I hand out a paper on which are listed the ten major religious traditions we will be studying. While students have often encountered some of these religions in high school classes such as Global Studies, the answers they provide on this survey are telling. Among some of the "worst" responses students have provided: Hinduism—"the five pillars" (Nice try but wrong religion); Buddhism—"worship a happy fat guy with a bald head"; Daoism— "That yin yang thing"; Zoroastrianism— "worship a guy with a mask whose sidekick is Tonto" (This earned the creativity award and was admittedly an attempt at humor by a student who had no idea what it was); Judaism— "don't believe in Jesus"; Christianity—"believe in Jesus"; Islam— "suicide bombers who get lots of virgins when they die." The simplistic views of the religions, the resort to humorous but derogatory terms in the face of ignorance, and the number of totally blank answers left on the survey sheets bespeak the need for these students to take this course. However, some students also shine on this survey, and occasionally I have students who ask for more paper and time, despite my reminder that this is just a quick "initial perceptions" survey to see what the class does or does not know so I can adjust the course accordingly.

The next step is to expose students to language that is meant to color their perceptions of a particular culture, before I provide the summary of initial perceptions responses for discussion. Students are assigned Horace Miner's essay, "Body Ritual Among the Nacirema," and asked to think about the culture he describes (1956). What students aren't told is that this prominent social anthropologist wrote this essay as something of a criticism of 19th century anthropologists and their superior, ethnocentric way of describing "Other" cultures as inferior or primitive. They also aren't told that "Nacirema" is "American" spelled backwards. In other words, the culture Miner describes is their own American culture (although mid-20th century). In the essay, he describes Americans' preoccupation with and negative perceptions of their own bodies. He includes rituals such as teeth brushing, toilet training, shaving, hairdressing (where women bake their heads in ovens once a month), visiting a hospital, and seeing a psychiatrist. Although one or two students catch on, for the most part the students do not, and the discussion in the next class inevitably begins with comments about how strange and primitive this culture's rituals are. After allowing students the chance to express their feelings of repulsion towards this culture and its body rituals, I write the word Nacirema on the board and then write American under it. The proverbial light bulbs begin to go on, and students have a good laugh at themselves for being taken in by Miner's rhetoric. The real work then begins. Students are asked what made them think of this culture as primitive, backwards, disgusting, or whatever their conclusion was. Ultimately we look at Miner's use of language in describing familiar habits or "rituals" of our society in a way that makes us assume our own societal habits or rituals are superior and different from those he describes. Miner uses words such as "magic," "primitive," "superstitious," "potions," "ritual," "shrine," "secret," "initiation," "medicine men," and "holy mouth men" to create a sense of mystery and backwardness that makes most students feel repulsed about what ultimately describes their own society. Potions were medical prescriptions, shrines were bathrooms, the initiation was toilet training, and holy mouth men were dentists. Students begin to see language about the Other turned upon them. At this point, I turn to their initial perceptions surveys, and we talk about the language they used to describe something unfamiliar to them.

As students become more conscious of the language they use to frame the cultures, religious practices, and concepts that are unknown to them, they also begin to understand the importance of asking more productive and thoughtful questions about the Other. Students are now asked to write three questions about religions other than their own that they would like to attempt answering by the end of the semester, and the difference in the language used is telling. For example, in the initial perceptions survey, one student wrote that Islam is a religion of "suicide bombers who get lots of virgins when they die." After the exercise with the Miner essay, the same student wrote as one of his questions, "How is the clash of Christianity, Judaism and Islam going to effect our children's generations and so on?" Additionally, the difference is marked between the student comment that Buddhists "worship a happy fat guy with a bald head" and the student question, "Why is the denial of material possessions, and necessities even, so important in Buddhism?"

These exercises in language in the Religious Concepts course are effective in raising students' awareness of the impact of negative language on perceptions about, biases towards, and the denigration of the Other. The remainder of the course provides students with the language of the religions themselves and a basic understanding of their concepts provided in a nonjudgmental exploration of their religious concepts, rituals, practices, and sacred literature. All this is meant to counter the type of language and "hate speech" arising from ignorance and fear that "incites or encourages physical violence toward minorities" or the Other (Olson, 2007, p. 648). For as Dorfman (2009) challenges us, "You want to free the world, free humanity from oppression? Look...at the hidden violence of language. Never forget that language is where the other, parallel violence, the cruelty exercised on the body, originates" (p. 54). Educating people and providing them with more appropriate language, a language of understanding to replace or displace the language of ignorance, hate, and violence, is one initial step in creating societal conditions necessary to the realization of: "Never again."

A FOUR-YEAR COLLEGE EXPERIENCE—MOUNT SAINT MARY COLLEGE, SISTER MARGARET MURPHY, OP

When Stephen Prothero, Chair of Boston University's Department of Religion, discussed the issue of religious literacy at the Pew Forum's biannual Faith Angle Conference in Religion, Politics and Public Life, in December 2007, his points were a mixture of humor and poignancy. Having surveyed undergraduates about their religious literacy, he gathered some amusing responses: Joan of Arc was Noah's wife, for instance. However, we have all become aware of the serious consequences of this illiteracy. Prothero (2007a) cites the impact of religious illiteracy on foreign policy and its significance, arguing that he doesn't think we understand Iraq as a place where people are, in many cases, primarily motivated by religion.

Dr. Prothero began to realize that his students at Boston University didn't seem to get the references to religion he was making as much as he expected they would. In the last six years, he started noticing a shift. When he would say, "This is in Matthew..." he realized the students didn't know what he was talking about and discovered they were thinking Matthew Perry from the sitcom "Friends." He then began to explain very basically: Matthew, which is one of the four Gospels, which are books in the New Testament, which is a scripture in Christianity, which is one of the world's religions. He then began to give his religious literacy quiz, which I have also given in my classes, and which is available online. Prothero recounts an early student's response: "*Jesus* parted the Red Sea—somebody must have been able to do that. It was probably Jesus, you know." In my own attempts to show the impact of the Bible on Western civilization and our everyday lives, I tell my four-year college students that they may see a reference to David and Goliath in the *Wall Street Journal* in articles about company takeovers. However, most of my students wouldn't know the reference to David and Goliath.

Prothero writes of an Austrian colleague at Boston University who was teaching a course on Orthodox–Catholic relations. He had assumed that students would know the information about the history of Christianity. He said, "Americans are very strange. They all go to church—and they know nothing about Christianity. . . . I have to begin with there once was a man named Jesus." This helps illustrate the central paradox in Prothero's book, *Religious Literacy: What Every American Needs to Know* (2007b). Prothero (2007a) sees religious illiteracy not as a strictly religious problem but as a civic problem. We now have politicians on both sides of the spectrum who connect their public policy and initiatives to religious ideas. Hillary Clinton now, when she talks about immigration, is quite likely to talk about the Good Samaritan story. The international aspect is even more urgent. Madeline Albright, in her book *The Mighty and the Almighty* (2007), stated that when she was Secretary of State under President Clinton, she had a dozen economic advisors she would call on to explain the economics or political situations of Middle East countries. But she had no one she could call on to explain the impact of Hinduism or Islam. She also observed that there's neither a prerequisite nor a policy for U.S. ambassadors to Middle Eastern countries to have any training in Islam or for the ambassador to India to know anything about Hinduism. These notions grew, in my discussions with my community college counterpart, about the relevance of courses in world religions and resulted in our presentation title, "Education of Peacemakers." Despite the differences in our colleges, one a public community college and the other a private four-year college, and the different socioeconomic populations that attend them, we found ourselves confronted with the same religious illiteracy among our students. Given these examples and Prothero's work, the relevance of offering world religions courses as part of undergraduate education becomes clear.

Our real goal in this presentation, then, is to share how we have seen the importance of religious literacy education lived out with our students. While the concentration in Professor Bliss's presentation has been on the importance of language, mine will be on providing students with real-life stories and experiences of diverse religious believers. In my own course at Mount Saint Mary College, several examples are relevant. For instance, in my class presentation on Judaism, I include an excerpt from an interview with Connecticut State Senator Joseph Liebermann, found in our textbook, *Living Religions,* by Mary Pat Fisher (2005). Liebermann spoke of his orthodox practice and his love of the weekly ritual of Sabbath from sundown Friday to sundown Saturday, noting it "is the time when the worldly concerns of the rest of the week are put on hold so that we can focus on appreciating all that God has given us." He shared, "I don't even wear a wristwatch on Sabbath" (Fisher, 2005, p. 268). One of my undergraduate students responded, "I'm amazed that religion could play such a part in people's lives." As another example, one of my guest lecturers for Hinduism, Dr. Supharna Bhalla, Assistant Professor of Biology, shared her home altar and her practice of daily puja (home worship). Seeing this respected scientist discuss her belief system was an important life-giving experience for my students. Another guest speaker, Muhamad al Filali, Director of the Passaic, New Jersey Islamic Center, spoke openly and candidly with my students. The students consistently mentioned their surprise at his encouragement to them to ask any question, noting that there are no politically incorrect subjects. His openness to discussions of the status of women, Jihad, and his own practice added tremendously to students' understanding of ethnicity and religious practice. His candor in sharing the struggle of the 5 a.m. prayer period teaches more than any text can about self-discipline and devotion. Personal stories and guest speakers have proven quite effective.

As an experiential assignment, one of the assignments for my course is a visit to a worship service other than the student's own. Students who attend mainline Protestant or nondenominational services consistently report surprise at the welcome, inclusion, and acceptance they experience. Four students attended the evening service at Congregation Shir, a Reform Jewish temple in Poughkeepsie, New York and had the experience of helping the children's group to construct a *sukka* (booth) for Sukkot in the backyard of the temple. They described for the class their experience of participation and their growth in respect for Scripture and the customs of Judaism. The fragile "booth" home reminds the faithful that their real home is in God, who sheltered their ancestors on the way from Egypt to the Promised Land of Canaan. "Sitting in the temporary shelter reconnects modern people to the natural order and to the transitory nature of our carefully constructed forms of material security" (Lerner, 1994, p. 365). For students, the experience of a religion other than their own expands their knowledge and their willingness to respect the Other, rather than to construct negative judgments based on ignorance.

Many are familiar with the film *Paper Clips* (2006), which describes the Holocaust education experience of a junior high school class in Whitwell,

Tennessee. In one of the opening scenes, the school principal remarks, "We're not too multicultural here. Most of our students have never seen a Catholic or a Jewish person." This school population was transformed by Holocaust education, and tours of their exhibit continue to be given by eighth-grade students to elementary groups from many neighboring states. I have shown this film each semester in World Religions as we discuss the Holocaust. A significant learning occurs when, after viewing the film, my students are shocked to realize that, attending a Catholic college and being primarily of Roman Catholic background, they are the Other in other areas of our country.

My young adult students also respond significantly to the story associated with the Holocaust Memorial in Miami Beach, Florida, a photo of which appears in their textbook, *Living Religions*. In Treister's book about the memorial, *A Sculpture of Love and Anguish* (1993), the story students find so touching was related by a Catholic priest and a teacher who took their high school seniors to the memorial. After instructing them to walk alone and in silence around the memorial, they studied the reactions of their students, mostly Cuban-Americans. The author tells of one girl who stood motionless in front of the sculpture of a nude elderly couple saying their last goodbyes: "It was a cold day, and after minutes of rapt staring, she took off her jacket and covered the bare shoulders of the woman" (Treister, 1993, p. 18). Such a symbolic act motivated by compassion and understanding in today's society truly resonated with my students.

Finally, students in the Mount Saint Mary College course, World Religions, are reminded that on the tragic day of the World Trade Center bombing in 2001, we witnessed the work of countless heroes, many of whom were our neighbors here in the Hudson Valley. As those firemen went up to assist in the buildings as others were coming down, no one asked, "Are you Jewish?" Or "Are you Muslim?" We were human beings together. As one measure of that, each year the students of Mount Saint Mary College sing with a large group of senior citizens and families of all ages from the Newburgh, NY Jewish Center during the annual Yom Ha Shoah commemoration at the College. This is our hope for peacemakers of the future. The commemoration ends with this song, sung in Hebrew and English:

Jerusalem of Gold

The Olive trees, they
Stand in silence
Above the hills of time.
We hear the voices
Of the city
As bells of evening chime.

The Shofar sounding
From the temple

Calling the world to prayer
So many songs,
So many stories.
We pray for peace everywhere.

THE HOPE THAT FOLLOWS

Our presentation title—Education of Peacemakers—has become more real to us as we reflect on the hope that we both experience as we share observations and ideas about our courses and students' responses. Students truly grow in understanding and respect for the Other as they gain the language and experiences necessary to discuss and interact with the Other in more positive ways. Our use of assignments, activities, and experiences that increase their awareness of the impact of language in describing the Other, and of common elements of humanity while appreciating cultural and religious uniqueness, work towards that end. Equally important is that a learning atmosphere that is nonjudgmental and open to questions and discussion is created. Through the courses we teach on world religions, our students become more open and willing to learn about the Other. That in turn gives us hope that we can accomplish a small step towards the goal of "Never again," whether that applies to global events such as the Holocaust or local events such as school bullying or community violence, of educating peacemakers that bear witness to the encouraging words of Pope John Paul II: "Hatred will never have the last word in this world."

REFERENCES

Albright, M. (2007). *The mighty and the Almighty: Reflections on America, God, and world affairs.* New York, NY: Harper Perennial.

Bartlett, A. (2008). The power to name in Darfur. *Peace Review: A Journal of Social Justice, 20*(2), 149–157.

Berlin, E., and J. Fab. (2006). Paper Clips. [DVD]. New York, NY: Arts Alliance America.

Dorfman, A. (2009). You want to free the world from oppression? Look inside, look at the hidden language of violence. *New Statesman, 138*(4931), 54.

Fisher, M. P. (2005). *Living religions* (6th ed.). Upper Saddle River, NJ: Pearson/ Prentice Hall.

Lerner, M. (1994). *Jewish renewal: A path to healing and transformation.* New York, NY: Harper Collins.

Miner, H. (1956). Body ritual among the Nacirema. *The American Anthropologist, 58,* 503–507.

Murphy, M., & Bliss, D. (2010). Education of peacemakers: Challenges and opportunities in interreligious dialogue in undergraduate education. Holocaust

Education Conference. In C. Rittner (Ed.), *Learn, teach, prevent: Holocaust education in the 21st century.* Greensburg, PA: National Catholic Center for Holocaust Education, Seton Hill University.

Olson, K. (2007). Opposing hate speech. *Journalism and Mass Communications Quarterly, 84*(3), 648–649.

Pearson, M. (2013, March 3). Steubenville teens treated girl "like a toy," prosecutor says. CNN. Retrieved from http://www.cnn.com

Prothero, S. (2007a, December). *Religious literacy—What every American should know.* Paper presented at the Pew Forum Faith Angle Conference, Key West, FL.

Prothero, S. (2007b). *Religious literacy: What every American needs to know.* New York, NY: HarperCollins.

Schwartzman, R. (2009). Using "telogology" to understand and respond to the Holocaust. *College Student Journal, 43*(3), 897–909.

Tolson, J. (2007, April 1). Q & A: Stephen Prothero. *U.S. News & World Report.* Retrieved from http://www.usnews.com/usnews/news/articles/070401/9qa.htm

Treister, K. (1993). *A sculpture of love and anguish.* New York, NY: Shapolsky.

Wessler, S. (2011). Confronting racial and religious tension. *Educational Leadership, 69*(1), 36–39.

PART III

CHALLENGES

Adolescence and Emerging Adulthood

Paul Schwartz

In many ways, contemporary youth experience the same truths we all experienced as adolescents, the importance that parents, peers, school and community play in their lives—clearly, these constants haven't changed. However, the world as we know it has changed significantly and because of it, many of today's youth and emerging adults are decidedly different from their parents. Like the universe, the developmental stage called adolescence is expanding, beginning earlier and ending later! Adolescence was an almost nonexistent stage of development 100 years ago. Compulsory education laws and working restrictions for juveniles put adolescence on the map. Until recently, adolescence was a brief developmental period of life and was seen as a transitional moratorium that separated the innocence of childhood from the demands and responsibilities of adulthood.

Today's adolescent doesn't just jump into adulthood as in the past; it's now a slow and gradual weaning process. The implications of this shift are significant. Young children are displaying behaviors well before they are ready to act on or understand their meaning, and older adolescents are

Adolescence in the 21st Century, pages 167–169
Copyright © 2014 by Information Age Publishing
All rights of reproduction in any form reserved.

staying perpetual children. Adolescence has become one of the longest developmental periods, with theorists struggling to agree on when it begins and ends. Elementary school children seem to acquire mature knowledge younger, but yet they remain in an adolescent stage for a longer period.

Technology has dramatically altered the way adolescents and young adults communicate with each other socially. Face-to-face communication for many adolescents has been eclipsed by online relationships. The famous American psychologist Harry Stack Sullivan believed that the peer group and social acceptance are the precursors of healthy self-esteem and identity formation for adolescents, but he didn't foresee that an adolescent can have literally hundreds if not thousands of cyber "friends" and never experience the intimacy that many theorists believe necessary for the development of mature adult relationships. Some psychologists, like Daniel Goleman, believe that this generation of adolescents is losing the ability to interact with people in a "meaningful" way. Changes in acceptable sexual behaviors and loss of interpersonal intimacy are compounded by a sense of entitlement that permeates all aspects of their lives, at home, in school, and on the job, as well as in their relationships. What has created this exaggerated sense of their self-importance or egocentricism?

However, there is plenty of good news regarding today's youth as well. Cigarette smoking is down among today's youth as well as the use of most drugs and alcohol. Additionally, kids have related that they are more cognizant of the dangers that these drugs provide. The incidence of teen pregnancy and sexually transmitted diseases among adolescents are down as well and contraceptive use has increased. They might be a consummately self-absorbed generation, but they are also the most well-informed generation in history.

At the third annual CARD conference in April, 2012, Dr. Jeffrey Arnett spoke about his seminal work on emerging adulthood. For over a decade he has conducted research on emerging adults concerning a wide variety of topics, involving several different ethnic groups in the United States. He related that the lives of people from age 18 to 29 have changed so dramatically that a new stage of life has developed, emerging adulthood. This stage is distinct from both the adolescence that precedes it and the young adulthood that they will soon be entering. Rather than marrying and becoming parents in their early twenties, most people in industrialized societies now postpone these transitions until at least their late twenties, and instead spend the time in the continuous self-focus and exploration of adolescence as they try out different possibilities in their careers and relationships.

Dr. Arnett identified the characteristics of this newly defined developmental period as exploration, instability, possibility, self-focus, and a sustained sense of still being in transition. He further discussed how this generation of young people, more than prior generations, emphasizes having meaningful and satisfying work. They are not satisfied with jobs just to make a living.

In light of Arnett's work, the chapters in the final section of this book address the challenges and issues that adolescents and emerging adults face in the current social, political, and economic environment. In many ways, these challenges are similar to those faced by prior generations of youth. However, the venues have shifted and reflect the postmodern world of the 21st century.

The final chapters in Part 3 explore the challenges facing adolescents today and the ways in which they approach and overcome those challenges. Conformity and resistance are not new to adolescence, but in Chapter 10, Kristen Hawley Turner deftly focuses on the digital age and chronicles how the venue for adolescent resistance has changed and expands on the insights explained by David Gallagher in Chapter 4. In Chapter 11, a team of researchers (Jordan, Mazur, Athan, and Miller) explore the problems of a specific target group, perhaps not examined before in the literature of adolescent development. Their exploration of the coming of age of homeless adolescent mothers is both compelling and informative. In Chapter 12, Rae Fallon presents an equally compelling picture of one emerging adult for whom the future might seem particularly bleak. Instead, Fallon presents the success story an amazing young woman, 20 years after she was prenatally exposed to cocaine. In Chapter 13, Susan Conte examines the phenomenon of self-destructive behavior in adolescence and how adolescent women struggle to overcome the challenges that led to those behaviors.

Finally, coming to terms with changing and confusing emotions has always been part of the rite of passage during adolescence. How these new and impulse-ridden emotions can be regulated is discussed in Chapter 14, a provocative chapter by Janice Stapley.

Throughout the final chapters, adolescent voices help the reader understand the forces in play in the path to adulthood. In sum, these final chapters move beyond conventional understanding of this path to a clearer understanding of the factors and forces affecting adolescent development in contemporary environment of the 21st century.

CHAPTER 10

THE CHALLENGE OF ACCEPTANCE

Digitalk and Language as Conformity and Resistance

Kristen Hawley Turner

In the 1950s, adults were appalled by Elvis and his gyrations. While teens embraced the new sounds and movement, parents feared that rock and roll would lead their children to delinquency. Tensions between generations ran high, and a culture war ensued. For the adults, rock and roll was inappropriate. It was wrong. And teens resisted by joining the revolution and contributing to the evolution of music, of dance, and of language.

Historians of youth culture of the latter part of the 20th century trace similar tensions between generations with the rise of the Beat generation, Goth culture, or the hip hop movement. In every era, it seems, teens look for acceptance; they experiment; they evolve. Erikson (1968) suggested that adolescence, characterized by *identity vs. role confusion*, represents a stage of social experimentation in which teens "seem much concerned with faddish attempts at establishing an adolescent subculture" (p. 128). This

Adolescence in the 21st Century, pages 171–185
Copyright © 2014 by Information Age Publishing
All rights of reproduction in any form reserved.

subculture resists both childhood and adult identities, carving out new ways of being for the in-between crowd. Adults often do not embrace the social changes that ensue because, as Erikson asserted, "In regard to the social play of adolescents, prejudices similar to those which once concerned the nature of childhood play are not easily overcome. [Adults] alternately consider such behavior irrelevant, unnecessary, or irrational" (p. 164).

Today's generational gaps are no different from those of the past. At this point in time, however, information and communication technology (ICT) plays a vital role in the breach between teens and adults. Adolescents, sometimes classified as "digital natives" (Prensky, 2001) who were born into a world that is saturated with ICT, have had access to computers, cell phones, and other devices from a young age. They are comfortable with the tools of technology, and they have adapted these tools for educational and social purposes. This Net Generation is "always on" (Baron, 2008, p. xi) in their formative years in a way that most adults have not come to understand until later in life, if at all. Teens in the 21st century have created subcultures that exist in virtual spaces. Unlike their counterparts in the mid-20th century, today's adolescents do not congregate at the drive-in to share their language, their music, and their specific ways of being. In the contemporary era, these conversations happen digitally, almost entirely through written words. Consequently, adolescents have embraced a new form of resistance. Digitalk (Turner, 2010) is the blend of conversational and written languages that adapts standard conventions for communicative purposes and bonds teenagers, even as it represents a divide between generations.

"Texting is ruining the English language." This sentiment is heard in casual conversations, in popular media, and in academia. In all of these contexts, adults judge teenagers who abandon standard conventions as part of their daily habits of communication. What many critics fail to realize, however, is that adolescents experiment in digital writing, breaking from standard written English (SWE) in purposeful ways, and this linguistic diversion is significant in their personal growth. Why do adolescents make the language choices they do when they write digitally? Though the response to this question is multifaceted, this chapter focuses on the development of identity as one essential answer. Digitalk allows for the expression of both a community identity and an individual identity; adolescents have embraced its power to navigate Erikson's (1968) stage of *identity vs. role confusion*.

LITERACY AND IDENTITY

Erikson (1968) identified adolescence as a period of transition, where teens are "preoccupied with what they appear to be in the eyes of others as compared with what they feel they are" (p. 128). They are in "search for a new sense of continuity and sameness" (Erikson, 1968, p. 261) as they develop an "ego identity" (p. 261), which "is the accrued confidence that the inner sameness and continuity prepared in the past are matched by the sameness and continuity of one's meaning for others" (p. 261). Adolescents, then, struggle to understand themselves within the context of their communities. They search for belonging (community identity) even as they strive to understand themselves as individuals (individual identity). Though these two desires may appear to be contradictory, in Erickson's view, they are actually corresponding drives.

Though Erikson (1968) focused his discussion of adolescence mostly on the exploration of ideology, he did acknowledge in passing the powerful role of language in the development of children. He said,

> Speech not only increasingly commits [a child] to his own characteristic kind of voice and to the mode of speech he develops, it also defines him as one responded to by those around him with changed diction and attention. They in turn expect henceforth to be understood by him with fewer explanations or gestures. (p. 162)

At first consideration, this passage in Erikson's lengthy book might seem inconsequential; however, it assumes more importance in light of literacy theorists who have connected speech and language to cognitive development (e.g., Vygotsky, 1978) and identity (e.g., Gee, 2008).

Vygotsky (1978) suggested that through participation in a culture, individuals internalize the language and tools of that culture. Thus, adolescents in the 21st century, whose world is saturated with tools of communication technology, have internalized the tools and language associated with a digital world. Like those of prior generations, teens today talk to their friends on the phone; however, they are even more likely to communicate with each other via instant messaging (IM), texting, or social networking tools. As they exchange words and ideas, they develop social norms; they establish communities of practice (Wenger, 1998) in a virtual world. According to Wenger (1998), developing competence in the norms of such a community and understanding the practice of others in that community contribute to an individual's identity.

The work of Gee (2008) further elaborates the connections between language, identity, and community. In his discussion of literacy, Gee (2008) argued that language cannot be divided from "its social context" (p. 2). He outlined the difference between lowercase *discourse*, which represents language, and "big D," or uppercase, *Discourse* (p. 2), which includes language as well as "ways of behaving, interacting, valuing, thinking, believing, speaking, and often reading and writing" (p. 3), all of which contribute to identity. Gee theorized that these "ways of being in the world" lead to "socially situated identities" (2008, p. 3). In other words, identity develops from the interactions an individual has within a community of practice. The interactions between humans occur with, through, and because of language, or lowercase discourse. This language depends upon the "purposes and occasions" (Gee, 2008, p. 3) of the members of the community, and it is not uncommon for individuals to adopt different registers within different communities. The community identity is defined, in part, by this lowercase discourse, the language its members use.

Vygotsky's (1978) theory of internalization suggests that the interactions within a Discourse support an individual's understanding, use, and appropriation of language. Language, then, as a means for interaction, becomes a tool for identity formation. Moje (2004) has claimed that "all spaces are spaces of identity enactment, and these enactments shape and are shaped by literate practices" (p. 16). Digitalk, as a blend of formal and nonstandard languages, has developed as a code specific to virtual spaces. Adolescents' identities, therefore, are defined in part by the writing they do in texts, IMs, and digital social networks. For teens who navigate a primary Discourse that is saturated with technology, language play contributes to both group and individual identities.

Because digitalk allows writers to break from standard rules, teens have the ability to create their own community conventions. Crystal (2001) has suggested that this practice helps to "demonstrate their solidarity by evolving (consciously or unconsciously) measures of identity" (p. 60). Digital communities develop "guidelines, principles, rules, and regulations relating to the way people should linguistically behave" (Crystal, 2001, p. 68), and individuals can be marked as outsiders by the language they use. For adolescents digitalk contributes to "groupness" (Moje & Luke, 2009), yet individuals are free to experiment, a practice that offers them agency (Moje & Luke, 2009), an ability to choose their level of engagement and participation. In their digital writing, adolescents decide how to represent themselves via language. The norms of convention and the need for self-expression play key roles in the choices they make, and their use of digitalk secures their identities as individuals within a community. For adolescents who constantly negotiate identity, playing with language in virtual settings is both necessary and desirable.

COMMUNITY CONVENTIONS

Over a decade ago Cherny (1999) analyzed the linguistic conventions of particular multiuser dimension (MUD) virtual worlds, and since that time, other researchers have contributed to the understanding of language practices in instant messaging (Baron, 2008; Haas, Takayoshi, Carr, Hudson, & Pollock, 2011), texting (Crystal, 2008), and other Internet activity (Crystal,

2001). However, the majority of studies have focused on older populations within one of these media, and teens, who navigate multiple technologies on a daily basis, have been conspicuously absent from this body of research. This chapter reports data collected in an attempt to fill this void.

Researchers in this study collected samples of digital writing from 81 adolescents (ages 13–18) in order to understand how this community adapts language for communicative purposes. By analyzing the writing for (1) orthographic, (2) graphic, (3) lexical, (4) syntactic, and (5) discursive features of language, researchers identified 17 community conventions among this population (see Table 10.1). For a specific feature of language to be included on this list, 50% of the population demonstrated its use, and it was evidenced across digital media where teens regularly "talk" with each other (i.e., texting, instant messaging, and social networking), since it is within these communicative media where teens most frequently break from the rules of SWE (Turner, 2011).

This list of conventions begins to define the language practices of a community of adolescent digital writers. It is a blend of standard (e.g., complete sentences, apostrophe used) and nonstandard (e.g., nonstandard capitalization, multiple consonants) language. As a consideration of "groupness," there are two interesting points to make about the practices of the teens in

TABLE 10.1 Percentage of Participants Using Conventions of Digitalk

Convention	All Participants
Complete Sentence	97%
End Period Not Used	96%
Nonstandard Capitalization	94%
Acronym	76%
Question Mark Used	74%
Standard Capitalization	72%
Abbreviation (Cut off End)	71%
Logograms (Letters for Sounds)	68%
Apostrophe Not Used	65%
Fragment	65%
Lowercase i	63%
Run-On	63%
Compound Words	62%
Multiple Consonants	60%
End Period Used	59%
Ellipses	54%
Apostrophe Used	54%
Multiple Vowels	50%

this sample: (1) When separated by geographic subgroup, the data reveal distinct community conventions, and (2) writers in these communities do not learn the conventions by rote memorization of linguistic features, but rather by participating in the community of practice.

Geographic Subgroups

Data were collected and coded by "urban" or "suburban," and interestingly, across all data, the conventions were relatively uniform. In both suburban and urban samples, the top three conventions, each used by at least 94% of the subgroup participants, included (1) complete sentence, (2) end period not used, and (3) nonstandard capitalization (see Table 10.2.). The fact that nearly all of the participants used these three conventions shows that there exists a relatively consistent system of language use within the teen community that contributes to an adolescent subculture.

Although there is uniformity in the results across groups, the analysis of the data by geographical subgroup revealed distinctions between the urban

TABLE 10.2   Conventions of Digitalk and Percentage of Users by Geographic Subgroup

Conventions	Urban	Conventions	Suburban
Complete Sentence	100%	Complete Sentence	94%
End Period Not Used	97%	End Period Not Used	94%
Nonstandard Capitalization	95%	Nonstandard Capitalization	94%
Logograms (Letters for Sounds)	86%	Acronym	81%
Phonetic Spelling	84%	Run-On	74%
Question Mark Used	81%	Lowercase i	71%
Abbreviation (Cut off End)	81%	Apostrophe Not Used	68%
Standard Capitalization	76%	Standard Capitalization	68%
Acronym	73%	Question Mark Used	65%
Compound Words	70%	Multiple Consonants	65%
Slang	70%	Apostrophe Used	65%
Fragment	68%	Fragment	61%
Apostrophe Not Used	62%	Abbreviation (Cut off End)	58%
End Period Used	62%	Logogram (Noises for Actions)	58%
Ellipses	62%	End Period Used	55%
Lowercase i	57%	Multiple Vowels	55%
Multiple Consonants	57%	Compound Words	52%
Run-On	54%		
Abbreviation (missing vowel)	54%		
Capital I	51%		

and suburban communities—differences in language use that may contribute to a local, community identity. For example, as a group, the urban teens conventionalized (1) abbreviation: missing vowel, (2) phonetic spelling, and (3) slang. Lines like "just wanted u to kno u aint the only one in trbl these dayz" capture a distinct voice of the urban data. Abbreviations like "trbl," without the vowels, phonetic spellings like "dayz," and the use of slang like "aint" were much more common among the urban teens in the sample than they were among suburban users. In the suburban community fewer than 40% of participants displayed these features of language; the high percentage of teenagers from the urban community that used them accents a marked difference between the two groups. These differences may reflect urban vernacular structures and phonetic variations within these dialects, "lowercase discourse" (Gee, 2008) practices that contribute to identity.

In fact, teens themselves recognize these differences and can attribute particular conventions to distinct community use. For instance, when shown the following example, a 9th-grade class of students was able to correctly identify the author as "suburban."

> **"Hey!!! What are you doing tom?"**
> **Student 1:** Suburb
> **Student 2:** It's the burbs.
> **Student 1:** Cause he put the exclamation points and the "tom."
> **Teacher:** Okay, we've got suburb, suburb, suburb. Did anybody put the city?
> **Student 3:** Nobody in the city puts exclamation points.

The teens in this class confirmed what the data from the study participants demonstrated: suburban teens conventionalized the use of exclamation points whereas urban teens did not. As writers, these adolescents were aware of the conventions adopted by their communities of practice.

Participation in the Community

Though research has been able to describe what adolescents do in their digital writing, the lists of conventions presented here do not represent prescriptive rules. Rather, they were negotiated by users who chose to adopt them for communicative purposes. Acceptance into such a community requires, to some degree, use of the conventions because, like most social situations where there are norms and rules, "People who fail to conform . . . risk . . . being excluded from the group" (Crystal, 2001, p. 71). The following exchange demonstrated both the community expectation and the learning process.

Researcher: Why don't you use periods?
  Student 1: Because if you write proper it's like, "What? Who taught you how to write?"
Researcher: Who does teach you how to write in the texting world?
  Student 2: Nobody.
  Student 3: I learned from myself. Right? If I saw my friend using it, I tried it.
  Student 2: I just started using it out of nowhere.
  Student 4: I know what LOL means.
  Student 5: I didn't know it when I heard it. I had to ask someone.

Student 1 began this conversation with the expectation that "proper" writing is not the most accepted form in the adolescent community. It seems, as Erikson (1968) suggested, that adolescents have found a 21st-century resistance, a resistance to standard, adult language. In doing so, they have created their own code, and as the other students suggested, they learn that code from each other. They mimic, they experiment, and they find what works, both for them as individuals and for the community.

Audience plays a key role in this process. Throughout the data, teens suggested that their language choice "really depends on who's on the other side of the phone." The importance of audience became clear during the following discussion of "multiple letters."

  Student 1: Yeah, like, if you like someone, usually the more Y's you put, the more excited you are to talk to them kind of thing.
Researcher: You mean "like," meaning boy and girl?
  Student 1: Usually it's more, like, yeah, it's like if you want to go out with someone, but it can be, like, a best friend or something like that.
Researcher: So somebody that you don't know very well you would—
  Student 2: You just put "hey."
  Student 1: Or, like, even "hi."

Student 1 went on to explain that "It depends on your relationship with that person. If they're just a friend, usually it doesn't matter but if it's someone you like...sometimes I stress over, should I put two Ys or three Ys?" The "stress" this teen felt demonstrates the powerful role that community conventions play in adolescents' communication and relationships.

More importantly, however, use of the conventions separate adolescents from adults in critical ways. As one young man who participated in the study explained, "Only with my grandmother, that's when I text proper. She really doesn't understand the abbreviations. . . . If I said 'whatup' to my grandmother, she knows what it means, but she'll, she'll look at me like, 'Why you writing me like that?'" In the span of the study, researchers spoke at length with 24 teenagers, visited multiple high school classrooms, and surveyed over 100 individuals. Overwhelmingly, adolescents reported that digitalk is reserved for peers; it is language that is by and for teens, and as such, it represents an important aspect of adolescent identity development.

The fact that digitalk is a language of the adolescent community becomes even more clear when adults attempt to decipher it. Adults often stumble through an oral translation of the conversation below between Lily and Michael; however, teens, including those who might be labeled as struggling readers and writers, read it fluently.

> **Lily:** heyyyy (:
> **Michael:** wasz gud B.I.G. ?
> **Lily:** nm, chillennn; whatchu up too ?
> **Michael:** WatchIn da gam3
> **Lily:** mm, y quien ta jugandoo ?
> **Michael:** Yank33s nd naTi0naLs.
> **Lily:** WHAAAATT A JOKEEEEE, dime como yankees lostt
> againstt them yesterdaii.
> **Michael:** i n0e, th3y suCk.
> **Lily:** & the nationalsss won like only 16 games . . . one of the
> worst teams homieeegee.
> **Michael:** t3lL m3 b0uT it, i b3T y0u fIv3 d0lLaRs th3Y g00nA l0s3.
> **Lily:** AHA, naw gee thats easy $ for youu ! =p
> **Michael:** lol i waS plAyInG w| y0u. =D
> **Lily:** lol imma talk to you later . . . i got pizzaa awaitinggg
> meeeee (;
> **Michael:** iight pe3cE

Inevitably adults struggle in reading and comprehending this conversation because they have had little experience with the language. Fluency is built by practice, and adolescents read and write constantly as part of their interactions in a primary Discourse that is saturated with digitalk. They are motivated to gain competence in the discourse so that they may claim membership in their peer community. As Erikson might say, they seek "sameness" within the group.

INDIVIDUAL MARKERS AND IDENTITY DEVELOPMENT

Lily and Michael are representative members of the adolescent digital community. They adopt the language that contributes to their group identity, and teens from across geographical areas are able to read and understand their conversation. Even so, the differences in language use between Lily and Michael are recognizable. Each has a distinct voice that helps to create an individual identity within this community.

For example, students who have analyzed the conversation often identified Lily as "Hispanic," noting the ease with which she moved from English to Spanish in her writing. One classroom group characterized her as "girly" and "energetic and very happy," noting her use of multiple letters throughout the conversation. Michael, on the other hand, was often seen as a "thug" or "gangster," or at the very least "cool," a completely different character from Lily. The participants in the study were able to make judgments about Lily's and Michael's social identities because they recognized that digitalk represents both an individual identity and a community identity. Teenagers identified specific language variations (e.g., use of multiple letters, slang) as monikers of socioeconomic status, ethnic group, maturity/age level, or interest group (e.g., sports fan). All of these judgments derived from digitalk, and it is clear from the teens' characterizations of Lily and Michael that individuals create distinct voices—even as they participate in a larger community of adolescent digital writers who can easily read their messages.

Nearly every adolescent who studied the conversation noted that Michael replaced the letter "O" with the numeral "0" and the letter "E" with the numeral "3," using an adaptation of L33T, a code of computer programmers and hackers. This choice may reflect his identity with a particular group that has adopted L33T as a code, or it may represent his personal tag. Many of the teens who were surveyed and interviewed about their choices in digitalk indicated that they purposefully manipulated certain features of language to showcase their individuality, and in many cases, they associated particular patterns with individuals in their peer group. As Lebron noted of his friend Ray, "How I would know it was Ray is he doesn't write 'S's,' he writes '5's'." Ray confirmed this personal tag, saying he had adopted that language practice "just to have me there." Other students agreed that each user possessed a distinct voice. As one participant said, "People, they can pick up on the way you text, like a text style almost. . . . You can tell because the pattern changes a little bit." The pattern, as this student suggested, reflects the individual identity of the writer.

Though individual identity is important in the world of digitalk, it is not fixed. Experimentation allows for evolution, and the teens in the study admitted that their language practices changed over time. As one student said of his use of multiple consonants, it was "something I did in the past." In this developmental stage of role confusion, it is not surprising that adolescents "grow out of" particular uses of language. In some cases, they abandon conventions because adults appropriate them, making them common vernacular outside the adolescent subculture. An acronym like "OMG," which now appears in *The Oxford English Dictionary*, is, as CNN stated, "No longer just a teenage expression, but officially a word found in the dictionary" (Stewart, 2011, para. 1). Charlie and Alicia considered it "weird" when adults joined in their use of digitalk:

> **Alicia:** Want to hear something weird? Adults are picking up—
> **Charlie:** Yeah they're all, like, texting whatever. [My dad] responded with three E's which is how I usually say it. Like three E's. It was weird. I was like "why are you texting the way I text?"

To maintain a community identity, one that is specifically adolescent, teens may reject conventions when adults adopt them.

Overuse of the convention, either within or outside of their adolescent communities, may call for new trends. In addition, teens evolve on a personal level. Sarah's explanation revealed this growth. She began by describing her use of multiple letters, which her sister Cindy called "Sarah's thing."

> **Sarah:** Three H's, three T's, three D's. I would never, ever go beyond three. I still don't like the number four at all so there was never, like, anything that was the exception. Most of the time I would always do threes and then once in a while if I thought it was too much, I would, like, suffer and do two. But I didn't like it.
> **Researcher:** That's interesting. What do you like about the number three?
> **Sarah:** I don't know. I think I started liking it back in middle school. And well I've always liked the number three because that was, like, my number, just always my number. . . . It was back in middle school. I know that for sure.

Sarah's focus on her younger self continued as she discussed this particular convention, which she had written in a text message that was submitted to the research team during the previous academic year.

> **Sarah:** Yeah. I don't do that anymore. But I did do that a lot.
> **Researcher:** Why?
> **Sarah:** Because I don't know. I felt like last year, I kind of had this very outgoing, like, image going and, really fun and, like, carefree. And I thought that kept it. I was very obsessive keeping up that image . . . how I felt was, when I texted, like, more than one letter, it was just more exciting. Like if someone texted me that, I found them more of an open person, more of an exciting person. . . .

Researcher: Well what would happen if you just saw somebody who texted without multiple letters? What would that be? What kind of person would that be like?

Sarah: I mean now I don't think, I think I was totally immature last year. I was just, like, a little stupid last year. I was insecure last year.

Sarah characterized herself as "immature" during the previous school year, and in her eyes, her digitalk shifted as she matured. However, she had a difficult time explaining this growth.

Researcher: Something you said really caught my attention which is you think it's immature.

Sarah: I do.

Researcher: So but why? What would make if we just spelled N-E-W-S-S, spelled "newss," spelled N-E-W-S, why would that be mature and why would this be immature?

Sarah: I guess N-E-W-S, it's like simpler. It's just like, that is like, that's like how you do it. Like that's how you write it. That's the right way to do it. Like this is, this is not the correct way to do it. This is just, like, I mean, I don't know.

Though Sarah perceived that she "was just kind of stupid and dumb" in the past, she struggled to articulate why her use of multiple letters revealed her immaturity, eventually admitting to the researcher, "I don't know." During the interview she went on to admit that there is nothing in texting that makes language correct or incorrect. She said, "It's all a matter of perception." Even so, she perceived her own language habits in a negative light, admitting that she was "more mature" and no longer used those conventions.

This evolution in an individual's use of digitalk demonstrates a changing identity, and Sarah, as well as others in the study, were keenly aware that their sense of self, reflected in their digitalk, had shifted over time. In some cases this idea manifested itself in the data with statements like, "pre-teens do that all the time," or "that's something younger kids do." Interestingly, many of these comments were made in response to Lily and Michael's writing, a conversation written between two high school seniors. Lily and Michael's example, written approximately one year before the students began to analyze it, captured the community conventions of its time. Perhaps these conventions had already begun to evolve within the community—or perhaps the individuals who made such comments had already shifted their own identity, moving toward more adult roles in their lives, and consequently, in their use of language.

THE CHALLENGE OF ACCEPTANCE

Ray and Lebron made it clear that the adults in their lives "don't understand" the texting language that they use regularly with their friends. In their view, this digital language separates teenagers from adults, and the rest of the participants in this study confirmed that Ray and Lebron are right. Digitalk is a language of a digital generation. Though communities develop conventions that define users as members, these practices constantly shift. The fact that teens themselves create these shifts gives adolescents agency. It is this freedom to experiment, to evolve identity that marks the stage of adolescence. Digitalk serves this growth.

Erikson (1968) suggested that this period in youthful life brings with it resistance to adults even as adolescents explore desired social roles of adulthood. The blend of formal and nonstandard language patterns in digitalk mirrors these conflicting roles. To be accepted by their peers, teens must resist the rules associated with the adult world. To become adult, they must embrace them. In their digital communities teens navigate this tension by embracing the language of those around them, just as they do in the lunchroom and other spaces of identity enactment (Moje, 2004). Through these literate practices, they develop their individual identities, often evolving beyond trends that they come to see as immature.

In some ways adult society has fueled the spread of digitalk with pejorative views of lazy teenagers who do not take the time to write in proper form. In a study of over 100 print media reports on digital language, Thurlow (2006) found that the portrayal of digital language in public discourse is vastly negative. According to the Pew Internet and American Life study, "A considerable number of educators and children's advocates . . . are concerned that the quality of writing by young Americans is being degraded by their electronic communication, with its carefree spelling, lax punctuation and grammar, and its acronym shortcuts" (Lenhart, Arafeh, Smith, & Macgill, 2008, p. 3). In light of these views, it seems appropriate for adolescents to push back, to resist. However, despite these fears that are prominent among many adults, a growing body of research has shown that digitalk is not detrimental to literacy. In fact, the practice of manipulating language may both support the development of and illustrate the presence of advanced literacy skills (Kemp & Bushnell, 2011; Plester, Wood, & Bell, 2008; Plester, Wood, & Joshi, 2009; Wood, Jackson, Hart, Plester, & Wilde, 2011).

Baron (2008) suggested that college students "have neither time for nor interest in . . . linguistic posturing" (p. 70), and the teens in the present study also indicated that they matured in their use of language, viewing some conventions of digitalk as "immature" or reserved for younger individuals. Future research might explore this development, noting the effects of prolonged use of digitalk during adolescence on an individual's linguistic choices as an adult. At what point, if at all, do adolescents abandon digitalk entirely? Or in what cases do adults continue to use conventions of digitalk for purposes of efficiency or individual voice? The answers to these questions remain to be seen as the current generation, the first that is deeply entrenched in the discourse throughout their formative years, emerges into adulthood.

Like those in Elvis's generation, adults today may view adolescent subculture as inappropriate—or wrong. Digitalk, however, is neither. It serves a communicative purpose for teens; it allows them to belong to a community of peers; it encourages them to experiment as they develop their identities. In short, digitalk is a tool that serves adolescents in this age of *identity vs. role confusion*. It is a difference that draws a line between generations, fostering both the conformity and resistance that defines adolescence.

REFERENCES

Baron, N. S. (2008). *Always on: Language in an online and mobile world.* New York, NY: Oxford University Press.

Cherny, L. (1999). *Conversation and community: Chat in a virtual world.* Stanford, CA: CSLI Publications.

Crystal, D. (2001). *Language and the internet.* New York, NY: Cambridge University Press.

Crystal, D. (2008). *Txtng: The gr8 db8.* New York, NY: Oxford University Press.

Erikson, E. (1968). *Identity: Youth and crisis.* New York, NY: Norton.

Gee. J. P. (2008). *Social linguistics and literacies: Ideology in discourse* (3rd ed.). New York, NY: Routledge.

Haas, C., Takayoshi, P., Carr, B., Hudson, K., & Pollock, R. (2011). Young people's everyday literacies: The language features of instant messaging. *Research in the Teaching of English, 45*, 378–404. Retrieved from http://www.ncte.org/journals/rte/issues/v45-4

Kemp, N., & Bushnell, C. (2011). Children's text messaging: Abbreviations, input methods and links with literacy. *Journal of Computer Assisted Learning, 27*, 18–27. doi: 10.1111/j.1365-2729.2010.00400.x

Lenhart, A., Arafeh, S., Smith, A., & Macgill A. R. (2008). Writing, technology and teens. Pew Research Center. Retrieved from http://www.pewinternet.org/PPF/r/247/report_display.asp

Moje, E. B. (2004). Powerful spaces: Tracing the out-of-school literacy spaces of Latino/a youth. In K. Leander & M. Sheehy (Eds.), *Spatializing Literacy Research and Practice* (pp. 15–38). New York, NY: Peter Lang. Retrieved from http://www-personal.umich.edu/~moje/publicationsChapters.html

Moje, E. B., & Luke, A. (2009). Literacy and identity: Examining the metaphors in history and contemporary research. *Reading Research Quarterly, 44*(4), 415–437. dx.doi.org/10.1598/RRQ.44.4.7

Plester, B., Wood, C., & Joshi, P. (2009). Exploring the relationship between children's knowledge of text message abbreviations and school literacy outcomes. *British Journal of Developmental Psychology, 27,* 145–161. doi:10.1348/026151008X320507

Plester, B., Wood, C., & Bell, V. (2008). Txt msg n school literacy: Does texting and knowledge of text abbreviations adversely affect children's literacy attainment. *Literacy, 42*(30), 137–144. doi: 10.1111/j.1741-4369.2008.00489.x

Prensky, M. (2001). Digital natives, digital immigrants. Retrieved from http://www.marcprensky.com/writing/

Stewart, A. (2011). OMG! Oxford English Dictionary adds new words. *CNN Living.* Retrieved from http://articles.cnn.com/2011-03-25/living/oxford.new.words_1_new-words-oxford-english-dictionary-usage?_s=PM:LIVING

Thurlow, C. (2006). From statistical panic to moral panic: The metadiscursive construction and popular exaggeration of new media language in the print media. *Journal of Computer-Mediated Communication, 11,* 667–701. doi:10.1111/j.1083-6101.2006.00031.x

Turner, K. H. (2011). Digitalk: Community, convention, and self-expression. In J. Rowsell & S. A. Abrams (Eds.). *Rethinking identity and literacy education in the 21st century* (pp. 263–282). New York, NY: Teachers College Record Yearbook.

Turner, K. H. (2010). Digitalk: A new literacy for a digital generation. *Phi Delta Kappan, 92*(1), 41–46.

Vygotsky, L. (1978). *Mind in society.* Cambridge, MA: Harvard University Press.

Wenger, E. C. (1998). *Communities of practice: Learning, meaning and identity.* New York, NY: Cambridge University Press.

Wood, C., Jackson, E., Hart, L., Plester, B., & Wilde, L. (2011). The effect of text messaging on 9- and 10-year-old children's reading, spelling, and phonological processing skills. *Journal of Computer Assisted Learning, 27,* 28–36. doi: 10.1111/j.1365-2729.2010.00398

CHAPTER 11

HOMELESS ADOLESCENT MOTHERS

Engaging Strengths Emergent in Parenthood

Alexandra Jordan, Marina Mazur, Aurelie Athan, and Lisa Miller

INTRODUCTION

According to estimates from the National Health Care for the Homeless Council (Ammerman et al., 2004), between 750,000 and 2 million young adults between the ages of 18 and 24 experience an episode of homelessness each year. Due to the recent financial crisis and its impact on the job market, these numbers are expected to have risen significantly (Hibbard, 2010). It is clear that homelessness in young adults is a real crisis. The current chapter aims to better understand and treat a subset of this population: homeless adolescent mothers.

Literature examining the experience of motherhood in homeless adolescents is limited, despite the finding that adolescents in low socioeconomic brackets are more likely to get pregnant and give birth than those in

Adolescence in the 21st Century, pages 187–198
Copyright © 2014 by Information Age Publishing
All rights of reproduction in any form reserved.

middle and upper brackets (Trent & Crowder, 1997). Extant research, such as the finding that teens with children have elevated school dropout rates and lower socioeconomic statuses (Maynard, 1996), likely contributes to the casting of adolescent parenthood in a negative light. Teen mothers are often considered woefully underprepared for their new role of mother, an assumption echoed through research findings that teen mothers have been surprised by the difficulties associated with parenthood (Clemmens, 2003).

These findings present a bleak portrait of homeless adolescent motherhood. Yet the universality of the motherhood experience would suggest that, amidst the difficulties experienced by homeless adolescent mothers, there also exist its benefits and rewards. Motherhood allows teens to develop maturity and a sense of responsibility. And while teenage motherhood is perceived as a negative experience, recent studies have shown that teenage mothers can cope as well as adult mothers across multiple areas of functioning (Wrennick, Schneider, & Monga, 2005).

When conceptualizing treatment plans for this population, it is critical to understand their experience from a developmental perspective, taking into account their status as adolescents. Yet it is equally important to honor their status as mothers, with that role's attendant struggles and gifts. By understanding homeless adolescent mothers as unique yet deeply ingrained in the universal world of mothers, the present study aims to share a new perspective toward treatment of this population.

TREATMENT OVERVIEW

Setting

Two facilitators provided weekly group psychotherapy with rolling membership at a crisis shelter that offers housing to homeless adolescent mothers and their children for 30 to 60 days. The group offered potential participants a space for mothers to speak about life stressors, particularly their experience of the transition to motherhood, and was provided for eight months. In all, 96 mothers attended at least one session. The adolescents met in the lounge of the homeless shelter one evening per week for one hour and 30 minutes.

Client Demographics and History

The young women in the psychotherapy group ranged from 18 to 21 years of age and primarily were of African American or Latin descent. All shared two experiences: homelessness and motherhood. Upon intake, most mothers reported histories of abuse (51.1%—emotional abuse, 37.4%—physical abuse, 20.0%—sexual abuse). Their paths to homelessness differed, but the young women fell into two groups: those who were pushed out of their homes (i.e., by a family member who did not approve of the pregnancy) and those who left their homes to escape abusive situations. Mothers who were kicked out of their homes by their guardians were forced into a decision about how best to move forward in creating a more sustainable environment for themselves and their children. For those who ran away from home, leaving represented an act of decisiveness: a step away from an abusive situation due to their deep belief that they could create a better life for themselves. Often, this initiation was precipitated by pregnancy or childbirth, as suddenly there was another person to consider. For sake of illustration, we have compounded strong themes across young women into two cases, those of "Desiree" and "Marisol."

CASES

Case of Desiree: Creating a Family

Desiree came to the homeless shelter with her son having nowhere else to turn. She had been living with her grandmother, but was pushed out of her home soon after the birth of her son. Her grandmother was her only remaining family member: Desiree's parents had died when she was six, and a year later, Desiree's only sibling, her beloved older brother, was fatally shot. After being forced out of her home by her grandmother, Desiree had stayed with friends for several months. When she found that she had no other place to go, she came to the homeless shelter with her child.

Desiree arrived at the group as a silent, unknowable presence, exuding a quiet anger that suggested deep reserves of emotion below the surface. Though only nineteen years old, she projected a wariness that suggested knowledge far beyond her years. In her first two sessions, she did not speak. Yet Desiree revealed signs of humor and personality in small ways: she laughed heartily at other members' jokes before returning to her silent stance, and she wore bright blue fuzzy animal slippers to group that made everyone smile. At first, it was only through these small signs that Desiree communicated at all. In her second and third group sessions, silent Desiree began to show more engagement through her body language: where she had been leaning far back in her seat with her arms crossed, seemingly attempting to gain as much distance as possible from the group, now her hands lay on her lap and her rigid posture relaxed. She began to follow the movement of group conversation with her eyes and the tilt of her head, as if opening herself to the stories of the young women around her.

A more profound shift occurred during Desiree's third group session: her entire demeanor changed, and it seemed that she was ready to reveal herself. The shift occurred during a group session that several young women afterward referred to as "very emotional," wherein dialogue about familial relationships became a session of processing and sharing difficult interpersonal experiences with parents and siblings. The emotion that had seemed deep within Desiree began to emerge, quickly and powerfully: She was still sad, but a new openness was present as well. Desiree began to speak about the most difficult part of her past:

> My parents died when I was six, but I always had my brother—he was always around whenever I needed him. Since he was older, it was kind of like I was his kid. I never felt scared when he was around 'cause I knew he had my back. When I was seven he got shot accidentally—he was just walking by the wrong place at the wrong time. Since then, nothing's been the same. It's like my life changed that day and never went back.

Desiree's abandonment through death by both her parents and her brother had left her with conflicting desires: she wanted to protect herself from further pain, but she also wanted to find someone else on whom to rely. Desiree had hoped that her grandmother would be a safe haven, and for many years she was.

> My grandma took us in when my parents died, and I always got along with her. She was real strict, even more after my brother died, but I always thought she cared about me. When I got pregnant she was so mad, and she told me I wouldn't be able to live with her with the baby. That scared me, but I knew I wanted to have the baby because it was something that was mine. I wanted my son.

When her grandmother abandoned her due to her pregnancy, Desiree looked to her budding maternal role as one that could satisfy her need for family by allowing her to create anew.

When she began her story, Desiree's voice was soft and hesitant; it grew in strength as she progressed, so that she was nearly shouting by the end. Even as she began to cry when discussing her brother's death, her voice never wavered; the only sign was her tear-covered cheeks. It appeared almost as though she was birthing something: her true identity, emergent through her son and expressed through simultaneous vulnerability and strength. From the group's focused attention and empathic reaction to her story, Desiree seemed to perceive a sense of safety that allowed her to continue to show her true self. A more relaxed, engaged, and introspective Desiree emerged, one who was willing to explore loaded concepts like trust and betrayal by offering material from her own lived experience.

Over the course of several weeks Desiree continued to attend group sessions. She got to know other regular group members better and began to demonstrate one of her most defining qualities: her fierce loyalty to those she cared about. When several regular group members were scheduled to be discharged from the shelter due to their allotted time in the program coming to an end, Desiree was as frustrated with the system's lack of assistance in securing housing as she would have been for herself. Yet Desiree's loyalty was not blind. She gave it to those who were of a similar makeup: serious about their roles as mothers, serious about creating better lives for themselves in the future.

Other members began to look to Desiree for a kind of guidance, so that she became an elder in the group. She dispensed wisdom in a tough-love package, shaking her head and giving a rueful laugh when she thought a member was going astray. She was vocal with her criticism of other members, particularly mothers who were violent in front of their children. Yet she also was generous with her appreciation, building other mothers' self-esteem and providing motivation during their moments of self-doubt. It was clear that Desiree felt connected to the other group members by the sacred bonds of motherhood. The more she revealed of herself, the more her status as a mother emerged as a central organizing aspect of her identity. In the session where members drew self-portraits, Desiree's featured her child's name in large letters, with a rainbow and sunshine surrounding it to represent her feelings about being a mother.

Having suffered abandonment, an experience common among young homeless mothers, Desiree found that group offered the opportunity to make connections with fellow members on honest and fair terms. These relationships offered Desiree a "safe space" where she could forge authentic connections, allowing for meaningful content to emerge. In fact, it was through Desiree's bravery in addressing difficult content that many critical themes emerged in the group's work. In this way, she served as a spokesperson for the group, introducing critical topics on behalf of the young mothers.

One issue that Desiree addressed, which turned out to be of the utmost importance to nearly every member, related to respect and its importance in the lives of the teenage mothers. When the whole group was upset about the actions of a resident, Shauna, who had instigated a fight with several members, Desiree explained that Shauna's critical misstep was in making derogatory comments about people's children: "It's fine for us to have words with each other, but we don't bring the children into it. That's just not right." Despite the frequency of disagreements within the shelter's culture, a line was drawn at the children: there was an unspoken pact that the kids were to be kept out of any fight. Desiree felt that Shauna was disrespectful and admitted that there were times she wanted to resort to violence: "When someone disrespects you, it's so hard to just walk away." Yet each time, as she told the group, she reminded herself that the conflict was not worth losing her bed at the shelter (violence was not allowed). More importantly, she said, she did not want her child exposed to violence.

Desiree's artful description of the situation with Shauna brought to life for the facilitators the importance of respect for this population, who admitted that they often did not feel respected within the homeless shelter environment and by society more broadly. Likewise, it introduced the idea of motherhood, and more specifically anticipated consequences for one's child, as a reason to disengage from conflict; this too ended up being a pertinent theme in group.

Desiree's upward trajectory within group was reflective of her overall growth during her time at the homeless shelter. During her stay, she completed a job-readiness program, received her G.E.D., and procured employment as a secretary. She found a stable living environment for her child and herself, gaining entry into a competitive housing program. When it was time for her to leave the shelter, she reflected on her time as a group member and described what made it a different space than other gatherings within the homeless shelter: "I never realized how much we all have in common. We've got real different perspectives and ways of thinking about things. But in here, it doesn't matter that we're not all best friends. We still help each other and listen and kind of get it." Desiree gave herself the gift of connection within the group, stepping outside of her fierce independence to open up to those around her. Once thus connected, she flourished.

Case of Marisol: Looking to the Future

Marisol came to the homeless shelter with her two young daughters after ending her relationship to their father. Her story reveals the classic concerns of the young group members: being perceived as substandard mothers and learning to disengage from violence in a world rife with conflict. The force of Marisol's salvation, and the salvation of many others in group, came through her astonished discovery of the depth of her love for, and commitment to, her young children. From her first time with the group, Marisol was very vocal, exuding a seemingly boundless optimism that belied her difficult history and life circumstances. Speaking with a heavy Spanish accent, she projected an easy confidence by volunteering her experiences freely, despite the fact that she was new to the shelter and did not yet know the members of the group. She was always good-humored, often laughing at herself in a way that was incredulous: "Can you believe I have two babies under two years old?" Her manner had a way of drawing in the group, allowing for the exploration of difficult topics in a gentle, low-risk manner. She seemed open to discussing anything, even the ways her body had changed since having a baby. In this way, she served as a direct line to the group's experiences. She modeled the safety of sharing by disclosing first.

At her first group, Marisol expressed her frustration with how others perceived her:

> People tell me they can't believe they're both mine. Just because I look younger than I am, people think I'm fifteen with a baby and a toddler. Plus, my babies look so different, people judge me because they think they're from two different fathers. They're from the same father, but either way it's nobody's business! And everyone thinks because I look so young that I don't know what I'm doing. But I'm careful with my girls. They always have what they need: they're clean and I dress them well. Look at my baby—she's so round! She eats well. I don't like when people try to tell me what I'm doing wrong. I make some mistakes, but I'm a good mother.

Despite her cheerful manner, Marisol had learned through her emergent mother identity to manage her anger without resorting to defensive violence. During one group session, Marisol's good nature showed vulnerability as she recounted an altercation on the subway. A woman made a rude remark in reaction to Marisol's daughter crying, and Marisol punched the woman in the mouth. Almost immediately, she felt remorseful: She didn't want her daughters to learn that type of behavior. As soon as possible, she left the train with her children to avoid exposing them to further conflict. From the start, Marisol showed us the primacy of motherhood to her personal identity. She referred to motherhood as "the best thing that ever happened to me," ushering in a discussion of identity pre- and post-motherhood, which became a frequent topic of group conversation. She illustrated a fundamental shift that took place within her through the story of her reaction to her second pregnancy:

> I got pregnant with my second child two months after my first was born. I didn't even realize it could happen so fast; I thought I couldn't get pregnant while I was breastfeeding. I remember exactly where I was when I found out. I was standing in my bathroom holding the pregnancy test, and my baby was waking up in the other room, and she was crying. I started crying, too.
>
> I called my babies' father—we were engaged then. He was such a good daddy to our daughter. When I called him I expected him to be upset, but he wasn't. He said this was a blessing for our family. Later I explained to him I couldn't do it again, not when I didn't have enough to give to our daughter already. He told me that it was my decision.
>
> I made an appointment at the abortion clinic, and I was there filling out all my paperwork and sitting in the waiting room thinking. I knew something didn't feel right but I couldn't figure out what it was. When I got taken back into a little room, I took off my clothes and put on the gown. I was sitting

and waiting for the nurse to come in, and all of a sudden it hit me that I couldn't be there—I couldn't do it. I thought to myself, "I'm a mother. I can't kill a child." I put my clothes on so fast and ran out of there. I didn't want them to try to talk me out of it. I called my baby's father back and was crying, saying, "We're gonna have another baby." I was so happy. It hit me in that moment, I think.

The force of maternal love superseded adolescence and poverty to become a central guiding force. Marisol spoke often of the motivating nature of motherhood, particularly as related to her willingness to sacrifice her needs and wants for the benefit of her children. She referenced her own upward momentum in a self-portrait drawn in group, wherein she drew herself from below the knees, her high-top sneakers climbing a step. Three arrows accompanied the picture, with "past" toward what would be behind her, "present" straight ahead, and "future" pointing up. She described it:

I drew this because this is how I feel like I'm doing: I'm moving forward and going up at the same time. I know I'm not trying to go down or go back to my past. I'm doing my present and constructing my future.

Marisol maintained this full engagement in the present and rarely spoke about her experiences before having her daughters. She often encouraged the group to discuss current situations and maintained that this was where they had the control to influence their outcomes. She was convinced that, though she had no job and had been looking for months, life was going to get better for herself and her children. She said, "I'm focused on my daughters' future; if they're good, I am too."

Through Marisol, the group harnessed the force of motherhood, moving toward a new strategy for resolving previously unacknowledged anger at other people, such as their children's fathers or their own mothers. In several letter-writing exercises, Marisol was able to access a more vulnerable side of herself than what she displayed in conversation with the group. Though not required to do so, Marisol always shared her letters with the group. It seemed that, through the letters, she could reveal her deeper feelings. When participants were invited to compose a letter to a person in their future, Marisol chose to write to the husband she would have one day:

Dear Hubby, I'm glad you came into my life. It's like you came at the right time, because I was going through a lot. We went through our rough patch, but I'm proud to say that you blessed me with two beautiful kids. I'm glad you're in my life.

She read her letter to the group, explaining that she had recently broken off her engagement with her children's father. She expressed her shock and confusion when, after his initial excitement about their second child, he disappeared from their lives following the baby's birth. Marisol held out hope for the relationship, but she also expressed a realistic view of it, and revealed her profound disappointment. The letter seemed to allow her to access the feelings of betrayal that lay behind her optimism.

During another letter-writing exercise, Marisol wrote a letter to her mother, who had abandoned her after Marisol had her children. In the letter, she told her mother how hurt she was by her rejection, and how much she wished her children knew their grandmother. Yet at the conclusion, Marisol told her mother that she still loved her, that she forgave her, and that she wished that they could speak again. Marisol read the earnest, heartfelt letter aloud, causing most group members to cry. Marisol's letter led to a long discussion about group members' relationships with their own mothers; it had made it safe to share about one of the most intimate topics for these young mothers.

While in the group, Marisol became more comfortable expressing all of her emotions, moving beyond her optimism to make room for the insecurities and pain that existed alongside it. She made improvements in the rest of her life, embodying her illustration of herself climbing the step to her future. The day she secured her full-time position as a cashier at a nearby branch of a high-end grocery chain, she came to the group with a broad smile, wearing an employer-issued shirt inscribed with the company logo. She told the rest of the group about her interview: the manager had spoken to many people, but he told her that he admired her motivation and trusted her assertions that she would devote herself to customer service. She shared her feelings of gratitude, especially because the job offered benefits that would cover her children as well as herself. She was excited to start work the next morning, and wanted to take on as many shifts as possible. This served as a kind of allegory for the approach to life shared by many group members and truly embodied by Marisol: moving forward to create the life she wanted for her children and herself.

CLINICAL IMPRESSIONS

Accelerated Transition to Adulthood

Through our experiences working with homeless adolescent mothers, we have come to find that the teen mother is a walking contradiction. While a teen may be considered the pinnacle of immaturity—focusing on the self, guided by desire over reason—the mother is prized as selfless and mature. In many ways, the teen mother is like no other, with these distinctive elements of adolescent and mother blended together. Working with her, we see that she has largely moved away from teenage narcissistic self-focus. Yet we encounter very teen parts of her, such as her sensitivity to rejection or her shifting friendships, and these remind us that she is still, at least in part, her age. When examined in the context of emerging adulthood, one may see this unique being—this half-child, half-adult—as one who is moving more swiftly toward adulthood than others her age. While she is still in the process of becoming an adult, she seems very much ahead of her non-mother peers. The thrust of motherhood largely supersedes the adolescent maturation process, such that it propels a mother forward in her own development at an accelerated rate.

What might a mother gain and lose from this accelerated transition to adulthood? As noted above, through motherhood, our participants shared that they gained motivation, perspective, clarity of purpose, compassion, and an ability to step away from conflict. Yet they lost something, as well, by bringing adulthood on more swiftly than their contemporaries. They showed us, through their descriptions of how they moved from dependence on their families to the same on their children, how they lost the precious time of individuation that more typical teenage life provides. Likewise, due to a lack of time and an all-consuming focus on their children, they lost the luxury of forging bonds outside of the mother–child dyad. As one mother stated, "I wish I could have some type of relationship with someone other than my child."

The early adulthood rush into motherhood results in a loss of freedom to experiment with defining oneself during these years. This may be considered a significant deficit, as identity formation may be understood as some of the most critical work of adolescence (Arnett, 2000). Conversely, as remarked upon by the teens themselves, the acceleration of motherhood may also confer a quality of maturity, fulfillment, purpose, and healing that few other life paths may have provided as efficiently.

The issue of identity formation is an interesting one through which to examine the process of an adolescent mother. While typically a teen may rely on a mother figure to facilitate the process of maturity, looking to her as a safe home base from which to take flight, these teens have *become* a mother to bring about their personal evolution. As noted previously, often they shared with us a sense of abandonment by their own mothers; though the stories were different, the experience of the loss of that maternal presence was common throughout. Though these young women may not have felt they could rely on their own mothers for true mothering, they have looked to themselves through the process of becoming a parent. They were searching for a safe adult and created that identity within themselves.

Integration of the Motherhood Role

Though the teenage mothers seemed in some ways to have had their identities overtaken by motherhood—they were defined by wiping, feeding, and managing of childcare—they did not appear to integrate the role of mother into their identities in the deepest, most meaningful sense. For this reason, the group's emphasis on the transition to motherhood was critical. Group members expressed their desire for a maternal identity through their eagerness to discuss what they felt they had gained from motherhood: They had never before been given the chance to talk about their embodiment of the mother role (Athan & Miller, 2005), perhaps because our society does not allow teen mothers to claim the positive aspects of the mother identity. Though teen mothers are expected almost at conception to become mature and deal with the everyday demands of mothering, many pressing issues (such as financial support for the child, the mother's education, etc.) distract from the notion of how the teen is *experiencing* motherhood, so that this largely is forgotten. Due to this lack of emphasis on their own personal evolution, teen mothers are denied the critical step of integrating motherhood into their own identity. They find it to some extent in groups of like-minded peers, such as at the shelter for homeless adolescent mothers, yet in the eyes of the wider world they do not get to *own* their motherhood.

IMPLICATIONS FOR FUTURE TREATMENT

In young adulthood, homelessness may impact the process of individuation. Jeffrey Arnett's (2000) literature on emerging adulthood has illustrated that the period between the ages of 18 to 25 is a unique time of role exploration in certain cultures, including the United States. According to Arnett (2000), "Identity formation involves trying out various life possibilities and gradually moving toward making enduring decisions" (p. 473). As homeless young adults are undergoing their identity formation process in tandem with the experience of housing instability, they would benefit from a supportive group to assist them in their transition to adulthood.

Homeless adolescent mothers may require an individualized therapeutic response due to their embodiment of three distinct roles: teen, mother, and survivor of trauma. Rather than being approached individually, these identities may be understood as a continuum across which to apply treatment. This tripartite model was utilized with the homeless adolescent mothers who partook in the therapeutic intervention described in this chapter. The teenage-specific aspect of the treatment focused on conflict and impulsivity, most often manifested within romantic relationships or female friendships.

This portion of the work developed out of the understanding that these young women were still teenagers, and as such wanted to talk about topical, relevant issues. The motherhood aspect of the treatment focused on the transition to motherhood, specifically what had been lost and gained from the assumption of this new role. This segment of the treatment allowed for an emphasis on how motherhood impacted each young woman's sense of self and how it impacted her emerging adult identity. The trauma component of treatment addressed any present psychopathology, particularly as it related to past traumatic experiences that often remained unaddressed throughout these young women's lives.

It may be posited that, if homeless adolescent mothers are provided a space through which to understand and integrate their role as mothers, the benefits of this treatment can extend to each mother's child. These children become the recipient of more mindful, present, intentional parenting. In this way, treating homeless adolescent mothers can be considered an investment in future generations, so that each child has a greater chance of achieving the dreams begun in the mind of each mother the moment she decided to keep her baby.

REFERENCES

Ammerman, S. D., Ensign, J., Kirzner, R., Meininger, E. T., Tornabene, M., Warf, C. W., Zerger, S., & Post, P. (2004). *Homeless young adults ages 18–24: Examining service delivery adaptations.* Nashville, TN: National Health Care for the Homeless Council.

Arnett, J. J. (2000). Emerging adulthood: A theory of development from the late teens through the twenties. *American Psychologist, 55*(5), 469–480.

Athan, A., & Miller, L. (2005). Spiritual awakening through the motherhood journey. *Journal of the Association for Research on Mothering, 7*(1), 17–31.

Clemmens, D. (2003). Adolescent motherhood: A meta-synthesis of qualitative studies. *American Journal of Maternal/Child Nursing, 28,* 93–99.

Hibbard, R. (2010). Generation homeless: The new faces of an old problem. *AOL News.* Retrieved from http://www.aolnews.com/2010/10/19/generation-homeless-young-adults-put-new-face-on-old-problem/

Maynard, R. A. (1996). *Kids having kids: A Robin Hood Foundation special report on the costs of adolescent childbearing.* New York, NY: Robin Hood Foundation.

Trent, K., & Crowder, K. (1997). Adolescent birth intentions, social disadvantage and behavioral outcomes. *Journal of Marriage & the Family, 59,* 523–535.

Wrennick, A. W., Schneider, K. M., & Monga, M. (2005). The effect of parenthood on perceived quality of life in teens. *American Journal of Obstetrics and Gynecology, 192,* 1465–1468.

CHAPTER 12

PRENATAL COCAINE EXPOSURE— TWO DECADES LATER

A Case Study

Rae Fallon

ABSTRACT

This is a longitudinal, qualitative case study of a child born with a positive toxicology to crack cocaine. The study is designed to follow the young child through infancy, toddlerhood, preschool, school years, adolescence, and into young adulthood. With a brief background on "Hope" (not her real name) and her family and her early years, and the impact of the drug cocaine on the developing child, we will concentrate on Hope as an adolescent and young adult and her challenges and triumphs. The current investigation studies the young adult Hope and examines her current life as to her ability to adapt to her school, home, and community. In the late 1980s and early 1990s these children were given up for lost with virtually little hope of ever living normal lives. The dire predictions at the time were a real concern for social services and law enforcement as well as the medical and educational communities. Since the use of cocaine and its derivatives occurs in all segments of Ameri-

Adolescence in the 21st Century, pages 199–207
Copyright © 2014 by Information Age Publishing
All rights of reproduction in any form reserved.

can society regardless of race, ethnicity, or socioeconomic status, this subject captured the attention of the American people. This follow-up study explores the life of a young woman and helps to further understand the phenomenon of prenatal cocaine exposure and the value of public funding thoughtfully applied to our youngest "at risk" children.

INTRODUCTION

Walking elegantly and confidently across the college stage, a lovely young woman with a radiant smile accepted her Bachelor of Science diploma with style and grace. Like so many of her fellow graduates, she had a sense of accomplishment and gratitude for her family and friends who supported her efforts, but unlike so many of them, it was not predicted that she would even be able to live a normal life, let alone achieve so much.

Hope (not her real name) was a child born in the early 1990s with a positive toxicology to the drug crack-cocaine. At that time, a whole generation of children born with cocaine in their systems were considered "doomed and damned" and given up for lost (Mayes, Graner, Borstein, & Zuckerman, 1992). Based on little scientific evidence, early reports of the effects of cocaine on children were exaggerated (Mayes et al., 1992). The first wave of research took society by surprise and the concerns for these children were seen in many areas of society. Hawley, Halle, Drasin, and Thomas (1995, p. 3640) contend that the "crack epidemic" struck the academic, health, political, government, and legal communities. In the late 1980s and early 1990s, newspaper headlines referring to infants affected by cocaine warned the school system to prepare for the coming of these children in great numbers (Rist, 1990).

At the time of Hope's birth, the influx of these so called "crack babies" was beginning to be seen in New York City. The hospitals were overcrowded with "boarder babies"—infants who were not allowed to go home with their drug-seeking mothers. A similar situation was occurring in the Hudson Valley as well. At that time, there was very little known about the long-term effects of this drug on the developing person, but the predictions were anything but positive. These initial predictions, fueled by the media, gained national attention. Because the use of cocaine and all of its derivatives occurs in all segments of American society, regardless of race, ethnicity, or socioeconomic status, the subject captured the attention of the American people.

The initial scare of the effects on this drug on the infant focused attention on the health and development of the children who were drug-exposed. While accompanied by some misinformation, the scientific community did exert some effort to learn more about this phenomenon and correct some of the misrepresentations of the initial studies. In a meta-analysis of articles published between 1975 and 1989, Lutiger, Graham, Einarson, and Koren (1991) searched for a relationship between gestational cocaine use and pregnancy outcome. Cocaine was associated with a higher risk of spontaneous abortion, shorter gestational age, smaller head circumference, shorter birth length, and lower birth weight.

Subsequent research by Karmel and Gardiner (1996) did find that attention and state deficits were found in these children. Animal studies also suggest that cocaine exposure might have an impact on functional systems thought to control arousal and attention modulation, the regulation of anxiety and other emotional states, the regulation of reactivity, the level of arousal induced by novel stimulation, and the reinforcing of properties of stimuli (Eyler, Behnke, Conlon, Woods, & Wobie, 1998; Mayes & Bornstein, 1995; Vogel, 1997). At birth, characteristics of infants exposed to cocaine include a tendency to be irritable and tremulous, with sudden startle responses, even though they are not going through actual withdrawal of the drug (Chasnoff, Burns, & Schnoll, 1985; Lester, LaGasse, Friere, & Brunner, 1996; Volpe, 1992).

These physiologic and behavioral findings suggested that cocaine-exposed infants may initially be incapable of responding appropriately to their caregivers. The reciprocity normally present in the process of bonding would not be possible for the infant (Brazelton, Koslowski, & Martin, 1974; Eyler et al., 1998). A negative cycle may be developed in which the poorly organized, high-risk infant may suppress the care-giving patterns necessary to facilitate optimal development. In addition to the physiological and behavioral patterns of these newborns, environmental and socioeconomic factors place the child at risk. The maternal psychopathology, the maternal-infant relationship, lack of parenting skills, and the chaotic and transient nature of a drug-seeking family all compound the early neurobehavioral deficits of the newborn. Some researchers propose that parents often view these children as demanding yet unresponsive to attempts to comfort them (Chasnoff, 1989; Finklestein, 1994).

For many women addicted to crack cocaine, the demands of parenting a newborn are insurmountable, and the added demands of a high-risk infant are untenable. Many of these children were placed in foster homes to provide a safe home for the infant and respite for the drug-abusing parent. At the time, crack-exposed children were placed in emergency foster placements, and the foster parents had little help in learning "best practices" for dealing with the very demanding children, since these children were a relatively new phenomenon.

A STORY OF HOPE

It was during this time of fear and uncertainty that Hope (all names in this chapter have been changed) was born in a hospital in the Hudson Valley of New York State. Hope was her biological mother's third child born with a positive toxicology to cocaine. Her older half-brother, Sean was born two years previously and, after a series of inappropriate foster homes, was found to have developmental delays and was placed in the home of Betty and John Brook (a pseudonym), a middle class bi-racial couple. The couple ran a licensed day care center at their home and cared for other children in their home. It was in the Brook home that Hope began her life as a foster child at 3 days of age. Hope, an African-American child, was born at 7 pounds, 7 ounces. It is not known whether or not the child was full-term. Hope was born with evidence of cocaine in her blood. Hope's biological mother was 26 years of age and reportedly a user of street drugs and in frequent scrapes with the police. Her first child, Sara, was placed in an adoptive home, and after her second child, Sean, was placed with the Brook family, it was thought at social services that the best placement for Hope would be with her half-brother in the Brook home. The biological mother agreed with the placement.

Mrs. Brook reported that initially Hope experienced all-over tremors and needed to be tightly swaddled in a receiving blanket. The child screamed and cried constantly, and there was almost nothing they could do to calm her. She was described by her foster mother as insatiable for food. Mrs. Brook reported that the left side of Hope's body would become so stiff and rigid that it couldn't move. There was no position that Hope was comfortable: not stomach, back, or side. Hope also did not want to be held or cuddled and would push away whenever they tried. The Brooks finally discovered that by swinging Hope in a vertical movement she was temporarily comforted. Mrs. Brooks reported that only through "love, patience, and incredible will" they got through those first months.

When Hope was three months of age, Mrs. Brook contacted social services for a screening for possible intervention services for Hope. The consultant for the county health department's early intervention office conducted an initial screening at the Brooks' home. Hope was found to need a full evaluation in the areas of cognition, speech-language, physical therapy, and occupational therapy.

The Brook family enrolled Hope in an early intervention program to address her needs, and from the time of her entrance to the program, she made good progress. She adjusted to the program, the staff, routines, and therapists. Hope seemed to become more relaxed and was progressing in her speech and language. Hope attended the program consistently, and her behaviors were increasingly more and more age appropriate. By her first birthday, Hope's coping behavior was effective more often than not. She had a mild delay in expressive language skills and was at age level in her receptive skills.

By 24 months, Hope appeared to be functioning at near age-appropriate levels for receptive-expressive language skills. At 24 months, Hope transitioned to a toddler class where the teachers reported that she seemed very withdrawn for the first few months in the class. She had a very difficult time adapting to the new class and took several months to "warm up." Most of Hope's difficulties seemed to be in her interactions with adults and the other children. She withdrew to a point where she would refuse to initiate any kind of interaction with an adult or child, or just the opposite, where she would act out, yell, throw a toy, or be totally noncompliant with any request. It took almost 10 months in that class before she was a full participant in group activities such as music and exercises.

At 36 months of age, Hope was evaluated by the educational team that serviced her since entry to the program. Her team of professionals agreed that Hope had made significant progress and no longer required a center-based special educational program. The Brook family, who had almost completed the adoption of Hope at that time, were convinced that the infant intervention program had made a great difference in Hope's life. Mrs. Brook reported that in September a "regular" nursery school would be the place for Hope.

Mrs. Brook reported that Hope was "a love and a beautiful child." She was now able to "talk and move and behave normally, although she still liked to have her own way at times"; Mrs. Brook's main concern for Hope was the possible long-term effects of her drug exposure at birth. At four years of age, Hope, now adopted by the Brook family, entered nursery school and was able to fully participate in all activities with her peers. She was able to cope with her environment and to comply with the demands of both her home and school in an effective manner. Her literacy skills in emerging reading, writing, speaking, and listening were evident in both her home and preschool.

ELEMENTARY SCHOOL

At seven years, four months of life, Hope was a second grade student at the local elementary school. She was the top reading student in the top reading group in her class, and both her teacher and her mother report that she was doing "marvelously." She took gymnastic classes as well as dance classes in tap, jazz and ballet. Her teachers stated she was a "natural." Betty laughed at that remark, knowing the difficult path that Hope had in her first days, months, and years of life. Both her gymnastic teacher and her dance teacher both exclaimed how "flexible and natural" her movements were. Betty did not share with them about the "wired, stiff infant" that came into her life and the years of physical therapy that Hope had from her earliest months. Betty described Hope as an "affectionate, loving joy of a child." She visibly shuddered when she recalled Hope as an infant who could not tolerate her touch and cried insatiably. Hope was now in the second year of Brownies, and she won the Student of the Month award and the Perfect Attendance Award in first grade.

It was during this observation at the Brook home that Betty shared an incident that had recently occurred at home. When Betty and Hope were watching a local news program about a drug arrest, the drug crack cocaine was mentioned several times. Hope looked at Betty in what Betty considered a hostile way and blurted out, "Why did you take me from my real mother?" Betty recalled that she was really shocked since that was the first time Hope had said anything like that to her. Betty, trying to remain as calm and relaxed as she could, explained, "I didn't take you from your mother, Social Services did. Your mother was sick with drugs and was a crack addict. She couldn't take care of you and Sean. You wouldn't want to live with a crack addict, would you?"

Betty said that Hope's face was still very angry looking and in what seemed like a very long time, probably a full minute, Hope just stared at Betty. Seeing Hope's face change from anger to resignation, Hope, in a very calm voice said, "I guess, I will just stay with you in my own house." This exchange with Hope, although Betty felt it was inevitable, was nonetheless disconcerting. Betty asserts that she has told the children all along that they are adopted and has always made their adoption day a "big deal" of celebration in the family. She has explained their story "over and over" to them and has never hidden anything but the most sordid details from them. Betty has explained that she has the social history of their mother and will share it with both Sean and Hope when she feels they will be able to handle it. Betty said that this exchange with this seven-year old was frightening especially the anger she saw in Hope's face and heard in her voice. Betty laughingly said she was "not especially looking forward to Hope's teen-age years."

Hope continued to excel in her third grade class and seemed to be able to cope very well with the demands of school. When she entered fourth grade there was a dramatic change in her school behavior. The demands of fourth grade and the difficulty of the teacher–child interaction proved to be very challenging to Hope. She could no longer seem to concentrate and was no longer able to pay attention to her school work and learn in her usual efficient manner. It was determined that she might need medication in order for her to pay attention to her teacher and her school work. It was determined that she had attention deficit hyperactivity disorder (ADHD) and was placed on medication to help her cope. This disorder is largely characterized by trouble focusing, an inability to pay attention to details, and disorganization. The use of the medications (Concerta and Adderall) was not an easy decision since all were concerned with her previous prenatal exposure and the possible negative effects, but Hope seemed to calm down and excel in her work again. Hope reports that the medication helped her to "really focus." She was again able to cope and continued to be an excellent student for the rest of her elementary school days.

ADOLESCENCE

For Hope, her middle school years were very productive for her, especially in her joining of ROTC. She feels that this was just what she needed to help her with her self-discipline and her need for structure. In eighth and ninth grade, she became assistant flight commander, then flight commander and squadron commander. She continued with her ROTC work in high school where she became a communication officer and led her drill team to win the first place medal. Her friends were chosen very carefully, since she wanted to be with people who were focused and high achieving. She worked part time in the field of retail, since she was very much interested in the field for her future. While completing all of this, she managed to win the scholastic award in eleventh grade and in senior year won the senior athlete award as well as the Daughters of the American Revolution Award. Hope Graduated from high school in the top 15% of her class with a 3.2 grade average.

THE COLLEGE YEARS

With her excellent grades and accomplishments, Hope was accepted to a private four-year college and was able to become a business major and again distinguished herself in her work. Hope excelled in her classes and was able to conquer college and successfully adapt to all the demands of college life. She is very grateful to her parents and credits them with being her driving force in her success. Over the years her parents were able to adopt five other children (all prenatally exposed), and her family is filled with pride and admiration for her as she is for them.

CONCLUSION

In a rush to judgment over twenty years ago, a child born with a positive toxicology to crack cocaine was seen as "doomed and damned" and given up as lost (Mayes et al., 1992). Subsequent research by Karmel and Gardiner (1996) did find that attentive state deficits were found in these children, and more recent studies with adolescents have findings consistent with findings among younger children. The prenatal cocaine exposure increases the risk for small but significant differences in adolescent functioning (Howes, Berger, Scaletti, & Black, 2013). Other recent research has linked risk of cardiometabolic disease in late adolescence to prenatally exposed children (Messiah, Lipshultz, & Bandstra, 2011). Subsequent research on these children and young adults is crucial to determine long-term risks of cocaine ingestion during pregnancy.

This longitudinal case study of Hope is a "best case" scenario and cannot be generalized to all children born with a positive toxicology to cocaine, but it is important to understand that a facilitative care-giving environment is critical. This child, thought of as one of many who had no chance of living a full and successful life, is a testament to what is possible. A child prenatally drug exposed, although initially delayed in development, through a stable foster home, early intervention, and a supportive, facilitative environment, may be able to overcome the initial insult and become a highly functioning, successful member of her community. The young woman who accepted her four-year degree diploma with grace and dignity is a reminder to us all that emerging adulthood may show us some delightful surprises indeed!

REFERENCES

Brazelton, T. B., Koslowski, B., & Marten, M. (1974). The origins of reciprocity: The early mother-infant interaction. In M. Lewis & A. Rosenblum (Eds.), *The effects of the infant on its caregiver* (pp. 335–341). New York, NY: Wiley.

Buckingham-Howes, S., Shafer Berger, S., Scaletti, L. A., & Black, M.M. (2013). Systematic review of prenatal cocaine exposure and adolescent development. *Pediatrics, 131*(6), E1917–E1936.

Chasnoff, I. J. (1989). Drugs and women: Establishing a standard of care. *Annual of the New York Academy of Science, 562*, 208–214.

Chasnoff, I. J., Burns, W. J., & Schnoll, S. H. (1985). Cocaine use in pregnancy. *New England Journal of Medicine, 313*, 666–669

Eyler, F. D., Behnke, M., Conlon, M., Woods, N. S., & Wobie, K. (1998). Birth outcomes from a prospective matched study of prenatal crack/cocaine use: Interactive and dose effects on neurobehavioral assessment. *Pediatrics, 101*, 237–241.

Finkelstein, N. (1994). Treatment issues for alcohol and drug dependent pregnant and parenting women. *Health and Social Work, 19*, 7–15.

Hawley, T. L., Halle, T., Drasin, R., & Thomas, N. (1995). Children of addicted mothers: Effects of the "crack epidemic on the caregiving environment and the developing preschoolers." *American Journal of Orthopsychiatry, 65*, 364–379.

Karmel, B., & Gardner, J. (1996). Prenatal cocaine exposure on arousal-modulated attention during the neonatal period. *Developmental Psychobiology, 29*, 463–480.

Lester, B., LaGasse, L., Friere, K., & Brunner, S. (1996). Studies of cocaine-exposed infants. In I. Wetherington, V. Smerglio, & L. Finnegan (Eds.), *Behavior studies of drug-exposed offspring* (Methodological Issues in Human and Animal Research, CNIDA Research Monograph 164, NIH, 96-4105, pp.175–210). Rockville, MD: National Institute of Health.

Lutiger, B., Graham, K., Einerson, T. R., & Koren, G. (1991). Relationship between gestational cocaine use and pregnancy outcomes: A meta-analysis. *Teratology, 44,* 405–414.

Mayes, L., Granger, R., Bornstein, M., & Zuckerman, B. (1992). The problem of prenatal cocaine exposure: A rush to judgement. *JAMA, 267,* 406–408.

Messiah, S. E., Lipshultz, S. E., Miller, T. L., Accornero, V. H., & Bandstra, E. S. (2012). Assessing latent effects of prenatal cocaine exposure on growth and risk of cardiometabolic disease in late adolescence: Design and methods. *International Journal of Pediatrics,* 1–13. doi: 10.1155/2012/467918.

Rist, M. (1990). The shadow children. *The American School Board Journal, 117,* 18–24.

Vogel, G. (1997). Cocaine wreaks subtle damage on developing brains. *Science, 278*(5335), 38–40.

Volpe, J. (1992). Effects of cocaine use on the fetuses. *The New England Journal of Medicine, 32,* 397–407.

CHAPTER 13

MY BODY, MY BIOGRAPHY

The Use of Narratives of Self-Injury as a Path for Healing

Susan Anne Conte

In my work with young women who self-injure, I searched for a metaphor to describe what they have taught me. Recently, that metaphor appeared in bold letters on a sign in The Gap's showcase window: *My Body. My Biography.* There it was: a way to understand the meaning of self-injury from the perspective of the young women's life stories.

This chapter emphasizes the value of a narrative to unlock the meaning of self-injury. Highlights from the stories of three women who self-injure—Maya, Stacey, and Ariel—will be used to illustrate the power of narrative. Excerpts from the experiences of Heather and Stacey will underscore the role of professional help in the treatment of self-injury.

THE POWER OF A NARRATIVE

Telling one's story, in the safety of a therapeutic relationship, can empower its author to find her own path for healing and wholeness. The process of

Adolescence in the 21st Century, pages 209–224

narrative is, in itself, therapeutic. In telling her story, the narrator creates space between herself and the symptom, "externalizing" it. In so doing, the symptom no longer identifies her (e.g., as a self-injurer, or worse, as a "cutter"). Within the therapeutic process, the author of the story can begin to internalize her sense of personal agency. The author sees herself in an active rather than in a passive role in her story (Hoffman & Kress, 2008; Muelenkamp, 2006; Smith & Nylund, 1997). It is the listener's response to the story, with interest and empathy, and without judgment, that further empowers the narrator to reframe her story and to tap her own resources for healing. By highlighting the power of an individual's narrative as a path for healing, it is not my intention to devalue the range of effective interventions for self-injury. What I am suggesting is that listening to a patient's narrative as it unfolds over time is a valuable experience for the narrator as well as for the listener.

In order to provide a framework for the young women's narratives, I will give a brief overview of the research literature on self-injury. I will introduce excerpts from the stories of young women to illustrate the unique meaning and function of self-injury, and to provide guidance for parents, teachers, and helping professionals who struggle to understand this puzzling—and frightening—behavior.

REVIEWING THE RESEARCH, DEFINING SELF-INJURY

Self-injury is not a "fad." Under other names—"moderate-superficial self-mutilation," "delicate self-cutting," "deliberate self-harm" (DSH), "self-harm behavior" (SHB), "trauma-re-enactment syndrome" (TRS), "self-inflicted violence" (SIV), "self-injurious behavior" (SIB), and so on—self-injury has been in the research literature for close to a century. In this chapter, the term "self-injury" will be used to reflect the name articulated by the adolescent girls and young women who engage in it.

The research demonstrates a spectrum of self-injurious behaviors (Favazza, 1996; Menninger, 1938). For our purposes, "self injury" will be limited to self-cutting or self-burning that is intentional but not suicidal. It typically begins in adolescence and has a prolonged duration. For some, self-injury can be addictive, due in part to the release of endogenous opioids and endorphins stimulated by pain (Winchel & Stanley, 1991). Although it has increased among "mainstream" adolescents and young adults, self-injury is not culturally sanctioned, nor does it include tattooing or piercing. It is precisely because of its adolescent onset and chronicity that self-injury is of critical concern for clinicians, healthcare professionals, teachers, and family members who seek to help young people to prevent and/or to decrease the behavior.

Self-injury has been studied among males and females in diverse populations and in varied settings, including in correctional facilities, in boarding schools, in hospital emergency rooms, in drug treatment facilities, and, most commonly, in psychiatric hospitals. Because research indicates that self-injury is more common in females and that it may persist for many years in a woman's life, this chapter will focus exclusively on teenage girls and young women in the general population. For the sake of simplicity, the term "young women" will denote females ranging in age from 13–22 years. Throughout this chapter, the author's qualitative (interview-based) research and narrative approach to clinical work will inform our discussion.

PREVALENCE OF SELF-INJURY AMONG ADOLESCENTS

In a lead article in *The New York Times Magazine* in the late 1990s, the journalist J. Egan hailed self-injury as "anorexia of the 1990s," implying that the behavior would become an "epidemic" that defied treatment (Egan, 1997). Although experts report that the prevalence of self-injury in the United States has increased by 150% in the last 20 years, these estimates are based on diverse populations and may not reflect self-injury among adolescents (Walsh, 2012). A recent summary of research studies on adolescents who self-injure indicates that approximately 15% of teenagers report "some form" of self-injury (Kerr, Muehlenkamp, & Turner, 2010, p. 241).

THE IMPETUS FOR MY WORK: THE FRANTIC FIVE

They called themselves the *Frantic Five*. They were intelligent, popular high school students, involved in sports and in community activities. Not one of them had a psychiatric history. Each of them was escorted to my office by a friend, a horrified teacher, a frustrated coach, or a desperate parent. As she rolled up her sleeve, one after the other revealed a series of self-inflicted cuts or burns. In my years of work with adolescents, this was something new. My administrator further fueled my need to understand this growing issue in our community with her direct challenge: "Why are they hurting themselves? Make them stop!"

It was the *Frantic Five* who drove me to study self-injury. Countless other teenage girls showed up in my office with self-inflicted cuts and burns in the months and years that followed. I consulted with colleagues, read, and went to conferences. I learned that I was not alone. None of us had any idea how to "manage" what we were seeing.

CONTRIBUTING FACTORS AND
FUNCTIONS OF SELF-INJURY

In order to treat a symptom or behavior, it is essential to look for underlying issues or contributing factors. The research on young women who self-injure reveals that self-injury is a multidetermined behavior. That is, it is not directly caused by any one factor: for example, developmental issues, childhood trauma, family problems, peer influences, the media, or a single psychiatric diagnosis. The research illustrates multiple functions for self-injury, including these: a preverbal means of communication, a manipulative or attention-seeking gesture, a means of expressing emotional pain, or an insignia of membership in a secret peer group (Conte, 2004). What I have learned from listening to young women who self-injure is just that: It is important to listen. Their unique stories reveal what contributes to self-injury, what it means to them, and what effect it has on their lives.

A "Profile of the Typical Self-Injurer?"

Women who self-injure have been the focus of research since the early 1900s (Emerson, 1914). Based on a single case, Emerson's profile of the typical self-injurer, the unmarried young Caucasian woman with conflicts about her sexuality and problems with her menses was, for close to a century, the stereotype for women who self-injure. Emerson started another trend in the literature. His report of his patient's self-injuring behavior became a template for the phenomenology—or "lived experience"—of "stages of abuse," namely: a "precipitating event, escalating dysphoria, efforts to forestall the self-mutilation, the self-abuse, and the aftermath" (Weber, 1998, p. 37). In my clinical work with young women since the late 1990s, I have learned that there is *no* "profile of the typical self-injurer" and that the template does not fit their unique experiences.

Young Women in the General Population

Although the literature is replete with research on women who self-injure, the majority is based on small samples of psychiatric inpatients ("wrist cutters"). The young women who are the focus of our concern here are our daughters, students, and clients. To date, studies of these young women are few. However, there have been four studies conducted recently with young women in the general (nonclinical) population, based on large populations drawn from middle schools, high school, and colleges. These will be summarized here as relevant to our interests.

Ross and Health's (2002) study found that 13.9% of the 440 high school students surveyed reported self-injury. Of those, 64% were females; 36% were males. Of particular concern is that 59% of the self-injurers reported that they began to self-injure in seventh and eighth grades, reinforcing the observation that self-injury is beginning among younger-age children. In Whitlock, Eckenrode, and Silverman's (2006) research on 3,069 college students, 17% reported self-injury; 56.3% were females and 43.7%, males. In this study, the mean age of onset was 14–15 years of age with an average duration of 5 years, indicating the chronicity of self-injury. Two studies emphasized childhood risk factors for self-injury. Gratz's (2006) study of 249 college students found that child maltreatment and emotional reactivity contributed to more frequent self-injury in their sample. Hilt, Nolen-Hoeksema, and Cha's (2008) study of public middle school students (n=96) highlighted depressive symptoms and negative peer interactions as risk factors. Although these studies indicate the need for additional large-scale research on community samples, they emphasize four significant hallmarks of self-injury among young people in the general population:

1. that adolescents are beginning to self-injure at younger ages
2. that females self-injure more frequently than their male peers do
3. that both internal (e.g., negative affect) and environmental factors (e.g., child abuse and maltreatment; negative peer interactions) may contribute to self-injury
4. that parents, educators, and helping professionals may assume a key role in teaching young people positive ways to regulate affect and to address destructive environmental influences.

Interpretations of Self-Injury: Why Not Ask the Young Women to Speak for Themselves?

The research literature illustrates countless ways to interpret self-injury. Among them are these: as a "conflict over menstruation and emerging sexuality" (Emerson, 1914; Rosenthal, Rinzler, Wallsh, & Klausner, 1972); as a "defense against suicide," as "localized self-destruction," or "focal suicide" (Menninger, 1938); as a "means to resolve conflict and ease tension" (Gardner & Gardner, 1975; Graff & Mallin, 1976; Pao, 1969); as "sadomasochism" (Cross, 1993); as a symptom of "adolescent developmental breakdown" (Laufer & Laufer, 1989); and as a "female perversion" (Kaplan, 1997). Each one bears the stamp of the researcher's theoretical orientation. Not one of them comes close to the interpretations of young women who self-injure. For me, these studies raised one question: "Why hasn't anyone asked the young women to speak for themselves?"

QUALITATIVE RESEARCH: LEARNING
FROM THE YOUNG WOMEN

That question was the impetus for my qualitative research and continues to direct my clinical practice. In my study, the young women shared details of their self-injury: precipitating factors, its effect on them and on others, who/what helped them. It was one of the most powerful experiences of my life.

In qualitative research, the emphasis is on understanding a little-known phenomenon, based on in-depth, repeated interviews with a small sample. The respondents in my study were 10 female college students who reported at least one experience of nonsuicidal self-injury since age 13. Consistent with research findings, each young woman reported that she began to self-injure in adolescence: the youngest, at age 12; the oldest, at 18, as a college freshman. Also consistent, and particularly disturbing, was that each one spoke about self-injuring over the course of many years. At the time of their interviews, 9 out of the 10 reported self-injuring for an average of 7 years. In response to my naïve question, "What helped you to stop?" all but one responded: "Who said anything about stopping?"

WHY TEENAGE GIRLS?

The young women spoke candidly about what contributed to their self-injury and about what—or who—helped them to decrease it. They reflected on what role gender and adolescent development may have played in their self-injury. Each one debunked the research that at puberty, teenage girls were more likely to self-injure than boys because they felt a lack of control over their bodies' emerging secondary sex characteristics (Cross, 1993). When I asked them what role their bodily changes had in their beginning to self-injure as adolescents, they all agreed: "That had *nothing* to do with it!" I also asked them about feminist interpretations of self-injury—specifically as a protest against the objectification of their bodies by the dominant (male) culture. They resounded: "No! That's not it!" I was at a loss. So I asked them what *they* thought. "Maya" was forthright. She explained that it was what was going on in her life as an adolescent, and not the bodily changes or the fear of loss of control over her body that contributed to her self-injury. She summed it up this way:

> For me, "adolescence" as in fitting in, being a part of a group, having friends, being cool was a part of it. It was not like ... adolescence as in, "I'm growing up and I hate my body." I mean, we cared about our bodies. We worked out; we liked to look good. So it wasn't about "I can't control what's happening to my body!" It was "I can't control what's happened in my life or what's going on in my family!" (Conte, 2004, p. 145)

LEARNING FROM THE YOUNG WOMEN:
MAYA, STACEY, AND ARIEL

The young women's personal experiences discredited the "profile of the typical self injurer" and emphasized that each person's struggle with self-injury is unique. In addition, the young women's narratives challenged existing theories about the meaning and function of self-injury. They expanded my understanding about what contributes to self-injury and pointed to paths for healing. The stories of three young women will be retold in some detail here. Each cited unique factors that contributed to their self-injury: Maya's traumatic experience of the sudden death of a parent, Stacey's self-hatred and internalized homophobia regarding her sexual orientation, and Ariel's self-punishment for childhood sexual abuse.

Maya began to self-injure when she was 16, one month after the death of her father. The youngest of his 6 daughters, Maya described herself as "Daddy's Little Girl:" She said:

> We were very close. My mom worked a lot, so my father was always around. My dad would cook us dinner.... He was always there; he would pick us up from school.... I think that his death was such a shock and so... unexpected that it hit me so hard. That's when I started cutting myself and wanting to hurt myself. (Conte, 2004, p. 141)

Maya's self-injury was symbolic for her. She described it as "a way of remembering my father:"

> Not that I would like... necessarily want... people to say: "You know, your father died," I just wanted.... It just wasn't brought up at home.... So I wanted to remember him every day and I was afraid that if I didn't do something, I would forget... Forget my father. So I would carve his initials into my arms... and my thighs.... So cutting was a way to remember him.... It makes sense to me now. It didn't then. (Conte, 2004, p. 174)

Maya's high school counselor suggested that she join the school's bereavement group. She gave the group credit for helping her to self-injure less frequently. "The other kids understood. It helped me to talk about my father; to cry about him. Sometimes I didn't know *what* I was feeling. No one there thought I was crazy. Although I kept cutting, I didn't need to do it so much. I'd lost if I didn't have my friends" (Conte, 2004, p. 182).

DISCOVERING "NEW" RISK FACTORS

The young women's stories shed light on risk factors involved in self-injury. Two of these were not present in the research literature. The first is that the sharing of cutting implements and the exchange of bodily fluids during a cutting ritual increase the risk for contracting blood-borne pathogens. The second is that lesbian, bisexual or transgender women may be at higher risk for self-injury than are their heterosexual peers.

Maya's story revealed a serious risk factor in self-cutting. She came to the surprising discovery herself while she was telling me about a "secret group" who self-injured together in high school:

> ...We used to do it in Art class...in a group, when everyone was working so they weren't looking up. And you kind of...it doesn't take that long. You just take the *Exacto-knife* and you just go: *SShhhht! SShhhht! (She demonstrated on her upper arm)* and then you pass it to the girl next to you. Everybody takes a turn; one at a time...*Maya looked up and said:* Oh, my *God!* What did I say? It just hit me! HIV! Hepatitis! What were we *thinking?* (Conte, 2004, p. 160, italics added)

Stacey spoke about her girlfriend who also cut and burned (branded) herself. One morning, she told me about an episode that occurred the previous night:

> My girlfriend and I were together last night and we were getting little drunk and "in the mood." So, I asked her to cut me, and then I cut her. And then we just sort of...sucked each other's blood. It was a high...like an orgasm...high. It was amazing. Even though it hurt, it was still kind of...kind of romantic. My guy friend and I used to do this together. It sounds weird, but we both "get off" on it. (Conte, 2004, p. 169)

The young women's reports of self-injuring with others emphasize the need to include the sharing of cutting implements and the exchange of bodily fluids (e.g., blood) in assessment protocols for young women who self-injure.

LESBIAN AND BISEXUAL YOUNG WOMEN WHO SELF-INJURE

The research literature indicates that adolescents and young adults who self-identify as gay, lesbian, bisexual, or transgender (GLBT) more frequently demonstrate at-risk and suicidal behaviors than do their heterosexual peers (D'Augelli & Herschenberger, 1993; Gay, Lesbian & Straight Education Network, 2012; Herschenberger & D'Augelli, 1995; Pilkinton & D'Augelli, 1995, Remafedi, 1987). Some of the young lesbian and bisexual women I have counseled have spoken about harassment, verbal abuse, and internalized homophobia as contributing to their negative self-esteem and to self-injury. Stacey traced the onset and duration of her self-injuring to her experience of herself as the target of her peers' verbal abuse in early adolescence. She recalled:

> ... So I started cutting myself when I was 13. That's probably when I found out I was a lesbian. I wasn't happy about that. And someone I trusted "outed" me in school. And I wasn't even o.k. with *myself* at that time. You know? ... Junior high! The kids were *mean!* And it's not like anybody *physically* hurt me, but I didn't feel safe there. Every day, kids would write things on my locker, like "Lesbo!" They would talk about me: "Don't sit with her. She'll attack you. You'll turn into a lesbian!" ... In the hallways, they would yell out "Yo, Dyke! Butch!" Those words hurt a lot. And I *hated myself* for being a lesbian. And I started to make up excuses for not wanting to go to school. My mother finally took me to a shrink. Guess what the shrink said? ... that I had "school phobia!" *What?*? And it just got worse. A lot of the same kids went to my high school. I could *never* fit in. And I even had transfer out of my first college for the same reason: not too "gay-friendly." Now I'm 21 and I'm still cutting myself. *Shows me scars from self-cutting and self-inflicted cigarette burns.* And now I have a girlfriend. She cuts, too. We're trying to help each other to stop. (Conte, 2004, p. 148)

Stacey' story emphasizes that, although it is well-documented that persons who are gay, lesbian, bisexual, or transgender are at higher risk for self-injurious and suicidal behaviors than are their heterosexual peers, additional research is needed on lesbian and bisexual women who self-injure. Of particular concern for us are the internalized and environmental factors that negatively affect the young woman's sense of self and create vulnerability for self-cutting and/or self-burning. Such findings will be invaluable to us to guide preventive and clinical interventions.

WOMEN AND SEXUAL ABUSE

The body of research on women who self-injure emphasizes childhood sexual abuse as a major contributing factor (Alderman, 1997; Briere & Gil, 1998; van der Kolk, 1987; van der Kolk, Perry, & Herrman, 1991; Vig, 1999). Although we cannot assume that all women who self-injure have been sexually abused, it is plausible that prevalence of self-injury among women may be attributed to the overrepresentation of women among persons who report sexual abuse. It is particularly important for us to assess for sexual abuse when counseling young women who self-injure.

Ariel's story illustrates the dynamic interplay between childhood sexual abuse, negative self-image, feeling powerless or lacking a sense of self-agency, and self-injury. At 20, Ariel came for counseling for help with anxiety that frequently led her to the emergency room "because I feel like I'm having a heart attack." She said that self-injury worked for her as a "quick fix," giving her temporary relief from "feeling panicky." Unlike the young women whose scarred wrists were visible, Ariel's self-injury was hidden. She had begun to cut her abdomen and upper thighs when she was a freshman in high school. Looking back, she explained, "When I started, I think it was a way that I could punish myself for my mother's drinking and wanting to 'off herself" with pills. I couldn't do anything to stop her, so I felt that it was my fault."

Towards the end of a year of working together, Ariel mentioned that she had "something I want to talk about but just can't." It was around that time that Ariel had become involved in a serious relationship. When the relationship became sexual, she started to have nightmares. We began to work with her dreams, as she tried to externalize them, writing about them in her journal or doing artwork to "get it out of my head."

Ariel's mother's abusive marriage ended in divorce when Ariel was two years old. Her mother got a weekend job and Ariel's father, who had moved back with his parents, agreed to take care of his daughter while her mother was working. During the week, Ariel hated to be separated from her mother, fearing that "something terrible'" would happen to her. When Ariel was in second grade, her teacher noticed that Ariel frequently masturbated in the classroom. She suggested that Ariel's mother take her to a counselor. Convinced that Ariel would "grow out of it," her mother didn't follow up. Ariel was "a good girl and a good student."

Ariel remembered: "As the weekends came close, I would scream and cry and refuse to go to my grandparents' house. I was terrified to tell my mother why I didn't want to go back there." Ariel was 20 years old before she could reveal the secret that she had been sexually abused by her grandfather beginning when she was two until she was nine years old. He would lock her in the bathroom, climb into the tub with her, and molest her while her grandmother stood by and watched. He threatened to kill Ariel's mother if she ever told anyone. So she never did. The abuse stopped when he died.

Telling her story was agonizing for Ariel. As she slowly connected her self-injury to what she had experienced and to her need to punish herself, her self-injury became less frequent and less severe. In the process, Ariel and I experimented with different forms of expressive therapy to help her to work through the trauma: drawing, painting, and writing poetry. She took a class in kick-boxing to help her to release her rage about her abuse. After working together for several months, she decided that she wanted to tell her mother. She asked for my help. We invited her mother to my office. Much to Ariel's relief, her mother believed her. One at a time, Ariel and her mother told key people in the family what had happened. Her mother eventually sought help for her alcoholism and Ariel joined Al-Anon. On campus, Ariel participated in *Take Back the Night* and painted messages on t-shirts for the *Clothesline Project* in solidarity with women survivors of sexual abuse and rape. Ariel graduated from college with honors. She now teaches children with special needs. She no longer self-injures.

WHO OR WHAT HELPED?

Consistent with the research on "help seeking," the young women confirmed that few young people in the general population seek professional help for self-injury (Brain, Haines, & Williams, 1998; Di Brino, 1999; Kerr et al., 2010). In my study, only two out of ten young women sought counseling. What is encouraging to note, however, is that the young women spoke positively about their high school or college counselors as the first professionals with whom they spoke about self-injury. Heather reflected on her experience with her high school counselor:

> By the time I was a junior in high school, my self-injuring . . . had been going on for four years and no one had called me on it. When my friend found out, she dragged me to the school guidance counselor. I had no idea how the counselor was going to respond. I was fearful . . . that maybe she would think I was crazy and I would end up in some hospital in lock-down. But she responded . . . with support . . . and understanding. She was like, "O.k., I see this is happening." And she also explained that we needed more intervention. The situation had increased in severity. We needed more help, so she had to get my parents involved. But the counselor always made it a point . . . to let me know that she was there to support me and to help me to follow through with the situation. (Conte, 2004, p. 188)

COUNTERTRANSFERENCE: A WORD FOR COUNSELORS

The literature indicates that countertransference can be a serious obstacle to maintaining a therapeutic relationship with a person who self-injures (Rayner, Allen, & Johnson, 2005). Countertransference, a counselor's unconscious reaction to a client and/or symptom, rooted in unresolved conflicts or issues of her/his own, can compromise a counselor's objectivity and her ability to focus on the client's needs. In treating self-injury, additional factors may add to a counselor's negative reaction to the client's symptoms, including fear, lack of knowledge, misdiagnosis, lack of experience, or the need to control the behavior. A counselor's fearful, uninformed, or negative response may directly contribute to a young person's decision to terminate counseling prematurely. Kristy, a college freshman, explained that her counselor's reaction to self-injury was an obstacle to continuing in therapy. She said:

> When my mother found out, she took me to a counselor. . . . But even my counselor at home . . . when she found out about my self-injury . . . she didn't want to talk about it. When I told her she said, "Well, that's over now, *right?* . . . Well you *stopped* that, right? . . . So she gave me the impression that she didn't want to hear about it. I think it scared her. She didn't want to go near that at all. So I never went back to counseling after that. (Conte, 2004, p. 195)

SUMMARY: GUIDELINES FOR SCHOOL COUNSELORS, PARENTS, AND HELPING PROFESSIONALS

The chapter has focused on the importance of narratives of self-injury in the healing process. Based on our discussion, I would like to conclude by offering some suggestions for those who are concerned about young people who self-injure:

1. "Watch your language": Because one of the tasks of adolescence is identity formation, it is crucial for us to avoid referring to a young person as a "cutter" or as a "self-injurer." The use of such descriptors may confirm the individual's identifying herself by her symptom and may also contribute to "normalizing" the behavior.

2. Avoid groups: Another key factor in adolescent development is the need to belong to a peer group. Maya's description of her high school bereavement group illustrates that groups are powerful treatment modalities, especially for adolescents. Groups such as these reduce isolation, provide for healthy social interaction, and model positive strategies for addressing varied issues. For these same reasons, groups are *not* indicated for young persons who self-injure. Recent research on the effect of websites and social media about self-injury suggests that these vehicles may be powerful means of social learning, contributing to the prevalence of self-injury in the general population (Lewis, Heath, St. Denis, & Noble, 2011). Closer to home, although members of the Frantic Five demonstrated the effect of social learning, each one of them denied that "friends who self-injure" had anything to do with their own self-injury: "I'm my own person! I don't believe in peer pressure." Although it was beyond the scope of this chapter to study social learning and modeling behavior—observed directly or through the media—as a factor in the increased prevalence of self-in-

jury among general populations of young women, it warrants further research and our clinical awareness.

3. Develop large-scale educational programs: In consulting with parent groups, faculty members, and staff in various middle and high schools, I suggest that schools develop workshops to educate parents, teachers, and students about adolescent developmental issues and risk factors. Finding collaborative ways to promote mental health, to teach positive strategies to regulate affect, and to address negative environmental factors are key to preventing the onset of self-injury as a coping mechanism.

4. Establish a school-based protocol: As school and community leaders, counselors are important resource persons. School counselors need to be prepared to offer resource materials and referrals for individual and family counseling.

5. Working with parents: Because students in our middle schools and high schools are minors, it is essential to involve parents in helping young people who self-injure. Since it typically falls to the school counselor to engage the parent, counselors need to create a protocol for addressing self-injury in the school environment. Counselors need to alert parents to notice possible "warning signs" of self-injury, including the wearing of long-sleeved shirts or long pants in hot weather, or the appearance of unexplained injuries. In the high school in which I have consulted, I have recommended that counselors and administrators create a policy to collaborate with the school nurse and the student's parents. In order to prevent "normalizing" or inadvertently contributing to direct modeling of self-injury, the behavior is addressed as a health issue. The counselor does not "treat" self-injury in the school, but engages the school nurse who notifies the student's parent and makes a referral for psychological evaluation and treatment using professional resources in the community.

6. School counselors: "It's all about you": Consistent with the research, our clinical experience confirms that the majority of young persons in the general population do not seek professional help for self-injury (Brain et al., 1998; Di Brino, 1999; Kerr et al., 2010). School and college-based counselors continue to report that they are the first adults with whom young people speak about self-injury. In this role, it is essential that school counselors be well-educated about self-injury, its contributing factors, and effective strategies to lessen the behavior.

7. Counselors' self-awareness and self-care: In order to strengthen our skill in working with young people, it is essential for us as counselors to practice self-care as we engage in a therapeutic process that may be time-intensive and challenging. By being self-reflective and aware of countertransference, a counselor facilitates the therapeutic alli-

ance. By availing ourselves of the techniques we offer to our clients (e.g., for relaxation or for affect regulation), we, as counselors, can add to our own repertoires for self-care. In addition, as we consult with colleagues, participate in professional conferences, and keep up with more recent community-based studies, we can strengthen our knowledge base and continue to inform our clinical practice. Attending to self-care as we attend to the needs of our clients will enable us to continue to provide the safe space in which the storyteller and the listener may continue to learn from this valuable experience.

REFERENCES

Alderman, T. (1997). *The scarred soul: Understanding and ending self-inflicted violence.* Oakland, CA: New Harbinger.

Brain, K., Haines, J., & Williams, C. L. (1998). The psychophysiology of self-mutilative behavior: A comparison of current and recovered self-mutilators. In R. Kosky (Ed.), *Suicide prevention: The global context* (pp. 211–222). New York, NY: Plenum.

Briere, J., & Gil, E. (1991). The long-term effects of sexual abuse: A review and synthesis. *New Directions for Mental Health Services, 51,* 3–13.

Conte, S. A. (2004). Speaking for themselves: A qualitative study of young women who self-injure. New York University School of Social Work, NY. *Dissertation Abstracts International, Section A: Humanities and Social Sciences, 65*(01), 286 A (UMI No. 3119926)

Cross, L. W. (1993). Body and self in feminine development: Implications for eating disorders and delicate self-mutilation. *Bulletin of the Menninger Clinic, 57*(1), 41–68.

D'Augelli, A. R., & Herschenberger, S. L. (1993). Lesbian, gay, and bisexual youth in community settings: Personal challenges and mental health problems. *American Journal of Community Psychology, 21,* 421–448.

Di Brino, C. J. (1999). *Self-mutilation in adolescence.* Unpublished doctoral dissertation, Adler School of Professional Psychology, Chicago.

Egan, J, (1997, July 27). The thin red line. *The New York Times Magazine,* pp. 21–25, 34, 40, 43–44, 48.

Emerson, L. E. (1914). The case of Miss A.: A preliminary report of a psychoanalytic study and treatment of a case of self-mutilation. *The Psychoanalytic Review, 1,* 41–54.

Favazza, A. (1996). *Bodies under siege.* Baltimore, MD: Johns Hopkins.

Gardner A. R., & Gardner, A.J. (1975). Self-mutilation, obsessionality, and narcissism. *British Journal of Psychiatry, 127,* 127–132.

Gay, Lesbian & Straight Education Network (GLSEN). (2012) *Strengths and silences.* New York, NY: Author.

Graff, H., & Mallin, R. (1967). The syndrome of the wrist cutter. *American Journal of Psychiatry, 124*(1), 36–42.

Gratz, K. (2006). Risk factors for deliberate self-harm among female college students: The role and interaction of childhood maltreatment, emotional inexpressivity, and affect intensity/reactivity. *American Journal of Orthopsychiatry, 76*(2), 238–250.

Herschenberger, S. L., & D'Augelli, A. R. (1995). The impact of victimization on the mental health and suicidality of lesbian, gay, and bisexual youth. *Developmental Psychology, 31,* 65–74.

Hilt, L. M., Nolen-Hoeksema, S., & Cha, C. B. (2008). Non-suicidal self-injury in adolescent girls: Moderators of the distress-function relationship. *Journal of Consulting and Clinical Psychology, 76,* 63–71.

Hoffman, R., & Kress, V. (2008). Narrative therapy and non-suicidal self-injurious behavior: Externalizing the problem and internalizing personal agency. *Journal of Humanistic Counseling, Education, and Development, 47*(2), 157–172.

Kaplan, L. J. (1997). *Female perversions.* Northvale, NJ: Jason Aronson.

Kerr, P., Muehlenkamp, J. J., & Turner, J. (2010). Non-suicidal self-injury: A review of current research for family medicine and primary care physicians. *Journal of the American Board of Family Medicine, 23,* 240–259.

Laufer, M., & Laufer, M. E. (Eds.). (1989). *Developmental breakdown and psychoanalytic treatment in adolescence: A psychoanalytic view.* New Haven, CT: Yale University Press.

Lewis, S. P., Heath, N. L., St. Denis, J. M., & Noble, R. (2011). The scope of non-suicidal self-injury on *You Tube. Pediatrics, 127,* 552–557.

Menninger, K. (1938). *Man against himself.* New York, NY: Harcourt, Brace.

Muehlenkamp, J. J. (2006). Empirically supported treatments and general therapy guidelines for non-suicidal self-injury. *Journal of Mental Health Counseling, 28,* 166–185.

Nock, M. K., & Prinstein, M. J. (2004). A functional approach to the assessment of self-mutilative behavior. *Journal of Consulting and Clinical Psychology, 72,* 885–890.

Pao, P. (1969). The syndrome of delicate self-cutting. *British Journal of Medical Psychiatry, 42,* 195–206.

Pilkington, N. W., & D'Augelli, A. R. (1995). Victimization of lesbian, gay, and bisexual youth in community settings. *Journal of Community Psychology, 23,* 33–56.

Remafedi, G. (1987). Adolescent homosexuality: Psychosocial and medical implications. *Pediatrics, 79,* 331–337.

Rayner, G., Allen, S., & Johnson, M. (2005). Countertransference and self-injury: a cognitive behavioural cycle. *Journal of Advanced Nursing, 50, 1,* 12–19.

Rosenthal, R., Rinzler, C., Wallsh, R., & Klausner, K. (1972).Wrist-cutting syndrome: The meaning of a gesture. *American Journal of Psychiatry, 128*(11), 1363–1367.

Ross, S., & Heath, N. (2002). A study of the frequency of self-mutilation in a community sample of adolescents. *Journal of Youth and Adolescence, 31,* 66–77.

Smith, C., & Nylund, D. (Eds.). (1997). *Narrative therapies with children and adolescents.* New York, NY: Guilford.

van der Kolk, B. (1987). *Psychological trauma.* Washington, DC: American Psychiatric Press.

van der Kolk, B., Perry, C., & Herrman, J. K. (1991). Childhood origins of self-destructive behavior. *American Journal of Psychiatry, 148*(2), 1665–1671.

Vig, A. (1999). *Age at sexual abuse onset and its effect on long-term symptomatology.* Unpublished doctoral dissertation. Pacific Graduate School of Psychology, Palo Alto, CA.

Walsh, B. W. (2012). *Treating self-injury* (2nd ed.). New York, NY: Guilford

Weber, M. T. (1998). *Identity construction in the in the interview narratives of self-abusive women.* Unpublished doctoral dissertation, University of Florida, Tampa

Whitlock, J., Eckenrode, J., & Silverman, D. (2006). Self-injurious behavior in a college population. *Pediatrics, 117,* 1939–1948.

Winchel, R. M., & Stanley, M. (1991). Self-injurious behavior: A review of the behavior and biology of self-mutilation. *American Journal of Psychiatry, 148*(3), 306–317.

CHAPTER 14

MUSIC AND EMOTION REGULATION AMONG EMERGING ADULTS IN COLLEGE

Janice C. Stapley

In the current economic climate, with students and parents alike questioning the wisdom of investing in higher education, increasing our understanding of the factors that promote successful college adjustment is crucial. There is a robust body of literature linking emotion regulation skills to overall healthy psychosocial functioning (e.g., Baumeister, Bratslavsky, Muraven, & Tice, 1998; Pulkkinen, Nygren, & Kokko, 2002; Silk, Steinberg, & Morris, 2003). More specifically, Tamir, John, Srivastava, and Gross (2007) found that college students' confidence in their ability to regulate their emotions was associated with their social and emotional functioning. Although emotion regulation is just one type of self-regulation (Baumeister, Zell, & Tice, 2007), it is a central one as demonstrated by longitudinal research (Gerdes & Mallinckrodt, 1994; Stapley & Mizrahi, 2003), and it may indeed be more influential in students' college adjustment than academic indices (Pritchard & Wilson, 2003). Based on Pritchard and Wilson's

Adolescence in the 21st Century, pages 225–238
Copyright © 2014 by Information Age Publishing
All rights of reproduction in any form reserved.

(2006) report of very little change in coping styles across the first semester of college, students may not spontaneously alter their emotion regulation strategies, regardless of how effective they are!

EMOTION REGULATION

The ability to regulate one's emotions can be conceptualized as an individual difference variable consistent with the basic tenets of the construct of emotional intelligence (Mayer & Salovey, 1997). It is important to be able to screen for deficits in college students' emotion regulation strategies because students who have difficulty in regulating their emotions are at risk of adjustment problems. It is also especially crucial based on the findings of Baumeister, Zell, and Tice (2007), who have shown that when students experience negative emotions, these feelings tend to reduce their overall ability to self-regulate and make choices that require delayed gratification.

A developmental, functionalist approach to the study of emotion regulation would suggest that college students' idiosyncratic strategies for managing their feelings and levels of self-awareness of their emotions are due to different childhood influences of family, culture, and gender socialization as well as individual differences in their temperament (Thompson & Meyer, 2007). Thus, by late adolescence, students hold widely differing expectations, some conscious and explicit and some implicit, regarding appropriate emotion expression and experience and their self-efficacy for emotion regulation. Some students might worry that their anxiety or sadness will overwhelm their ability to manage at college whereas others might have a history of feeling out of control of their anger and worry about the repercussions of losing control of their temper. In this chapter, a program of research examining emotion regulation among college students will be presented. A unique aspect of this line of research is that music was used as a window into emotion self-regulation strategies.

Consistent with Thompson and Meyer's (2007) developmental approach, emotion regulation, as examined here, includes managing positive and negative emotions (e.g., enhancing interest or joy as well as holding fear to a manageable level but not denying it). Furthermore, integrating a functionalist approach with the developmental lens sheds light on the complicated nature of evaluating emotion regulation strategies. The debate concerning the utility of regulation strategies such as distraction and rumination exemplifies the complex nature of emotion regulation.

Distraction is not always beneficial. Indeed, those with a functionalist perspective would argue that we should not avoid unpleasant emotions because they give us useful information about situations, such as relationships, that we might want to change (Parrott, 2002). Rumination might provide insight into a problem that we can solve and thus enhance our functioning in the long run (Ciarocco, Vohs, & Baumeister, 2010). However, there is an extensive literature documenting the debilitating effects of excessive rumination when experiencing sadness (Nolen-Hoeksema, Morrow, & Fredrickson, 1993; Nolen-Hoeksema, Stice, Wade, & Bohon, 2007). Although comprehensive discussion of the general efficacy of rumination is beyond the scope of this chapter, the proposition that there may be individual differences and context differences in its utility helps inform the current model of emotion regulation.

Perhaps the most important question is not what type of emotion regulation strategy does a student use most, but rather, does he or she have a feeling of self-efficacy in general about emotion regulation? Tamir et al.'s (2007) longitudinal study revealed that college students' confidence about whether they were able to regulate their emotions was associated with their social functioning during their transition to college. Similarly, research regarding college students' emotion regulation advice to their peers (Stapley, Wolff, & Noonan, 2009) revealed that those who were able to give any suggestions for regulating emotions to their peers were managing better at college than those who could not offer any helpful advice. But what is it about college that strains the self-regulation abilities of young people?

EMERGING ADULTHOOD AND THE COLLEGE TRANSITION

Traditionally aged college students are in emerging adulthood, characterized as a time of instability (Arnett, 2000, 2007). We have argued for more than a decade (Stapley & Scalzo, 2000; Stapley, Stedman, & Botti, 2002) that emerging adults' self-regulation skills in general and emotion regulation skills in particular are challenged by the new developmental tasks with which they are presented when they begin college. More recent adolescent neurological research has shown that during this period, emerging adults' prefrontal lobe executive functions are still developing, so they are not yet as efficient at making decisions as adults (Spear, 2010). Emerging adults in college have very little adult supervision and a relatively unstructured schedule, which is often a drastic change from their daily life in high school. Anecdotally, a question I am often asked at orientation sessions for incoming first year students is, "What do we do in between classes?" Whether they are commuting to college or living in student residence halls on campus, emerging adults have to develop a strategy for balancing their social life with peers, family of origin social obligations, paid employment that may be on or off campus, coursework, and whatever other activities they are involved in such as clubs and sports. They need to make many decisions every day about how to spend their time and how to plan ahead to successfully complete their coursework.

Music as an Emotion Regulation Tool

When this program of research began in 2003, most research on music focused on the possibility that certain music genres, such as heavy metal, might be correlated with problem behavior (e.g., Arnett, 1991). There had also been research conducted on the relationship between psychosocial adjustment and the type or genre of music that adolescents prefer. Schwartz and Fouts (2003) categorized adolescents' musical preferences into heavy, light, or eclectic and reported that those who had the most flexible and eclectic tastes in music seemed to have the fewest adjustment problems.

Analogous to viewing emotional expression and experience in young people as being useful rather than being something to simply be controlled (Haviland-Jones, Gebelt, & Stapley, 1991), this line of research is designed to explore the adaptive uses of music for emotion regulation. The studies summarized in this chapter examine emerging adults' music choices when experiencing distressing feelings such as anger, sadness, and stress. Students' music choices while happy were also examined based on suggestions that regulation of positive emotions predicts psychosocial functioning (e.g., Bandura, Caprara, Barbaranelli, Gerbino, & Pastorelli, 2003). It may be as important for adaptive functioning to know how to induce feelings of happiness as to know how to dampen feelings of anger.

Schwartz and Fouts (2003) speculated that choice of music genre might be used to validate adolescents' feelings or modify their moods. The present line of research does not assess frequency of listening to various genres of music or try to classify students globally by the type of music that they listen to most frequently. This program of research examines students' choice of music described only by tempo, loudness, and emotional tone in relation to their moods and regardless of genre. Rentfrow and Gosling's (2003) questionnaire study of undergraduate students found that music is central in students' lives: they listen to it frequently and they believe that music choices are indicative of personality traits and dispositions. Similarly, Zentner, Grandjean, and Scherer (2008) argued that emotion regulation is a primary reason for listening to music. Greenwood and Long (2009), in discussing all media (e.g., television, reading, movies, as well as music), made a strong case for examining individual differences in mood regulation through the lens of media choice. Here we will use self-report regarding music choice, a particularly salient form of media for emerging adults, as a window into emotion regulation strategies.

Although there are many different emotion regulation strategies, music lends itself particularly well as a marker of two strategies that have been demonstrated to be important predictors of adjustment—namely, rumination and distraction. The purposeful use of music to regulate one's emotions is conceptualized here as an adaptive strategy. Specifically, the decision to either match one's current emotion with music choice or modify it is examined as an indicator of students' tendencies to either ruminate (focus on their current emotion) or distract themselves from their current emotion.

It has been suggested (e.g., Cooper, Frone, Russer, & Mudar, 1995; Magai, 1999) that addictive behaviors often develop because individuals have not learned other strategies to regulate emotion. More recently, Baumeister et al. (2007) expanded on this concept to include the proposition that "emotional distress can be linked to unpleasant self-awareness, and so it could motivate people to reduce or escape from self-awareness" (p. 413). They suggest that this is one of the motivations behind drinking alcohol, especially in the context of drinking when one is sad or angry. Drinking alcohol helps people reduce painful self-awareness. Since emerging adulthood is a highly self-focused time of life (Arnett, 2000), the desire to escape from self-awareness would be expected to be particularly prevalent in this age group. Thus, early studies in this line of research also assessed participants' tendencies toward problem drinking behavior.

MONMOUTH EMOTION LAB FINDINGS

All of the research conducted in the Monmouth Emotion Lab was reviewed and approved by the university's Institutional Review Board for Human Research Ethics and followed the ethical guidelines of the American Psychological Association (APA, 2002). Consistent with the nature of our participant pool, the samples were predominantly European American except as otherwise noted.

Since gender differences in emotion are pervasive (e.g., Brody, 1999; Pulkkinen et al., 2002; Stapley & Haviland, 1989), in the first study (Stapley, 2005) we held gender constant. We examined the relationship between music and emotion regulation among 86 female students (age M =19.93, SD = 3.01) who volunteered to participate from a psychology research pool. The research protocol began with a short demographic questionnaire and a questionnaire about participants' choice of music that assessed whether participants chose songs to match sad, angry, or happy feelings; chose songs to change these emotions; or didn't think their music choices were related to their emotional state.

Participants' problems in living created by their use of alcohol were measured by the Rapid Alcohol Problems Screen (RAPS4-QF, Cherpitel, 2002), which has been found to perform well among young adults, and the Beck Depression Inventory (BDI-II, Beck, Steer, & Brown, 1996) was used to assess depression.

A series of one-way ANOVA's assessing the relationship between music choices while sad, angry, and happy and participants' RAPS4-QF and BDI-II scores were computed. A significant difference in BDI-II scores was found for the item "I would usually listen to loud, upbeat songs to make me happy when I am sad" ($F(1, 83) = 7.63$, $p = .007$, $r_{effect} = .29$). Those who use music to distract themselves when they are sad had *lower* BDI-II scores.

Participants who reported that when they were angry they listen to loud angry songs to match their mood (rumination) had significantly higher problem drinking scores ($F(1, 83) = 4.53$, $p = .04$, $r_{effect} = .23$). Those who agreed with the item "I listen to soft and calming music when angry" (used distraction) had significantly lower problem drinking scores ($F(1,83) = 4.71$, $p = .03$, $r_{effect} = .23$).

Thus, for reports about anger, both rumination and distraction were associated with problem drinking scores in the directions expected for adaptive use of music. Also, participants who reported using music to change their mood when sad had lower depression scores than those who did not report using music to distract themselves when sad.

After our first study with gender held constant for a preliminary test of the relationship between the central variables, the remainder of the program of research was conducted with samples of college men and women. For study two (Stapley, 2005), volunteers were solicited from summer school classes. Sixty-seven females and 38 males (age $M = 20.81$, $SD = 2.09$) completed the same questionnaire protocol.

The previous finding, among females, that listening to loud angry songs to match their angry moods was associated with higher scores on the RAPS4-QF, was not replicated. The relationship between listening to soft music when angry and lower problem drinking scores was replicated (RAPS4-QF ($F(1,99) = 7.49$, $p = .007$, $r_{effect} = .26$). There was also a significant interaction between sex and choice of soft music when angry on RAPS4-QF scores, with a stronger effect among males than among females ($F(1,99) = 4.23$, $p = .04$).

These first two studies (Stapley, 2005) demonstrated preliminary support for the proposition that choosing music to distract oneself from unpleasant feelings is related to better adjustment among college students. This is consistent with previous studies that have found distraction to be an adaptive emotion regulation mechanism (e.g., Nolen-Hoeksema et al., 1993). In addition, consistent with previous research (e.g., Broderick & Korteland, 2002), the findings from the study of females also supported the hypothesis that rumination when sad is related to higher levels of depression. The most robust finding from these first studies is that using music for distraction when feeling angry predicts less problem drinking behavior.

In the next study (Stapley, 2007) we examined the relationship between college students' emotion regulation and adaptation to college, a positive behavioral criterion that was assessed by the Student Adaptation to College Questionnaire (SACQ, Baker & Siryk, 1989). We also included an open-ended questionnaire to learn about what emerging adults do when they feel sad, happy, angry, and stressed. The sample of 46 males and 105 females (age M = 19.2, SD = 187) most often reported reaching out to friends or family when feeling sad, closely followed by either listening to music or doing some activity to distract themselves. When they were feeling angry, the most frequently reported response was to talk to others or vent.

There were gender differences in these free-response data in this study (Stapley, 2007). College women reported ruminating when feeling sad more often than did the men (χ^2 (3, N = 141) = 17.91, $p < .001$). When angry, males were more likely to report exercising or other physical activity, whereas females were more likely to report choosing to be alone (χ^2 (4, N = 126) = 17.96, $p = .001$). The analyses of the music choice and emotion questionnaire used in the first two studies (Stapley, 2005) revealed that social adjustment scale scores from the SACQ were significantly higher if they reported listening to upbeat music when feeling sad (t (76) = 2.35, $p = .02$, $r_{effect} = .26$), angry (t (76) = 2.13, $p = .04$, $r_{effect} = .24$), or stressed (t (76) = 2.62, $p = .01$, $r_{effect} = .29$). Their social adjustment scores were also higher if they reported choosing soft music when angry (t (76) = 2.00, $p = .05$, $r_{effect} = .22$).

The data from this third study (Stapley, 2007) support the previous findings regarding the relationship between emotion regulation strategies and adjustment problems (Stapley, 2005) by showing that music choice by mood is related to a positive adjustment measure, as well as depression and problem drinking. Since students have less risk of adjustment problems and better social adjustment at college when they choose to modify their unpleasant moods with music and do not choose to match these distressing feelings with music, the next study in our program of research was a pilot test of a psychoeducational intervention using self-chosen music, designed to increase students' self-efficacy for managing their emotions.

Stapley and Jeffers (2011) chose to invite first-year honors school students living on campus to take part in the psychoeducational program at the beginning of their first semester of college. This sample was chosen to be fairly homogeneous to decrease individual differences. Three males and four females volunteered for the five-week intervention (pre-post design). They made playlists for happy, sad, and angry moods, using the music that they normally listen to on their Mp3 players. These first-year students emailed the research team daily to let us know whether they had listened to their emotion playlists and report on their satisfaction with regulating their feelings through their music. Intervention group participants' scores increased marginally pretest (M = 2.86, SD = 1.07) to posttest (M = 3.14, SD = .69) on the item "I feel I can control my emotions" (t (6) = −1.55, p = .086 [one-tailed]).

A second group of 11 first-year honors students living on campus (4 males, 7 females) served as the control group and completed posttests to control for time in semester effects. Did the intervention group just feel more in control six weeks into the semester than they had on the second week of classes when the pretest measures were completed? Participants in the intervention group had higher overall self-efficacy, as measured by the General Self-Efficacy Scale (GES, Schwarzer & Jerusalem, 1995) with an additional item for this study " I feel I can control my emotions" (t (15) = 2.56, p = .01 [one-tailed]).

Based upon the preliminary support we obtained through the within-group changes over time and the self-efficacy differences between the intervention group and the control group, a fifth study (Stapley, Gissubel, Kelly, Cinque, & Dillaway, 2012) was conducted to replicate the psychoeducational intervention in a different population.

We invited the sophomores from an EOF (Educational Opportunity Fund) program to participate, and all 34 students in the program volunteered (35% males, 65% females; age M = 19 years, SD = 0). Most of the participants (71%) were first-generation students. They were a diverse sample: 41% Hispanic, 35% European American, 18% African American, and 6% Asian American. The participants completed the General Self Efficacy Scale (GES, Schwarzer & Jerusalem, 1995) with the additional item for this program of research, "I feel I can control my emotions."

After our elation at 100% volunteer participation for this population at the Time 1 pre-intervention data collection, no one volunteered for the five-week intervention! Follow up debriefing revealed that students viewed the five-week intervention as too labor-intensive. While this is probably true for most undergraduates, it might be especially true for this sample, in contrast to our original pilot sample. These participants were predominantly first-generation students and nearly half were Latino, so this sample might be especially stressed and under time pressure to accomplish the myriad tasks on their plates. Sanchez, Esparza, Colon, and Davis (2010) have shown that Latino students often do not follow the common emerging adult patterns, as they take on more social and financial obligations for their families of origin. Although obviously disappointing, this lack of interest in the intervention program also demonstrated that students might not be willing to do it unless they feel in need of help with their emotion regulation. Perhaps we were able to get a small group of the honors school first-year students to participate because they were seeking help with managing their initial adjustment to college.

Despite abandoning the intervention phase of this study (Stapley et al., 2012), analyses of their self-report data replicated the rumination with music effect among this diverse sample of sophomores. Participants who usually chose sad, slow music to listen to while they are feeling sad (ruminators) had lower overall self-efficacy (GES) than those who do not ruminate with music when sad (t (32) = 1.85, p = .04, one-tailed).

DISCUSSION AND CONCLUSIONS

The program of research discussed here generally supports the use of music as a window into the customary ways that emerging adults in college manage their emotions. Furthermore, the relationship between students' use of distraction or rumination via music choice does appear to be related to important indicators of their adjustment to college. One of these indicators is the students' self-efficacy (e.g., Stapley et al., 2009; Tamir et al., 2007). Emerging adults' social adjustment to college was also found to be higher among those who either did not ruminate with music or did use music to modify their unpleasant emotions.

In contrast to the suggestion of Bandura et al. (2003), we did not find any relationship between regulation of happiness and the indices of psychosocial adjustment. It may be that regulation of the distressing emotions is more critical for adjustment, as prolonged experiences of the unpleasant emotions affects students' abilities to self-regulate in general (e.g., Baumeister et al., 2007). As emerging adults who are still immature in their neurological development, especially as pertains to decision making (Spear, 2010), their ability to balance their social life, family obligations, paid employment, coursework, and other activities is affected by their self-regulation skills.

The use of music to modify emotions was also related to depression and problem drinking, two of the most common problems in living among college students. Longitudinal research has demonstrated the predictive power of students' emotional regulation (Gerdes & Mallinckrodt, 1994; Stapley & Mizrahi, 2003) for explaining individual differences in the degree of success emerging adults have at college. Thus, these data may be useful for guiding practices in the college setting. Indeed, based upon their longitudinal data demonstrating the predictive validity of emotion regulation patterns for emotional adjustment, Berking, Orth, Wupperman, Meier, and Caspar (2008) suggested that emotion regulation skills should be enhanced to both prevent and treat affect related psychopathology. We argued decades ago (Haviland-Jones et al., 1991) that a key problem with emotional regulation skills in our culture is that people assume they are acquired naturally during development, rather than being explicitly taught.

The literature on the topic amassed since that time demonstrates the utility of developing explicit training in emotion regulation to foster adolescents' and emerging adults' adjustment and give them tools to help them negotiate the transition to adulthood.

Self-report of patterns of music choice may be useful as an assessment of emotion-regulation strategies. Self-report measures of the choice to match music to one's mood or use music to modify one's current emotion could be used either as a screening measure or in an individual counseling session for students experiencing problems in adjustment at college. Our attempts to conduct a psychoeducational intervention in which students are trained to create their own mood regulation playlists using the music that they enjoy yielded mixed results. The first pilot (Stapley & Jeffers, 2011) yielded preliminary support, albeit with a very small sample longitudinally and a small control versus intervention group comparison at the completion of the program.

Our second attempt at an intervention study (Stapley et al., 2012) revealed that even a highly cooperative group with 100% volunteer rates for a single-session data collection is not willing to commit to an intensive multiweek program. Future intervention research might be more successful if it is targeted to those who are actively seeking counseling for adjustment problems at college and thus more motivated to commit to learning and using a new technique. Follow-up debriefing in several focus groups also suggested that students found the five-week period too long and the daily contact by email to sound too intrusive. Short text messages on an every-other-day basis might improve volunteer rate for interventions as well.

Although emotion regulation is only one type of self-regulation, Baumeister et al.'s (2007) finding that students experiencing distressing emotions were rendered less capable of self-regulation in general supports the importance of assessing students' emotion regulation self-efficacy and success and offering guidance regarding effective emotion regulation for those experiencing college adjustment problems. Rather than assuming that emerging adults naturally acquired all the emotion regulation skills necessary for negotiating the challenges of college, information about effective emotion regulation should be incorporated into college orientation programming and the training sessions for academic advisors.

The centrality of self-regulation for optimal psychosocial functioning is a "hot topic" across many areas of psychology today. The program of research presented here can be used as a model for programs aimed at enhancing young people's self-regulation competency. Adolescence and emerging adulthood are periods of development that are critical for the development of self-regulation patterns as they include major developmental tasks and increased assumptions that these tasks will be handled independently. Following the suggestions in Aldao's (2013) recent review of the emotion regulation literature, future research should further the understanding of emerging adulthood by studying the context of their emotional experiences and the extent and flexibility of their emotion regulation repertoires.

AUTHOR'S NOTE

I would like to thank all of the student researchers who contributed to parts of this research program and co-authored earlier conference presentations and the participants who shared their thoughts and feelings with us so that we could better understand the emotional lives of emerging adults.

REFERENCES

Aldao, A. (2013). The future of emotion regulation research: Capturing context. *Perspectives on Psychological Science, 8,155-17.* DOI: 10.1177/1745691612459518

American Psychological Association (2002). Ethical principles of psychologists and code of conduct. *American Psychologist, 58,* 1060–1073.

Arnett, J. J. (1991). Adolescents and heavy metal music: From the mouths of metal-heads. *Youth and Society, 23,* 76–98.

Arnett, J. J. (2000). Emerging adulthood: A theory of development from the late teens through the twenties. *American Psychologist, 55,* 469–480.

Arnett, J. J. (2007). Emerging adulthood: What is it, what is it good for? *Child Development Perspectives, 1,* 68–73.

Baker, R. W., & Siryk, B. (1989). *SACQ Student Adaptation to College* (Manual). Torrance, CA: Western Psychological Services.

Bandura, A., Caprara, G. V., Barbaranelli, C., Gerbino, M., & Pastorelli, C. (2003). The Role of affective self-regulatory efficacy in diverse spheres of psychosocial functioning. *Child Development, 74,* 769–782.

Baumeister, R. F., Bratslavsky, E., Muraven, M., & Tice, D. M. (1998). Ego-depletion: Is the active self a limited resource? *Journal of Personality and Social Psychology, 74,* 774–789.

Baumeister, R. F., Zell, A. L., & Tice, D. M. (2007). How emotions facilitate and impair self-regulation. In J. J. Gross (Ed.), *Handbook of emotion regulation* (pp. 408–426). New York, NY: The Guilford Press.

Beck, A. T., Steer, R. A., & Brown, G. K. (1996). *Manual for the Beck Depression Inventory II.* San Antonio, TX: The Psychological Corporation.

Berking, M., Orth, U., Wupperman, P., Meier, L. L., & Caspar, F. (2008). Prospective effects of emotion-regulation skills on emotional adjustment. *Journal of Counseling Psychology, 55,* 485–494. DOI:10.1037/a0013589

Broderick, P. C., & Korteland, C. (2002). Coping style and depression in early adolescence: Relationships to gender, gender role, and implicit beliefs. *Sex Roles,46,* 201–213.

Brody, L. (1999). *Gender, emotion and the family.* Cambridge, MA: Harvard University Press.

Cherpitel, C. J. (2002). Screening for alcohol problems in the U.S. general population: Comparison of the CAGE, RAPS4, and RAPS4-QF by gender, ethnicity, and service utilization. *Alcoholism: Clinical and Experimental Research, 26,*1686–1691.

Ciarocco, N. J., Vohs, K. D., & Baumeister, R. F. (2010). Some good news about rumination: Task-focused thinking after failure facilitates performance improvement. *Journal of Social and Clinical Psychology, 29*(10), 1057–1073. doi:10.1521/jscp.2010.29.10.1057

Cooper, M. L., Frone, M. R., Russer, M., & Mudar, P. (1995). Drinking to regulate positive and negative emotions: A motivational model of alcohol use. *Journal of Personality and Social Psychology, 69,* 990–1005.

Gerdes, H., & Mallinckrodt, B. (1994). Emotional, social, and academic adjustment of college students: A longitudinal study of retention. *Journal of Counseling and Development, 72*(3), 281–288.

Greenwood, D. N., & Long, C. R. (2009). Mood specific media use and emotion regulation: Patterns and individual differences. *Personality and Individual Differences, 46,* 616–621. DOI:10.1016/j.paid.2009.01.002

Haviland-Jones, J., Gebelt, J. L., & Stapley, J. C. (1991). The questions of development in emotion. In P. Salovey & D. J. Sluyter (Eds.), *Emotional development and emotional intelligence: Educational implications* (pp. 233–253). New York, NY: Basic Books.

Magai, C. (1999). Affect, imagery, and attachment: Working models of interpersonal affect and socialization of emotion. In J. Cassidy & P. R. Shaver (Eds.), *Handbook of attachment: Theory, research, and clinical applications* (pp. 787–802). New York, NY: Guilford Press.

Mayer, J. D., & Salovey, P. (1997). What is emotional intelligence? In P. Salovey & D. J. Sluyter (Eds.), *Emotional development and emotional intelligence: Educational implications* (pp. 3–31). New York, NY: Basic Books.

Nolen-Hoeksema, S., Morrow, J., & Fredrickson, B. L. (1993). Response styles and the duration of episodes of depressed moods. *Journal of Abnormal Psychology, 102,* 20–28.

Nolen-Hoeksema, S., Stice, E., Wade, E., & Bohon, C. (2007). Reciprocal relations between rumination and bulimic, substance abuse, and depressive symptoms in female adolescents. *Journal of Abnormal Psychology, 116*(1), 198–207.

Parrott, W. G. (2002). The functional utility of negative emotions. In L. F. Barrett & P. Salovey (Eds.), *The Wisdom in Feeling* (pp. 341–359). New York, NY: The Guildford Press.

Pritchard, M. E., & Wilson, G. S. (2003). Using emotional and social factors to predict student success. *Journal of College Student Development, 44*(1), 18–28.

Pritchard, M. E., & Wilson, G. S. (2006). Do coping styles change during the first semester of college? *The Journal of Social Psychology, 146*(1), 125–127. Doi:10.3200/SOCP.146.1.125-127

Pulkkinen, L., Nygren, H., & Kokko, K. (2002). Successful development: Childhood antecedents of adaptive psychosocial functioning in adulthood. *Journal of Adult Development, 9,* 251–265.

Rentfrow, P. J., & Gosling, S. D. (2003). The do re mi's of everyday life: The structure and personality correlates of music preferences. *Journal of Personality and Social Psychology, 84,* 1236–1256. DOI: 10.1037/0022-3514.84.6.1236

Sanchez, B., Esparza, P., Colon, Y., & Davis, K. E. (2010). Tryin' to make it during the transition from high school: The role of family obligation attitudes and economic context for Latino emerging adults. *Journal of Adolescent Research, 25,* 858–884. DOI: 10.1177/0743558410376831

Schwarzer, R., & Jerusalem, M. (1995). Generalized Self-Efficacy scale. In J. Weinman, S. Wright, & M. Johnston (Eds.), *Measures in health psychology: A user's portfolio. Causal and control beliefs* (pp. 35–37). Windsor, UK: NFER-Nelson.

Schwartz, K. D., & Fouts, G. T. (2003). Music preferences, personality style, and developmental issues of adolescents. *Journal of Youth and Adolescence, 32,* 205–213.

Silk, J. S., Steinberg, L., & Morris, A. S. (2003). Adolescents' emotion regulation in daily life: Links to depressive symptoms and problem behavior. *Child Development, 74,* 1869–1880.

Spear, L. P. (2010). *The behavioral neuroscience of adolescence.* New York, NY: W. W. Norton & Company.

Stapley, J. C. (2005, February). *Music and emotion regulation among college students.* Poster presented at the Conference on Emerging Adulthood, Miami, FL.

Stapley, J. C. (2007, February). *Music and other emotion regulation strategies as predictors of adjustment among emerging adults.* Poster presented at the Conference on Emerging Adulthood, Tucson, AZ.

Stapley, J. C., Gissubel, K., Kelly, G., Cinque, A., & Dillaway, K. (2012, March). *Emotion regulation and self-efficacy among at-risk college students.* Poster presented at the Annual Meeting of the Eastern Psychological Association, Pittsburgh, PA.

Stapley, J. C., & Haviland, J. M. (1989). Beyond depression: Gender differences in normal adolescents' emotional experiences. *Sex Roles, 20,* 295–308.

Stapley, J. C., & Jeffers, M. R. (2011, October). *Psycho-educational training in emotion regulation using music among emerging adults transitioning to college.* Poster presented at the 5th Conference on Emerging Adulthood, Providence, RI.

Stapley, J. C., & Mizrahi, H. J. (2003, November). *A prospective study of psychosocial factors predicting college adjustment.* Poster presented at the Conference on Emerging Adulthood, Cambridge, MA.

Stapley, J. C., & Scalzo, C. (2000, April). *Emotional intelligence and adjustment to college.* Poster presented at the Biennial Meeting of the Conference on Human Development, Memphis, TN.

Stapley, J. C., Stedman, T. L., & Botti, A. (2002, June). *Emotional intelligence and other resilience factors as predictors of adjustment to college.* Poster presented at the Annual Adult Development Symposium, Society for Research on Adulthood, New York, NY.

Stapley, J. C., Wolff, G., & Noonan, J. (2009, October). *Students' coping advice as a predictor of college adjustment.* Poster presented at the Conference on Emerging Adulthood, Atlanta, GA.

Tamir, M., John, O. P., Srivastava, S., & Gross, J. J. (2007). Implicit theories of emotion: Affective and social outcomes across a major life transition. *Journal of Personality and Social Psychology, 92,* 731–744.

Thompson, R. A., & Meyer, S. (2007). Socialization of emotion regulation in the family. In J. J. Gross (Ed.), *Handbook of emotion regulation* (pp. 249–268). New York: The Guilford Press.

Zentner, M., Grandjean, D., & Scherer, K. R. (2008). Emotions evoked by the sound of music: Characterization, classification, and measurement. *Emotion, 8,* 494–529. DOI:10.1037/1528-3542.8.4.494

ABOUT THE CONTRIBUTORS

Aurélie Athan, PhD, is a full-time lecturer and program coordinator of the masters program in the department of clinical psychology at Teachers College, Columbia University. Her scholarly and clinical interests center on women's development across the lifespan, with a current emphasis on the transition to motherhood. She also contributes to the rationale of creating a new transdisciplinary field of study of reproductive and maternal mental health. Dr. Athan has presented in numerous conferences, published in journals such as the *Journal for the Association of Research on Mothering,* and sits on the academic advisory board of the Museum of Motherhood. Dr. Athan may be contacted at ama81@columbia.edu

Diane Bliss, MA, is currently a full professor in the English department at SUNY Orange Community College, Middletown, NY, where she teaches a wide range of courses from college writing to early English literature, ethics, and religious concepts. Her research interests include the development of students' critical thinking, cross-cultural perspectives, and an appreciation for the impact of language on attitudes and actions. She may be contacted at diane.bliss@sunyorange.edu.

Rosaria Caporrimo, PhD, is involved both in teacher education and the development of psychologists and the general student population. Her research interests include adolescent cognitive and social development, metacognition, student motivation, attention deficit disorder, and social justice. She may be contacted at DrCaporrimo@yahoo.com.

Adolescence in the 21st Century, pages 239–245
Copyright © 2014 by Information Age Publishing

Susan Conte, PhD, is an associate professor in the graduate school/human services division of the College of New Rochelle (CNR) teaching in the mental health counseling department and supervising student interns. As a clinical social worker, she also serves part-time in CNR's counseling and career services office and acts as a consultant to local high schools. Dr. Conte has had more than 20 years' experience in clinical work with adolescents and young adults in high school and college settings and in private practice. Dr. Conte has presented widely on the topic of nonsuicidal self-injury in the U.S. In addition to her teaching and clinical work, she has acted as a consultant in hospitals, in substance abuse treatment facilities, in universities, and in high schools and middle schools. Her research informs her teaching and her clinical work. She can be contacted at sconte@cnr.edu.

Gregory M. Eirich, PhD, is a lecturer-in-discipline for the quantitative methods in the social sciences (QMSS) program and also for the department of sociology at Columbia University. He researches the causes and consequences of socioeconomic inequality, with a particular focus on family processes. He has studied "rich-get-richer" dynamics in the CEO labor market and the cumulative academic consequences of reading ability groups in the early years of school. His dissertation examined the relationship between parental religiosity and children's educational attainment in the United States. Prior to teaching at Columbia, he was a senior consultant conducting health care research at the Advisory Board Company in Washington, DC. Dr. Eirich may be contacted at gme2101@columbia.edu.

David Elkind, PhD, is currently professor emeritus of child development at Tufts University in Medford, Massachusetts. He was formerly professor of psychology, psychiatry and education at the University of Rochester. Professor Elkind obtained his doctorate at UCLA and then spent a year as David Rapaport's research assistant at the Austen Riggs Center in Stockbridge, Massachusetts. In 1964–1965 he was a National Science Foundation senior postdoctoral fellow at Piaget's Institut d'Epistemologie Genetique in Geneva. His research has been in the areas of perceptual, cognitive, and social development, where he has attempted to build upon the research and theory of Jean Piaget.

Dr. Elkind's bibliography now numbers over five hundred items and includes research, theoretical articles, book chapters, and eighteen books. In addition, he has published more popular pieces such as children's stories in *Jack and Jill*, biographies of famous psychologists in the *New York Times Magazine*, as well as presentations of his own work in *Good Housekeeping*, *Parade* and *Psychology Today*. Some of his recent articles include "Computers and Young Children," "The Authority of the Brain," "The Cosmopolitan School," "On Becoming a Grandfather," and "Thanks for the Memory: Froebel and Montessori." Perhaps Dr. Elkind is best known for his popular books, *The Hurried Child, All Grown Up and No Place to Go, Miseducation, Ties that Stress,* and most recently, *The Power of Play: Learning What Comes Naturally.* In preparation is a new book tentatively entitled, *The Stages of Parenthood: Growing up with Our Children.*

Dr. Elkind is past president of the National Association for the Education of Young Children and has served on the editorial board of numerous scientific journals. He serves as consultant to state education departments, as well as to government agencies and private foundations. He lectures extensively in the United States, Canada, and abroad and has appeared in such popular venues as the *Today* show, *CBS Morning News, Twenty/Twenty, Nightline, Donahue,* and the *Oprah Winfrey Show.* Professor Elkind also co-hosted the Lifetime television series, *Kids These Days.* Dr. Elkind is a contributing Editor to *Parents* magazine and is currently the chief scientific advisor for JustAskBaby, an internet service for parents.

Rae Fallon, PhD, is an associate professor of psychology at Mount Saint Mary College, where she teaches a variety of psychology courses including Child Psychology, Drugs and Society, Autism Spectrum and Psychology of Stress. As a special education teacher and an early interventionist, Dr. Fallon has had many years working with children with special needs and their families. She may be contacted at rae.fallon@msmc.edu.

Debra Hrelic, PhD, RNC, is associate professor of nursing at Mount Saint Mary College, where she has been coordinator of maternal child nursing and as chair of the nursing division. She has also been a practicing registered nurse with greater than 33 years' experience in the specialty area of labor & delivery and maternal child nursing. Her research interests lie in nursing student success and retention in baccalaureate nursing programs and NCLEX success, as well as continued interest in mother–daughter communication. Dr. Hrelic may be contacted at debra.hrelic@msmc.edu.

J. David Gallagher, PhD, is associate professor of education at Mount Saint Mary College, where he teaches courses in literacy and curriculum planning. His research interests include new literacies and pedagogies addressing the needs of underserved populations.

Tatiana Ilinichna Gustomyasova, PhD, is associate professor of international law and cross-cultural communication (Volzhsky Institute of Humanities, VoLSU). Her current research interests include English Language Training (ELT) methodology, sociolinguistic competence, and information technology (e-mail-projects). Dr. Gustomyasova may be contacted at dis10589end@yandex.ru.

Alexandra Jordan, MA, is a doctoral student in clinical psychology at Teachers College, Columbia University. She received her BA in English from the University of Pennsylvania and her MA in psychology from Teachers College, Columbia University. Her research explores the impact of motherhood on identity development. Ms. Jordan may be contacted by email at alexandra.jordan@gmail.com.

David Kerner, MA, graduated in 2013 with a master's degree in general psychology from Montclair State University. During his tenure as a graduate student, his primary focus was in cognitive psychology, researching sound localization. Kerner also represented the American Psychological Association as an intern at the United Nations. He is currently a campaign manager for a Boston-based patient recruitment company, BBK Worldwide. Mr. Kerner may be contacted at dwkerner@gmail.com.

Olga E. Lomakina, PhD, is head of the international law and cross-cultural communication division at Volzhsky Institute of Humanities, a subunit of Volgograd State University. She teaches classes in cross-cultural communication, law mediation, ELT methodology and has managed international development projects for Volzhsky Institute of Humanities for the last 10 years. She is also head of the Centre for Intercultural Communication, a part of London Chamber of Commerce and Industry (LCCI), International Qualifications since 2005 and is in charge of organizing the Children's University at Volzhsky Institute of Humanities. Dr. Lomakina may be contacted at lolga1177@gmail.com.

Marina Mazur is a fourth-year doctoral student in clinical psychology at Teachers College, Columbia University. She graduated cum laude with a bachelor of arts in psychology and religion, and after working in the field for two years she went back to earn her doctorate. Currently her research interests focus on the transformational power of motherhood, especially among adolescent mothers, and post-traumatic growth. Ms. Mazur may be contacted at Marina.Mazur@gmail.com.

Lisa Miller, PhD, is professor and director of clinical psychology at Columbia University, Teachers College, where she also founded and directs the Spirituality Mind Body Institute, to innovate, disseminate and train healers in foundationally spiritual treatments. Dr. Miller is co-founder and co-editor-in-chief of *Spirituality in Clinical Practice* (APA Press) and Associate Editor of *Psychology of Religion and Spirituality*. For the APA Society of Spirituality and Psychology, she previously served as president and now serves as an APA council representative. Dr. Miller is a fellow of the APA and was awarded in 2011 the Virginia Sexton Mentoring Award. Dr. Miller edited the *Oxford University Handbook of Psychology and Spirituality* (2012) and has published over seventy articles and chapters on spirituality in mental health and wellness, as well as being the principle investigator on several million dollars of grants from corporate and family foundations as well as NIMH. She is a graduate of Yale University and University of Pennsylvania. Dr. Miller may be contacted at lfm14@columbia.edu.

Sister Margaret Murphy, D Min, is a professor of religious studies at Mount Saint Mary College, focusing her research interests on interfaith dialog and Holocaust studies. In particular, she is interested in the interplay between culture and spirituality in the lives of undergraduate students, Catholic–Jewish relations, and contemplative practice. She may be contacted at Peggy.Murphy@MSMC.edu.

Susan Riemer Sacks, PhD, is professor of psychology at Barnard College where she teaches adolescent psychology and educational psychology. Her research focuses on transitions from adolescence to adulthood, preteens to teenagers, and students to teachers, examining the facilitating factors to support change. As chair of the education program for over 30 years, she worked with New York City public school teachers and Columbia University undergraduates entering teaching and studied role transitions and mentoring in urban classrooms. Presently she is engaged in research on girls' attitudes toward science. Dr. Sacks may be contacted at ssacks@barnard.edu.

Paul Schwartz, PhD, is a professor of psychology and co-director of the Center for Adolescent Research and Development (CARD) at Mount Saint Mary College. During his 36-year career, Dr. Schwartz has taught, counseled, lectured about, researched, written about, and developed programs for adolescents and held workshops for both parents and teachers. He has collaborated on research projects with Dr. David Elkind, professor emeritus of Tufts University and author of *The Hurried Child.* He developed the Center for Adolescent Research and Development in collaboration with Dr. Spielhagen, Dr. Maynard, and Dr. Uzelac as a means of providing a research and evaluation base for schools and agencies working with adolescents, as well as providing an information clearinghouse for parents and all those interested in adolescent development. His research interests include adolescent development and culture, especially the transitional aspects of adolescent development and emerging adulthood, and how adolescents develop meaning and purpose in their lives. His current research examines adolescent egocentrism and how adolescents and emerging adults use social networking sites. He additionally writes a monthly column on child and adolescent issues for *Hudson Valley Parent* magazine. Dr. Schwartz may be contacted at paul.schwartz@msmc.edu.

Frances R. Spielhagen, PhD, is associate professor of education and co-director of the Center for Adolescent Research and Development at Mount Saint Mary College, Newburgh, NY. She is a career educator, with 30 years' prior experience as a teacher in grades 7–12 and as coordinator of programs for gifted adolescents. Dr. Spielhagen is editor-in-chief of the *Middle Grades Research Journal* and member of the Middle Level Education Research SIG of the American Education Research Association. She was co-chair of the NAGC Education Committee (2009–2011) and president of the Sociology of Education Association (2007–2009). Her publications include peer-reviewed articles in the *Journal for Advanced Academics,* the *Middle Grades Research Journal, Research in Middle Level Education,* and *American Secondary Education,* as well as several book chapters. She has also edited and authored three books, *Debating Single-Sex Education: Separate and Equal* (Rowman & Littlefield, 2007, 2013), *The Algebra Solution to Mathematics Reform: Completing the Equation* (Teachers College Press, 2011), and *Adolescence in the 21st Century: Constants and Challenges* (in production, Information Age Press). Her research interests include transitions in adolescence, particularly in early adolescence, and civic engagement among young adults. Dr. Spielhagen may be contacted at frances.spielhagen@msmc.edu.

Janice C. Stapley, PhD, is associate professor of psychology at Monmouth University, West Long Branch, NJ. Her research program during her 23 years of college teaching has primarily focused on emotional development during adolescence and emerging adulthood. Her other areas of research include the socialization of gender, gender differences in emotion, college adjustment and academic advising, and gender and age differences in technology use. As an applied lifespan developmental psychologist, her expertise includes mixed-methods research and qualitative research, as well as research ethics. Dr. Stapley may be contacted at jstapley@monmouth.edu.

Moira Tolan, PhD, is a professor of business at Mount Saint Mary College in Newburgh, NY, teaching courses in management, organizational behavior, and international business. Her research interests are in the area of management education. She is currently involved with an ongoing study involving the aspirations and workplace values of "New Millennial" students. She is also working to develop improved methods for teaching business students about environmental sustainability. Dr. Tolan may be contacted at moira.tolan@msmc.edu.

Kristen Turner, PhD, is an associate professor in the Fordham Graduate School of Education. A former high school English and social studies teacher, Turner works with in-service and pre-service teachers across content areas to build students' literacy skills. Her research focuses on the teaching of writing and the effects of technology on written composition. She is a teacher consultant for the National Writing Project and director of the Digital Literacies Collaborative at Fordham University. Dr. Turner may be contacted at krturner@fordham.edu.

Irene Van Riper, EdD, is an assistant professor of special education at William Paterson University, where she teaches pre-service teacher candidates who are entering the field of special education. Her research focuses on instructional strategies for individuals with developmental disabilities, specifically individuals on the autism spectrum. Dr. Van Riper may be contacted at vanriperi@wpunj.edu.

CPSIA information can be obtained at www.ICGtesting.com
Printed in the USA
LVOW07s0304120914

403618LV00001B/21/P